SECESSION AND SELF-DETERMINATION

NOMOS

XLV

NOMOS

Harvard University Press
I   *Authority* 1958, reissued in 1982 by Greenwood Press

The Liberal Arts Press
II   *Community* 1959
III   *Responsibility* 1960

Atherton Press
IV   *Liberty* 1962
V   *The Public Interest* 1962
VI   *Justice* 1963, reissued in 1974
VII   *Rational Decision* 1964
VIII   *Revolution* 1966
IX   *Equality* 1967
X   *Representation* 1968
XI   *Voluntary Associations* 1969
XII   *Political and Legal Obligation* 1970
XIII   *Privacy* 1971

Aldine-Atherton Press
XIV   *Coercion* 1972

Lieber-Atherton Press
XV   *The Limits of Law* 1974
XVI   *Participation in Politics* 1975

New York University Press
XVII   *Human Nature in Politics* 1977
XVIII *Due Process* 1977
XIX   *Anarchism* 1978
XX   *Constitutionalism* 1979
XXI   *Compromise in Ethics, Law, and Politics* 1979
XXII   *Property* 1980
XXIII *Human Rights* 1981
XXIV *Ethics, Economics, and the Law* 1982
XXV   *Liberal Democracy* 1983
XXVI *Marxism* 1983

XXVII	*Criminal Justice* 1985	
XXVIII	*Justification* 1985	
XXIX	*Authority Revisited* 1987	
XXX	*Religion, Morality, and the Law* 1988	
XXXI	*Markets and Justice* 1989	
XXXII	*Majorities and Minorities* 1990	
XXXIII	*Compensatory Justice* 1991	
XXXIV	*Virtue* 1992	
XXXV	*Democratic Community* 1993	
XXXVI	*The Rule of Law* 1994	
XXXVII	*Theory and Practice* 1995	
XXXVIII	*Political Order* 1996	
XXXIX	*Ethnicity and Group Rights* 1997	
XL	*Integrity and Conscience* 1998	
XLI	*Global Justice* 1999	
XLII	*Designing Democratic Institutions* 2000	
XLIII	*Moral and Political Education* 2001	
XLIV	*Child, Family, and State* 2002	
XLV	*Secession and Self-Determination* 2003	
XLVI	*Political Exclusion and Domination* (in preparation)	

NOMOS XLV
Yearbook of the American Society for Political and Legal Philosophy

SECESSION AND SELF-DETERMINATION

Edited by

Stephen Macedo, *Princeton University*
and
Allen Buchanan, *Duke University*

NEW YORK UNIVERSITY PRESS　•　*New York and London*

NEW YORK UNIVERSITY PRESS
New York and London
www.nyupress.org

Library of Congress Cataloging-in-Publication Data
Secession and self-determination /
editied by Stephen Macedo and Allen Buchanan.
p. cm. — (Nomos ; no. 45)
Includes bibliographical references and index.
ISBN 0–8147–5689–1 (cloth : alk. paper)
1. Self-determination, National.   2. Separatist movements.
3. Minorities—Legal status, laws, etc.   I. Macedo, Stephen, 1957–
II. Buchanan, Allen E., 1948–   III. Series.
KZ1269.S43   2003
341.26—dc21   2003014074

New York University Press books are printed on acid-free paper,
and their binding materials are chosen for strength and durability.

Manufactured in the United States of America
10 9 8 7 6 5 4 3 2 1

CONTENTS

Preface   ix

Contributors   xi

Introduction   1
ALLEN BUCHANAN

PART I: THE RIGHT TO SECEDE

1. International Responses to Separatist Claims:
   Are Democratic Principles Relevant?   19
   DIANE F. ORENTLICHER

2. A Right to Secede?   50
   DONALD L. HOROWITZ

3. Democratic Principles and Separatist Claims:
   A Response and Further Inquiry   77
   DIANE F. ORENTLICHER

PART II: INTRASTATE AUTONOMY

4. An Historical Argument for
   Indigenous Self-Determination   89
   MARGARET MOORE

5. Indigenous Self-Government   119
   JACOB T. LEVY

6. Exploring the Boundaries of Language Rights:
   Insiders, Newcomers, and Natives   136
   RUTH RUBIO-MARÍN

7. Can the Immigrant/National Minority Dichotomy
   Be Defended? Comment on Ruth Rubio-Marín   174
   ALAN PATTEN

   PART III: CONSTITUTIONALISM AND SECESSION

8. Domesticating Secession   193
   WAYNE NORMAN

9. The Quebec Secession Issue:
   Democracy, Minority Rights, and the Rule of Law   238
   ALLEN BUCHANAN

10. Secession, Constitutionalism,
    and American Experience   272
    MARK E. BRANDON

   Index   315

PREFACE

This forty-fifth volume of *NOMOS* emerged, as do they all, from a meeting of the American Society for Political and Legal Philosophy (ASPLP), this time held in San Francisco in conjunction with the December 2000 annual meeting of the Association of American Law Schools. The topic "Secession and Self-Determination" was selected by the voting membership of the society, and as the essays contained here make clear, the subject could not be more timely. Many people deserve thanks for their efforts in making that initial meeting a success, especially Managing Editor John Holzwarth, who made the arrangements along with former Secretary-Treasurer Judith Wagner DeCew. Most of all, thanks to those who presented original papers and commentaries, since revised and refined into their present form.

The editors at New York University Press, Stephen Magro and Despina Gimbel, deserve praise for their efforts on our behalf. Coeditor Allen Buchanan helped think this volume through, edited several of the essays, and wrote the introduction. I have learned a lot from him. Working with him has been a great pleasure.

Managing Editor John Holzwarth has taken time out from his busy life as a Princeton graduate student in political theory to assist me for three years. He has helped organize every detail of the meetings and has helped conceptualize and edit the volumes. Were it not for his skill, intelligence, and steady attention, this volume and the previous two would have been much tardier in seeing the light of day. His work has been consistently excellent. As he passes on the baton with this volume, we all owe John a great debt of gratitude.

Thanks to all of the officers of the ASPLP, whose efforts ensure the continued success of the series. In particular, we thank Judith

Wagner DeCew, who took on the time-consuming and usually thankless role of secretary-treasurer back in 1997 and served in that capacity with great care and conscientiousness until 2002. Thanks, finally, to Jacob T. Levy for taking on these duties.

STEPHEN MACEDO

CONTRIBUTORS

MARK E. BRANDON
Law, Vanderbilt University

ALLEN BUCHANAN
Law and Philosophy, Duke University

DONALD L. HOROWITZ
Law and Political Science, Duke University

JACOB T. LEVY
Political Science, University of Chicago

STEPHEN MACEDO
*Politics and University Center for Human Values,
Princeton University*

MARGARET MOORE
Political Studies, Queen's University

WAYNE NORMAN
*Philosophy and Centre for Research in Ethics,
University of Montreal (CREUM)*

DIANE F. ORENTLICHER
Law, American University

ALAN PATTEN
Political Science, McGill University

RUTH RUBIO-MARÍN
Law, University of Sevilla and New York University

INTRODUCTION

ALLEN BUCHANAN

The many questions raised by movements for secession and self-determination are both practically urgent and theoretically perplexing. This volume provides an unusually comprehensive consideration of these challenges and offers theoretical insights that provide guidance for policy. Among the questions considered here are: Should the international community recognize a right to secede, and, if so, what conditions must be satisfied before the right can be asserted? Should secession and its conditions be recognized within domestic constitutions? Secession is the most extreme form of political separation, and there are modes of self-determination short of it, including indigenous peoples' self-government and minority language rights. To what degree can these intrastate autonomy arrangements help ameliorate the injustices faced by indigenous groups? When should the majority recognize and support minority language rights?

All of the contributions to this book expand the limits of current thinking about secession and self-determination. The chapters in Part I constitute a sophisticated and nuanced debate about the pros and cons of an international legal right to secede. By exploring the international implications of secession, these chapters reject the view, which is all too common in the normative literature on secession, that it is a two-party problem, a question that concerns only the interests of the state and those who seek to secede from it. Both Diane Orentlicher and Donald Horowitz make it clear that the international community has a legitimate interest in how secession is handled and that whether an international legal right to secede is desirable depends not only upon the content of the right but also upon how it fits with other principles of the international legal order, what sorts of institutional processes it is embedded in, and what sorts of incentives it creates. Even though Orentlicher is more optimistic about the prospects for an international legal right to secede than Horowitz, she agrees with him that there are other ways in which the international legal order can constructively respond to demands for self-determination.

Part II explores the resources and limitations of institutions to foster self-determination for groups within the state rather than through the creation of new states. Margaret Moore's and Jacob Levy's chapters respectively provide what may be the best available justification for intrastate autonomy for indigenous peoples and the most balanced evaluation of the strengths and weaknesses of this alternative to independent statehood. Ruth Rubio-Marín's and Alan Patten's chapters suggest that without appropriate minority language rights even substantial powers of self-government may not be adequate, and they go on to explore at a new level of complexity the difficult issue of how special language rights are to be allocated among a plurality of minorities. Both of these chapters demonstrate the inadequacy of the most common rationale for attempts to allocate special language rights, namely, by reliance on a simple distinction between immigrant minorities and national minorities, and both make a strong case that a more complex balancing of legitimate interests is needed.

The chapters in Part III by Wayne Norman, Allen Buchanan, and Mark Brandon provide what may be the most comprehensive examination to date of the relationship between constitutionalism and secession. Taken together, the first two of these lay to rest the view that secession is inherently at odds with constitutional principles by showing how secession can be constructively controlled within constitutional structures. While Norman focuses on the role of domestic institutions, including the constitution, Buchanan expands the discussion by considering a role for international mediation of constitutionalized secession. These two chapters also represent an advance in another sense: they make it clear that the relationship between the moral justifications for secession and the ways in which institutions, whether domestic or international, should respond to secession is neither simple nor direct. Finally, Brandon's chapter deepens the inquiry into the relationship between constitutionalism and secession by exploring the relationship between the justification for secession and the way the creation of a constitutional order is conceived, arguing that secession is not merely compatible with constitutionalism but inherent in the very idea.

PART I: THE RIGHT TO SECEDE

Diane Orentlicher's essay approaches the issue of how international law should respond to assertions of the right to secede by probing the relationship between secession and democratic principles. She argues that international law already includes a right to democratic governance and seeks to understand the bearing of this right on the problem of secession. The central question of her essay, therefore, is this: "What, precisely, are the implications of democratic principles for assessments [in international law] of separatist claims?"

After providing a concise recent history of international law concerning secession, self-determination, and democracy, Orentlicher argues that there can be no straightforward inference from democratic principles to a right to secede. Instead, democratic principles can, depending upon circumstances, count for or against international legal recognition of secessionist claims. Although Orentlicher stops short of explicitly endorsing a normative theory of the right to secede, she suggests that the strongest justification for assertions of the right to secede are remedial: in general, international law should recognize a unilateral right to secede (as opposed to a right that is created through negotiation or through a constitution) only where secession is a remedy of last resort for serious injustices. In addition, Orentlicher advocates a more ambitious role for international and regional institutions both to help prevent or resolve secessionist conflicts and to help ensure that when secession does occur, the rights of minorities on both sides of the new border are respected. Because she believes that international law already includes a right to secede when a minority within a state suffers the injustice of exclusion from political participation, Orentlicher sees her proposals for how international law ought to deal with secession as logical extensions of reforms that have already taken place rather than as proposals for radical change.

Donald Horowitz's essay provides a sharp counterpoint to Orentlicher's. Horowitz denies that international law already recognizes a right to secede when groups are excluded from political participation. However, on this point there may not be as much disagreement between his position and Orentlicher's as he supposes. Orentlicher can agree with Horowitz that existing international law does not recognize a right to secede when minority groups are denied participation in government if this means that they are not granted *group rights* of participation: that is, they are not given rights of political participation as collectivities. Her point, on this interpretation, instead would be that there is an international legal right to secede in cases where the individuals that compose a minority group are excluded from political participation in the state as individuals: for example, by being denied the right to vote or to participate in political parties or to run for office. Holding that international law recognizes a right of a minority to secede when the individual rights of political participation of its members are violated is compatible with denying that international law recognizes a right on the part of minority groups to corporate representation within the state.

The disagreement between Horowitz and Orentlicher is clearer and deeper on the issue of whether international legal recognition of a right to secede is desirable. Horowitz argues that secession almost always replicates the problems it is supposed to solve, at least when secession is put forward as a solution to ethnonational conflicts. He correctly observes that secession is almost always a failure as a solution to this problem because the new entities created by secession will invariably include ethnonational minorities who will be vulnerable to discrimination by the new majority.

Even here, however, the disagreement may not be as stark as it first appears, depending upon how one understands Orentlicher's support for an international legal right to secede. Her point, presumably, is that international legal recognition of a right to secede for minorities that are persecuted or denied access to political participation is desirable *if* it is accompanied by effective measures to ensure the rights of minorities in new states created by secession. The disagreement with Horowitz, on this interpretation, is not over whether international recognition of a right to secede under these conditions would be a good thing but rather over whether the conditions are likely to be realized. Horowitz is much less optimistic here than Orentlicher. He asks: If the international community can succeed in protecting the rights of minorities in new states created by secession, why can't it prevent secession by protecting the rights of minorities in existing states so that they don't need to secede?

Orentlicher might reply that new entities created by secession are more amenable to international influence than existing states because they crave international recognition as legitimate states. Thus the international community has greater leverage over secessionist entities than over existing states and may be able to do a better job of protecting minorities in the former than in the latter.

Nevertheless, the main thrust of Horowitz's chapter is extremely important. He makes a strong case that international legal recognition of a right to secede would by itself do little to resolve the ethnonational conflicts to which secession is often thought to be a solution. Recognizing a right to secede might even make matters worse unless it were accompanied by international commitments to protecting minorities, and those commitments may not be forthcoming. Orentlicher and Horowitz agree that democratic principles themselves do not provide a compelling case for international legal recognition of a right to secede, and both recognize that the balance of considerations will often weigh against international legal support for secession. Horowitz favors electoral systems that would reduce ethnonational conflict rather than recognition of a right to secede. Orentlicher could endorse Horowitz's strategy and add that the international community can play a constructive role in encouraging states that are prone to ethnonational conflict to create such systems in order to reduce the risk of secessionist strife. Yet she could still maintain that there is a limited role for international legal recognition of a right to secede when this strategy fails. The chief disagreement between Orentlicher and Horowitz, then, would concern how the international community should invest its energies: in pressuring states to adopt internal reforms that obviate the need for secession or in doing that and also working for international legal recognition of a right to secede when internal reform is not forthcoming, so long as the right to secede is embedded in international institutions that will ensure that its exercise will not result in violations of the rights of minorities.

PART II: INTRASTATE AUTONOMY

Jacob Levy's and Margaret Moore's chapters together constitute a comprehensive analysis of what may be the most compelling instance of autonomy for minorities within states as an alternative to secession: indigenous peoples' rights of self-government. Moore's chapter focuses on the moral justifications for states' granting rights of self-government to indigenous groups within their borders; Levy's articulates the limitations of self-government as a response to the problems of indigenous peoples.

Moore advances two closely related, historically based arguments for granting indigenous peoples rights of self-government within the state. According to both arguments, the historical injustices suffered by indigenous peoples ground their moral right to self-government. On the first argument, self-government as including authority over resources and territory is an important means of rectifying past injustices and their continuing ill effects on indigenous peoples. On the second, the case for indigenous self-government is grounded in the fact that indigenous peoples enjoyed self-government in the past but were unjustly deprived of it by conquest. Moore also makes the case that these arguments for indigenous self-government have significant advantages over an influential argument advanced by Will Kymlicka, according to which indigenous peoples are entitled to self-government because it is necessary to preserve their cultures, which provide a context for meaningful choice and hence make individual autonomy possible.

Moore has two objections to Kymlicka's argument. First, it depends on the premise that "societal cultures," understood as being institutionally complete, alone can provide a meaningful context for choice and hence for the flourishing of autonomy. Moore points out that often indigenous communities have been so damaged by conquest and colonization that they no longer possess a societal culture. Second, Kymlicka's argument is untrue to the aspirations of indigenous peoples: they see their claims for self-government not as being based on a liberal conception of individual autonomy but rather as being grounded in the historical injustices that they have suffered.

Levy's chapter provides a more qualified and less enthusiastic endorsement of self-government for indigenous peoples. His main thesis is that self-government for indigenous peoples poses "a number of theoretical paradoxes for arguments about self-government and self-determination." First, on remedial grounds indigenous peoples have the strongest case for a right to secede, but virtually none of these groups could establish viable independent states. Second, if the argument for indigenous self-government is that it is needed to protect indigenous peoples from injustices, the problem is that indigenous self-government is usually so weak that it cannot provide the needed protection. Third, the creation of indigenous self-government is likely to be the imposition of an alien institution and to constitute "a decisive break with customary understandings of the group, its relationship to its law, and its form of government."

In addition, Levy points out that not infrequently tribal governments are corrupt, attempt to stifle political opposition within the group, and use measures to protect the putative interests of the group that impose limitations on the freedom of individuals within it. Nevertheless, he concludes that with all these liabilities, self-government may still be the best response to the problem of remedying historical injustices against indigenous peoples and preventing violations of their rights. What neither Moore nor Levy explicitly considers is whether international institutions might play a constructive role in ameliorating some of the deficiencies of indigenous self-government: for example, by encouraging states to grant self-government to indigenous groups or by exerting pressure on them to abide by the terms of intrastate autonomy agreements. Buchanan's essay in Part III explores these possibilities.

While both Moore and Levy address explicitly only indigenous self-government, much of what they say applies to self-government for ethnonational minorities that do not qualify as indigenous peoples. Moore's first justification for indigenous self-government appears to apply to all groups that have suffered historical injustices. Levy's reservations about the efficacy of indigenous self-government appear to apply to self-government for national minorities generally. Taken together, these two essays supply a balanced and comprehensive appreciation of the attractions and liabilities of limited self-government as an alternative to secession.

Ruth Rubio-Marín and Alan Patten address the issue of special language rights for minorities. Although minority language rights can serve as an adjunct to minority self-government, these authors explore them in their own right. While it is true that minority language rights do not constitute autonomy in the sense of self-government, they can contribute to the individual autonomy of members of minority groups and can facilitate a degree of cultural autonomy for the group. For that reason, the editors have included these two essays in the part of the book devoted to intrastate autonomy. Like limited self-government within the state, minority language rights can be seen as alternatives to the more radical option of full independence for minorities. Both are attempts to accommodate the legitimate interests of minorities within the state rather than to equip them with their own states.

"Language rights for minorities" covers a wide range of types of rights. These include rights that constitute what Patten calls the "norm-and-accommodation" strategy for dealing with linguistic minorities. According to this strategy, one language is designated as official and linguistic minorities are granted special rights to enable them to accommodate to the dominance of the official language. For example, individual members of minority groups are given the right to have a translator when they appear in court or rights to bilingual education while they are developing competence in an official language. The other strategy Patten identifies is that of language equality: several languages are designated as official, thus recognizing the linguistic equality of those who use them. Individuals have rights to use any of these official languages and to receive public services in them. However, the second strategy does not solve the problem of linguistic discrimination because in many cases it will not be feasible to designate all languages spoken within the borders of the state as official. So the question arises: On what criterion should the distinction between official and nonofficial languages be drawn?

Rubio-Marín's chapter argues against one widely held proposal for determining how language rights should be allocated among different linguistic minorities: grant more robust language rights to national minorities than to immigrants. Presumably Rubio-Marín would also reject the national minorities/immigrant distinction as a criterion for determining which languages are designated official. One rationale for this proposal is that immigrants have voluntarily given up the right to full accommodation of their linguistic capabilities or preferences by choosing to immigrate, whereas national minorities have generally been forcibly incorporated into the state (or in some cases incorporated with a promise of equal status that has not been honored). Rubio-Marín argues that in many cases it cannot be said that immigrants voluntarily accept an inferior status for their language.

Often their choice to immigrate is not free but rather is compelled by economic need or political oppression, and in some cases the choice is less than fully informed because they tend to underestimate either the difficulty of adapting to the official language or the loss of cultural goods that goes with it.

Rubio-Marín's constructive contribution is a more complex proposal for how to allocate language rights. She proposes four criteria: (1) other things being equal, more numerous and geographically more concentrated groups should have more robust language rights; (2) language rights should be allocated in such a way as to protect the "nonexit option" for linguistic minorities (i.e., so as to make it feasible for people to continue to use their minority language and participate in the culture associated with it); (3) rights for new groups should be allocated so as to minimize negative impact on groups already established in the jurisdiction, other things being equal; (4) proposals for according language rights should be evaluated in the light of their tendency to encourage or discourage divisiveness (proposals that have less divisive consequences are preferable, all other things being equal).

Patten points out that Rubio-Marín may be wrong in suggesting that the use of these criteria would generally have the same policy implications as reliance on the national minorities/immigrant distinction. Patten notes, for example, that Rubio-Marín's first criterion, geographical concentration and numbers, implies that Cantonese immigrants in Canada should have more robust language rights than Cree Indians (who are a national minority). Because he believes that Rubio-Marín's proposal is more radical than she supposes and because he believes that the national minorities/immigrant distinction has considerable intuitive appeal as a criterion for allocating language rights, Patten undertakes to see whether a better rationale for using the distinction for this purpose can be developed than the implausible thesis that immigrants voluntarily accept greater limitations on their linguistic preferences by immigrating.

According to Patten, immigrants can be expected to make linguistic adaptations that it would be wrong to expect national minorities to make, not because the former have voluntarily accepted an inferior status for their languages by immigrating, but because members of the society to which they immigrate can legitimately impose conditions on immigrants that it would be inappropriate to impose on national minorities. Patten focuses, then, on the legitimate interests that members of the receiving society have in requiring immigrants to adapt to a new linguistic environment. These include their interest in "being able to control a particular territory . . . to ensure their own security, to protect the conditions necessary for democracy, and to maintain their own cultures and languages." Although Patten describes his view as an attempt to "resuscitate" the "consent theory" as a rationale for relying on the national minorities/immigrant distinction, it does not in fact rely upon the idea that immigrants voluntarily accept limitations on their linguistic preferences. Instead, it grounds the right to treat immigrants differently on the fact that it is reasonable to expect them to accommodate to the legitimate interests of members of the receiving society. In contrast, it would be wrong to expect national minorities to make the same compromises because their interests have the same status as those of the majority group in society.

Rubio-Marín's and Patten's approaches to language rights may not be as different as first appears. Employing Rubio-Marín's third criterion, which says that the allocation of language rights to immigrants should avoid negative impacts on established groups, assumes that established groups have legitimate interests that can justify limitations on the language rights of newcomers. This is precisely Patten's point.

Taken together, these two essays show that any reasonable attempt to accommodate minorities within the state must develop language rights regimes on the basis of a plurality of moral considerations and that more simplistic approaches are not true to the moral complexity of the situation. Even if, as Patten suggests, the national minorities/immigrant distinction is valuable to the extent that it indicates the importance of the legitimate interests of those who are already members of a society in determining the conditions of entry to it, those interests do not have absolute weight. A defensible allocation of language rights will, all things considered, have to take into account other interests as well, and Rubio-Marín's other three criteria can provide useful rules of thumb for accomplishing this.

PART III: CONSTITUTIONALISM AND SECESSION

In the literature on secession, the relationship between constitutionalism and the right to secede is relatively neglected. The three chapters in this part of the volume make a major contribution toward remedying this deficiency. Norman and Buchanan examine the attractions of constitutionalizing secession, of attempts to bring the potentially destabilizing and violent process of state breaking under the rule of law by subjecting it to processes provided for in a constitution. Brandon, in contrast, is concerned, not with how the process of secession can be brought within the scope of a constitution, but rather with how appeals to the nature of the founding of a constitutional order can serve to justify secession.

Like Horowitz, Norman favors constitutional design to cope with the problems that can lead to secession. But unlike Horowitz, Norman endorses constitutional provisions that make it possible to secede rather than (or in addition to) electoral procedures that reduce ethnic conflicts. However, the contrast between their approaches may not be so great as first appears because Norman explicitly limits his proposals to a small and in some respects very atypical set of potential secessionist situations: there is an advanced, reasonably stable, democratic system with a history of peaceful transitions of power; there is at least one territorially concentrated ethnocultural minority group with a a national or quasi-national identity and a political-territorial jurisdiction in which this minority forms a majority; there is a dominant secessionist movement within this group and this jurisdiction that is committed to the peaceful, democratic pursuit of independence; and there is a level of support for secession within the minority group, or within the minority group's region, that fluctuates somewhere between 20 and 60 percent. Norman cites Belgium, Canada, Switzerland (potentially), Spain, and the United Kingdom as satisfying these conditions. Horowitz might concede that constitutionalizing secession in these exceptional circumstances would be feasible but might stick to his generalization that secession does not solve the problems that give rise to it and that the latter are better addressed by designing electoral systems that encourage political parties to bridge ethnonational divides.

Norman first criticizes the view, advanced by Abraham Lincoln and Cass Sunstein among others, that legal recognition of a right to secede is incompatible with the principles of constitutionalism. According to Sunstein's version of this point, a chief object of constitutional design is to encourage citizens to commit to democratic deliberation, to engage in the hard work of principled political argumentation; but making secession a legal option would undercut this commitment by making exit an option and encouraging discontented minorities to use the threat of exit as a strategic bargaining tool rather than relying only on principled arguments to advance their preferences. Like Buchanan in an earlier discussion, Norman points out that these risks of the legalization of secession can be reduced to acceptable levels by appropriate proceduralization of the right, including constitutional provisions that make it difficult, though not impossible, to exercise. (For example, secession could be allowed only if a supermajority in the region in question voted in favor of it on two occasions, separated by a "cooling off" waiting period.)[1] If the constitutionally recognized right to secede is appropriately hedged, it will not encourage premature exit, and opportunities for strategic bargaining with the threat of secession will be reduced.

The remainder of Norman's essay is devoted mainly to showing that there are significant benefits to constitutionalizing secession and to distinguishing between different types of arguments for constitutionalizing it. One especially interesting feature of the latter discussion is Norman's conception of the relationship between the moral justification for secession and the way in which a right to secede should be constitutionalized. Like Orentlicher and Buchanan, he believes that the most compelling justification for secession is remedial, that it is justified as a remedy of last resort in response to serious and persistent injustices. Norman argues that it does not follow, however, that the proper way to constitutionalize the right to secede is to require secessionists to show that they have been subject to serious and persistent injustices. Following Buchanan, Norman holds that it would be unfair to the secessionists to require them to make a case that they have been aggrieved in a political system controlled by those against whom they make the charge of injustice.[2] To avoid this "biased referee problem," Norman suggests something like the political analogue of no-fault divorce: instead of establishing that they are the victims of injustice, secessionists must satisfy other, more normatively neutral procedural conditions, including a supermajority vote in favor of secession. Another advantage of Norman's distinction between the moral justification for secession and the conditions for exercising a constitutional right to secede is that it allows for the possibility of cases where an orderly constitutionally structured secession is desirable and morally permissible as well, even though the secessionists do not have a moral right to secede.

Norman's illuminating theoretical discussion of the relationship between secession and constitutionalism is complemented by Buchanan's analysis of a recent attempt by the Supreme Court of Canada to indicate how the secession of Quebec could be achieved by constitutional amendment. According to Buchanan, what is especially interesting about the Canadian Supreme Court's ruling is that it envisions a constitutionalized process of secession in the absence of both an explicit constitutional right to secede and a moral right to secede (understood as a remedial right to seek relief from injustices).

Buchanan argues that the Canadian Supreme Court's effort to show how secession by Quebec could be brought under the rule of law, though admirable, is incomplete. The Court held that the Canadian government would be obligated to enter into negotiations concerning secession if a "clear majority" in Quebec voted in favor of secession in response to a "clearly stated" referendum question on secession. However, the Court left the determination of the "two clarities" up to "the political actors," the Canadian government and the provincial government of Quebec, which proposed conflicting criteria for clarity. Buchanan argues that even if the initial hurdle of agreement on what counts as clarity is cleared, the process of negotiating the terms of secession may break down at a number of points. He suggests that a suitably composed, impartial international body could mediate negotiations concerning the satisfaction of the clarity conditions and the terms of secession. In addition, Buchanan argues that although the Court held that negotiated secession must be guided by the principle of respect for the

rights of minorities, the process that the Court outlined fails to provide an adequate voice for the indigenous peoples of Quebec. Norman and Buchanan both hold that under certain conditions it is
both desirable and feasible to use constitutional principles to bring
secession under the rule of law, but Buchanan goes on to suggest
that it may be necessary to supplement constitutional processes
with international involvement.

Brandon's contribution advances an intriguing hypothesis about
the relationship between constitutionalism and secession: constitutionalism as he understands it not only is compatible with secession
but implies its legitimacy. For Brandon, constitutionalism includes
the idea of the founding of the constitutional order, and this in
turn implies that constitutional orders are human creations that
can be replaced by new orders. Constitutionalism itself implies the
possibility of forming new political units out of old ones and in that
sense legitimizes secession. Secession, on Brandon's view, is inherently constitutional, even if there is no right to secede specified in
the constitution and even if the constitution's provisions for
amendment do not allow secession by constitutional amendment
as the Canadian Supreme Court envisions.

Furthermore, according to Brandon, the best—and indeed the
only cogent—justification for secession relies on beliefs about the
way in which the constitutional order was founded. The logic of getting into a constitutional order, as he puts it, supplies the logic for
getting out. In the American case, Brandon argues, both of the
main myths of the founding, properly understood, imply that states
can leave the union.

Brandon's conception of the justification for secession appears
to be directly opposed to the consensus shared by Norman,
Buchanan, and Orentlicher that the most cogent justification is remedial in character—that a group comes to have the right to secede when secession is the remedy of last resort for serious and persistent injustices. Instead, he hypothesizes that the best justifications are those that appeal to the logic of the founding myth.
However, depending on what is meant here by the "best" sort of justification, there may in fact be no disagreement. If Brandon's hypothesis about the importance of the logic of the founding myth
concerns only what people generally find to be a compelling justification for secession—that is, what most effectively motivates them

to secede or accept secession by others—then this is an empirical claim about motivation, not a normative claim about which justifications are cogent. Moreover, it may be somewhat misleading for Brandon to say that on his view the only compelling justification for secession is "constitutional," since his view seems to be that it is not the constitution, or even the actual nature of its founding, that counts but rather what the "dominant" founding myth is: that is, what most people *believe* to be the nature of the process by which the constitutional order was founded.

These essays do not "solve" the moral, political, and legal problems surrounding secession and self-determination, but we believe that they represent important advances in our thinking about them.

NOTES

1. Allen Buchanan, *Secession: The Morality of Political Divorce from Fort Sumter to Lithuania and Quebec* (Boulder, Colo.: Westview Press, 1991), chap. 4.

2. Ibid.

PART I

THE RIGHT TO SECEDE

1

INTERNATIONAL RESPONSES TO SEPARATIST CLAIMS: ARE DEMOCRATIC PRINCIPLES RELEVANT?

DIANE F. ORENTLICHER

Although a perennial feature of global politics, separatist movements had scant prospect of success for nearly half a century after World War II. And so the recent proliferation of new states has shattered settled expectations. In the 1990s, Yugoslavia fractured into five states, the Soviet Union split into fifteen, Eritrea separated from Ethiopia, Czechoslovakia divided into the Czech Republic and Slovakia, and East Timor won independence from Indonesia. The success of breakaway movements from Slovenia to Eritrea has given new impetus to a raft of other separatists across the globe.[1] And small wonder: the surge in state making in the 1990s marked a new departure.[2] Outside the context of decolonization, international law has long regarded separatist claims with disfavor. To be sure, international law and state practice remain deeply skeptical of separatist movements; few are likely to succeed. Even so, the recent success of several signifies the possibility of a broader realignment of law and policy.

An important barometer of change has been the nature of diplomatic responses to contested separatist claims. The breakup of the former Yugoslavia drew mediation efforts by the European

Community (EC), the Conference on Security and Co-operation in Europe, the United Nations, the five-nation Contact Group, and, finally, the United States. These and other mediation efforts have been shaped by and in turn are reshaping international law concerning recognition of new states.[3] With relevant principles now in flux, the question today is, What principles should guide international responses to separatist claims?

In this essay I explore an aspect of this question that has recently assumed special importance—the relevance of democratic principles. By focusing on this question, I do not mean to suggest that principles of self-government are the only—or even the most important—values that should be brought to bear in assessing separatist claims. Far from it. For good reason, concerns relating to international security and stability, as well as a core commitment to the territorial integrity of states, have long dominated international law's bias against separatist movements. That same bias is reinforced by the humanitarian aims of international law, whose antipathy toward ethnic separatism can be captured in a simple syllogism: If national groups enjoyed a presumptive right to statehood, national minorities would inevitably be captured within the boundaries of another nation's state—and would be vulnerable to repression. Equally important, postwar human rights law is imbued with the values of civic nationalism, which conceives citizenship not in terms of ethnic or national identity but in terms of equal protection of all citizens before a common law and shared institutions of governance.

Even so, recent developments in legal doctrine and state practice make clear, as I contend in the next section, that principles of self-government have already become relevant, both legally and practically, to the resolution of contested separatist claims. Much less clear, however, is the question I address in this essay: What, precisely, are the implications of democratic principles for assessments of separatist claims?

I. The Trajectory of "Self-Determination" in International Law

Although this question has at times loomed large in political theory and state practice, it has only lately become a substantial issue of international law. To appreciate the significance of this development, it is helpful briefly to recall how international law has treated separatist claims in the past.

A. *The Interwar Period*

The law governing separatist movements before World War I can be briefly stated: once a national movement secured independence, other states would acknowledge the established facts of statehood. International law did not, however, regard any type of self-determination claim as legitimate ex ante.

The Paris Peace Conference marked a significant, if limited, departure from the classic view. Although not yet considered a legal right, self-determination was a guiding principle for statesmen who remapped central and eastern Europe following World War I. To the extent consistent with other objectives, they gave effect to the "principle of nationalities": the boundaries of new and reconfigured states were to be drawn along national lines. The peacemakers also gave limited effect to another conception of self-determination, which supports the resolution of key political questions—including core questions of statehood—through democratic processes. For example, the fate of certain disputed territories, including Upper Silesia and Schleswig, would be determined by internationally supervised plebiscites.

It remained to be seen whether a general principle of law would emerge from the foundation laid at Versailles or whether, instead, the Peace Conference would remain a case-specific exercise of Great Power diplomacy. The answer came quickly. A proposal by Woodrow Wilson to incorporate the principle of self-determination in the Covenant of the League of Nations[4] was defeated.

If there was any lingering doubt about the legal status of "self-determination," it was put to rest in the reports of two commissions appointed by the League of Nations in connection with a dispute over the status of the Aaland Islands.[5] Both bodies concluded that international law did not recognize a right of national self-determination.[6] But their reports hinted at possible exceptions in circumstances implicating the rights of minorities. Most explicitly, the Commission of Rapporteurs suggested that secession might be available as a "last resort when the State lacks either the will or the power to enact and apply just and effective guarantees" of minority rights.[7]

The Aaland Islands remained in Finland, where their inhabitants now enjoy substantial autonomy. But the concept of remedial secession hinted at by the Commission of Rapporteurs continues to resonate in legal doctrine and political philosophy. As elaborated in the section that follows, in more recent incarnations the notion of a remedial right to secede has expanded to include situations in which a defined subpopulation is persistently excluded from full political participation.

B. Postwar Law: Decolonization

In the postwar period, self-determination was transformed from a principle into a legal right. With this, its meaning also changed. Now self-determination meant the right of colonized peoples freely to determine their political status. For a time, this meant that the postwar right of self-determination would have scant relevance beyond the context of decolonization. But in the view of many commentators, this generalization has long been subject to a key qualification: groups persistently denied meaningful participation in national political processes might be entitled to secede.

This view derives above all from the Declaration on Principles of International Law Concerning Friendly Relations and Co-operation among States in Accordance with the Charter of the United Nations ("Declaration on Friendly Relations"), adopted by the UN General Assembly in 1970.[8] The declaration made clear that the core meaning of the principle of self-determination enshrined in the UN Charter was the right of "the people of a colony or non-self-governing territory" freely to determine its political status.[9] Outside the special context of decolonization, established states would enjoy the right to territorial integrity. But the declaration famously hinted that this right might be forfeited if a state's government did not represent "the whole people belonging to the territory without distinction as to race, creed or colour."[10]

This language has been interpreted implicitly to confer the right of self-determination, exceptionally entailing secession, "only on *racial* or *religious* groups living in a sovereign State which are denied access to the political decision-making process; *linguistic* or *national* groups *do not* have a concomitant right" (italics in original).[11] But recent iterations of the principle enunciated in the Declaration on Friendly Relations have removed its restrictive terms. Where the 1970 declaration affirms the right of territorial integrity with respect to states whose government represents "the whole people belonging to the territory without distinction as to race, creed, or colour," UN declarations of 1990s vintage affirm the same right with respect to states "possessed of a Government representing the whole people belonging to the territory *without distinction of any kind*" (italics added).[12] The Supreme Court of Canada has characterized views to the effect that these instruments support an exceptional right of secession this way: "[W]hen a people is blocked from the meaningful exercise of its right to self-determination internally, it is entitled, as a last resort, to exercise it by secession."[13] In this view, secession is a remedy of final recourse that may come into play when it is the sole means by which a substate group can exercise its right of political participation on a basis of equality.

This view rests upon an implied assertion: everyone is entitled to participate, on a basis of full equality, in the political life of his or her nation. When the UN General Assembly adopted the Declaration on Friendly Relations in 1970, this claim was the sort of bromide from which few, if any, states would publicly dissent. But outside the special context of global concern with apartheid and decolonization, states were not prepared to back up this claim with the sanction of legal entitlement. And so any corollary right of secession had much the same force as a resolution proclaiming a definitive determination of the number of angels who could dance on the head of a pin. In this setting, there was scant reason for practitioners of statecraft to wrestle with the vexing questions bound up in a remedial right of secession: What manner of inequality in the exercise of political rights would justify remedial secession? How persistent must the shortcoming be? Are there measures short of secession that must be exhausted before the last-resort remedy can plausibly be claimed?

C. *The Democratic Entitlement*

But in the last decade of the twentieth century, the implied claim underlying the asserted last-resort remedy of secession—that everyone is entitled to participate, on a basis of equality, in self-government—gathered substantial support.[14] In addition to its external dimension, we were reminded, self-determination has an internal dimension, embodied above all in principles of democratic governance.[15]

This aspect of the right to self-determination received unprecedented attention beginning in the 1990s, but its core claim was already established in two widely ratified treaties. Common Article 1 of the International Covenant on Civil and Political Rights[16] and of the International Covenant on Economic, Social and Cultural Rights[17] asserts the right of "[a]ll peoples" to self-determination. The drafting history and text make clear that, while this provision encompasses the familiar right of peoples living under colonial rule to attain independence,[18] it has an internal dimension as well.[19]

Even so, rights relating to democratic government did not occupy a significant place in the domain of statecraft until recently. Now they occupy a pride of place. "Democracy," Thomas Franck wrote in 1992, "is on the way to becoming a global entitlement, one that increasingly will be promoted and protected by collective international processes."[20] The emerging law, Franck argued, "requires democracy to validate governance."[21]

The evidence supporting Franck's claim was impressive in 1992 and has become even stronger. In 1994, for example, the UN Security Council authorized a military intervention in Haiti for the express purpose of restoring "the legitimately elected President," who had been deposed in a coup.[22] These and other developments signal an unprecedented commitment by states to principles of democracy.

In the remainder of this essay, I explore the implications of that commitment for separatist movements. First, it might be helpful to highlight two possibilities latent in the preceding account of international law and state practice. One builds upon the plebiscite principle applied by statesmen at the Paris Peace Conference. The future status of several disputed territories, it will be recalled, was put to a vote of the territories' inhabitants. This conception of self-determination naturally raises vexing issues, which I want to set aside for now. Here I simply wish to note that diplomatic practice has at times affirmed the view that contested territorial claims should be resolved through a particular type of democratic process, balloting.

The second possibility latent in established legal doctrine is that a general right to democratic governance carries with it the right of a national subgroup to secede if this is the only means available to secure its members' right to self-government. In this view, secession is not a general entitlement for any particular type of collectivity but rather an extraordinary exception to the universal right of self-government. The latter right is conceived in terms that contemplate full realization *within* established states and not through withdrawal *from* them—except, that is, as a last-resort remedy.

In sum, then, international law has long disfavored separatist claims. But alongside this general disapproval, international instruments and other relevant sources have long reserved a possible exception: implicit in international law's core commitment to basic human rights and democratic principles is recognition of a last-resort, remedial right for a subnational group to secede when these rights are denied its members.[23]

II. Democratic Principles and Separatist Claims

A. The Relevance of Democratic Principles in Assessing Separatist Claims

Apart from the two possibilities just noted, to which I shall return later, does the international community's newly invigorated commitment to democracy have implications for separatist claims?[24] For many political and legal theorists, the answer is unambiguously "no." Questions of boundary, it is often said, stand wholly outside theories of democratic government.[25]

But this seems plainly wrong. An appeal to common sense suggests why. Suppose that, instead of opposing Quebec separatists, the rest of Canada overwhelmingly voted in support of their claim. In this counterfactual, Canadians outside Quebec simply would not wish to be politically yoked to Quebec any longer. Suppose also that a vast majority of Quebec's citizens, including all of its significant minority populations, voted for secession. If, with Professor Franck, we believe that an emerging body of international law "requires democracy to validate governance," most of us would conclude that the mutual desire of Canada's citizens to divide should be honored—perhaps *must* be honored—in the absence of overriding considerations. We may not readily agree, however, on the reasons behind this intuition. For some, the key point may be that, like any issue that has a significant impact on our lives and that therefore seems an appropriate subject of self-government, questions of boundary ought to be subject to democratic determination if they become substantial subjects of dispute. For others, a deeper principle may be at stake—the consent of "the people" to be governed by the political authority that exercises sovereign power over them. As Jamin Raskin has written, "[T]he very heart of the democratic idea" is "that governmental legitimacy depends upon the affirmative consent of those who are governed."[26] If, then, every substantial sector of Canadian society supported the independence of Quebec, this core principle might seem to be violated with respect to *all* of them—Quebecers and other Canadians—if they were forced to remain co-citizens.

Although its implications may seem radical, the second view is hardly novel. For some eighteenth-century nationalists—the intellectual progenitors of the emerging democratic entitlement—it seemed obvious that the right to self-government implied the right to choose one's fellow citizens.[27] The point seemed equally plain to John Stuart Mill. Affirming that "the question of government ought to be decided by the governed," Mill continued: "One hardly knows what any division of the human race should be free to do, if not to determine with which of the various collective bodies of human beings they choose to associate themselves."[28]

Again, an appeal to common sense clarifies the claim. It has long been settled that alien states may not lawfully impose their rule upon nonconsenting peoples. Put differently, international law no longer abides colonization or forcible annexation. But if these forms of nonconsensual rule cannot be reconciled with principles inherent in the right of self-determination, surely those same principles are challenged by a state's continued assertion of sovereignty over a defined population that has unambiguously rejected its authority. For if a significant, territorially bounded, national subgroup unambiguously expresses its will to secede, the legitimacy of the state's sovereignty over the rebel population is placed in question.[29]

The bald claim that democratic principles are beside the point in these circumstances seems to rest on several false assumptions. One is that to recognize the relevance of democratic principles in assessing separatist claims is to open up the boundaries of established states to perennial challenge. Yet the assumption that citizens provide ongoing, if tacit, consent to the boundaries of their state underpins the daily practice of democracy.

A more substantial fallacy is to equate the view that democratic principles may be relevant in judging separatist claims with the manifestly untenable claim that the will of any and every group that challenges established boundaries is entitled to prevail over that of others. The claim that principles of self-government may have *implications* for the resolution of boundary disputes does not imply that democratic values *generally privilege* separatist claims.

Earlier, I tried to make the point that an emerging democratic entitlement may have significant implications for separatist claims by invoking the proverbial easy case, a hypothetical situation in which all affected citizens would support such a claim. But few cases are easy; most separatist claims are contested. In this respect, the situation involving the Serbian province of Kosovo is typical: although a majority of Kosovars favor independence, most citizens of Serbia, including the minority Serb population in Kosovo, oppose independence for Kosovo. Plainly, in situations where the will of the affected polity is divided, democratic theories do not neatly dispose of contested separatist claims.

Even so, theories of democratic government point to considerations that may be relevant to the legitimacy and resolution of contested separatist claims, in part because some resolutions may promote democratic values better than others. By way of illustration, let us briefly consider the implications of two strands of democratic theory, utilitarianism and republicanism.

A utilitarian justification for democracy claims that self-government is more likely than its alternatives to secure the interests of the greatest number of persons subject to governmental authority. For eighteenth-century utilitarians like Jeremy Bentham and James Mill, democracy was desirable not as an end in itself but as a means for maximizing the realization of individuals' desires through the aggregation of private preferences. But this justification may begin to fray if a polity is divided along fault lines that entail profound differences in political choices.[30]

Under some conditions the republican tradition may also offer support for separatist claims—or at least it may seem to at the proverbial first blush. More particularly, values central to republicanism might be furthered by political divorce resulting in two or more states whose citizens were significantly better able than citizens of the previous, unified state to consider the common good in their democratic deliberations. Core principles of republicanism include citizen participation in the deliberative process, made possible by civic virtue; the equality of political actors; and a commitment to the common interest or good.[31] Republicanism not only tolerates but assumes some measure of diversity within the self-governing polity. As Cass Sunstein has written, republicanism rests on "a belief in the possibility of mediating different approaches to politics, or different conceptions of the public good, through discussion and dialogue" and sees disagreement as a creative force that promotes political deliberation.[32] Through deliberation, initial preferences change and political outcomes promote a common good rather than the preferences of the majority alone. This requires not only "a commitment to political empathy, embodied in a requirement that political actors attempt to assume the position of those who disagree,"[33] but also the ability to empathize with citizens whose interests are different than one's own. That capacity may be in short supply, however, when disagreements among citizens are rooted in profoundly different group identities.[34]

Similar considerations led John Stuart Mill to conclude that "it is in general a necessary condition of free institutions that the boundaries of government should coincide in the main with those of nationalities."[35] Indeed, the capacity to empathize was central to Mill's conception of nations: "A portion of mankind may be said to constitute a Nationality," Mill wrote, "if they are united among themselves by common sympathies which do not exist between them and any others—which make them co-operate with each other more willingly than with other people, desire to be under the same government, and desire that it should be government by themselves or a portion of themselves exclusively."[36]

There is no reason to suppose, however, that republicanism *tends* to favor separatist claims. Like other visions of democracy, republican principles are consistent with arrangements designed to resolve fundamental disagreements among disparate groups of citizens without changing national borders. Democratic institutions can be—and often have been—designed to foster interethnic accommodation within the boundaries of established states through such institutional devices as proportional representation and power-sharing arrangements.

So far I have tried to show how democratic principles might be relevant in assessing separatist claims through examples that may favor those seeking separation. And so I want to make clear that, in my view, democratic principles would be thwarted by a rule of international law generally favoring independence for state-seeking groups.[37] To begin, the very possibility of secession may subvert democratic deliberation by diminishing incentives for opposing groups to seek accommodative solutions. When secession is believed possible, minorities can distort the outcome of political processes by threatening to secede if their views do not prevail.[38] And as Abraham Lincoln argued, if a secessionist movement opposed by a majority of a state's citizens ultimately prevailed, its triumph would vitiate the principle of majority rule.[39]

Further, to the extent that separatist claims are fueled by nationalist sentiment, their success may result in the creation of states prone toward authoritarian social arrangements. Lord Acton had this in mind when he warned: "In a small and homogeneous population there is hardly room . . . for inner groups of interests that set bounds to sovereign power."[40] In his view, the multiethnic state "provides against the servility which flourishes under the shadow of a single authority, by balancing interests, multiplying associations."[41] If, with Locke, we believe that the principle of self-government follows from the intrinsic and equal worth of people, the authoritarian arrangements associated with ethnonational states imperil core values that democracy is meant to secure.

B. Democratic Processes for Resolving
Contested Separatist Claims

My argument so far has aimed at supporting a modest claim—that states' newly robust commitment to democracy has significant implications for separatist claims, even if those implications cannot be captured in a simplistic formula prescribing a uniform approach to all state-seeking movements. To illustrate, I have noted various ways in which democratic values might appear to favor one or another potential outcome of disputes arising out of separatist claims. Thus far, however, I have not addressed the distinct question of how these largely substantive considerations might be brought to bear in practice. The answer is hardly self-evident; after all, there is no standing body entrusted with the task of assessing separatist claims that might usefully be guided by the considerations explored in the previous section. Nor does my previous analysis touch on the related question of whether principles of democracy have more direct implications for the processes used to resolve disputes surrounding separatist claims. It is to these questions that I now turn.

My point of departure is the claim that, under virtually any vision of democracy, achieving a mutually consensual outcome is the preferred way to resolve disputes over separatist claims. In a utilitarian calculus, for example, a mutually consensual outcome suggests that the political preferences of all major segments of a divided polity have been realized to a degree that is acceptable to each of them. A mutually accepted outcome also affirms the republican faith in citizens' capacity to resolve their differences through dialogue aimed at promoting the common good. Thus democratic values, as well as other central commitments of international law, are best served when separatist claims are resolved through negotiation rather than by unilateral fiat.

Democratic values are placed in special peril when secession is accomplished without any meaningful input, through balloting or otherwise, by citizens left behind by successful separatist movements. In these circumstances citizens would be significantly—perhaps profoundly—affected by a decision in which they had no opportunity to participate.[42] Indeed, secession has at times had a tragic impact on groups stranded in the rump state. The effect of Croatia's and Slovenia's secession from the Socialist Federal Republic of Yugoslavia (SFRY) exemplifies the point. Until the two former SFRY republics seceded in 1991, multiethnic Bosnia and Hercegovina had no interest in seeking independence. To the contrary, it had a strong interest in preserving Yugoslav unity.[43] With no ethnic group forming a majority in Bosnia, its Muslim and Croat citizens feared for their welfare in a diminished Yugoslavia that did not include Croatia, while most Bosnian Serbs wished to remain attached to Serbia. Apprehensions about Bosnia's fate in a rump Yugoslavia proved to be justified, as I elaborate shortly. On the other hand, if the consent of all substantial substate groups were required before secession was allowed, any group opposing a proposed change in borders could block secession, even when separation would be the most prudent or democratically legitimate outcome of a dispute.

A commitment to address disputes over separatist claims through negotiated agreement entails two corollary claims. The first is that the negotiating partners must accept the possibility of secession as an outcome of their negotiations. The second is that, in general, disputes over separatist claims should not be resolved *solely* by plebiscite. If a contested separatist claim were resolved by balloting alone, the losing side would be governed by a political authority that it had avowedly rejected.[44]

Balloting may, however, play a legitimate role in resolving disputes within a broader context of negotiations. For example, an overwhelming vote in support of secession by residents of a specific region might be an appropriate way to trigger negotiations with other citizens of the state. A referendum might also be a valid mechanism for resolving disputes over separatist claims if the contending parties agreed in the course of negotiations to hold a referendum and accept its results. In the second situation, the result of balloting would represent a mutually accepted outcome. For similar reasons, balloting leading to political divorce would prima facie enjoy democratic legitimacy if the national constitution explicitly provided for secession under the conditions followed in the balloting process, assuming the constitution was adopted in a democratically legitimate fashion.

The Supreme Court of Canada took essentially the approach I have just outlined in a 1998 advisory opinion on the question whether Quebec had a unilateral right to secede. The Court

concluded that a clear expression of the democratic will of Quebecers to secede, presumably through a referendum, would confer legitimacy on their quest—though not a right to secede unilaterally.[45]
In the Court's view, Canada's constitutional commitment to federalism and democracy had crucial implications for separatist claims:

> The federalism principle, in conjunction with the democratic prin-
> ciple, dictates that the clear repudiation of the existing constitu-
> tional order and the clear expression of the desire to pursue seces-
> sion by the population of a province would give rise to a reciprocal
> obligation on all parties to Confederation to negotiate constitutional
> changes to respond to that desire. . . . The corollary of a legitimate
> attempt by one participant in Confederation to seek an amendment
> to the Constitution is an obligation on all parties to come to the ne-
> gotiating table. The clear repudiation by the people of Quebec of
> the existing constitutional order would confer legitimacy on de-
> mands for secession, and place an obligation on the other provinces
> and the federal government to acknowledge and respect that ex-
> pression of democratic will by entering into negotiations and con-
> ducting them in accordance with the underlying principles already
> discussed.[46]

Invoking the same constitutional values that informed this conclusion, the Court held that Quebec "could not purport to invoke a
right of self-determination such as to dictate the terms of a proposed secession to the other parties."[47]

At the heart of the Court's analysis is its vision of democracy as a
deliberative process—a project in which profound differences
within the national polity are resolved not through a winner-take-
all, one-time vote but through democratic negotiations. This approach provides an appealing strategy for addressing one of the
central problems presented by contested separatist claims—the impossibility of satisfying one group's aspirations without thwarting
the will of others.[48]

Assuming that the conditions surrounding a separatist bid have
not deteriorated to the point where genuine dialogue is impossible, the success of negotiations may turn in part on the institutional
context in which they are pursued. In some countries, that context
is defined by relevant constitutional provisions. With respect to others, intergovernmental bodies may provide the principal frame-

work for seeking peaceful resolution of boundary disputes. While it is beyond the scope of this essay to explore questions of institutional design in depth, several overarching principles can be derived from the previous discussion.

Ideally, negotiations over disputes relating to separatist claims should be carried out within a framework that simultaneously (1) builds in strong incentives for mutual accommodation, (2) minimizes the risk of deadlock, and (3) presents significant hurdles to secession. The first two interrelated goals are implicit in the goal of fostering mutually accepted outcomes. A key challenge in this regard is to ensure that one side cannot readily preclude a mutually acceptable outcome through intransigence. At the same time, an effective institutional design for negotiations must be able to address situations in which it is not possible to achieve a mutually accepted result, particularly where the very survival of a group is gravely imperiled.

While the third goal—erecting hurdles to secession—serves the same interests as the first two, it also provides insurance against the specter of political divorce resulting, at least in substantial part, from fortuitous political forces. This sort of risk is exemplified in the dissolution of Czechoslovakia. The negotiations that culminated in the division of Czechoslovakia initially were aimed at working out the allocation of power between the central government and the two constituent republics, though the focus of negotiations evolved significantly.[49] The course of negotiations was profoundly shaped by the two republics' diverging approaches on economic policy[50] and by the personalities of their respective leaders.[51] Importantly, too, the negotiations played out within a constitutional framework that fostered deadlock.[52] There were no structures in place to push the parties past impasse. Although less important than other factors, time pressures may have further contributed to the Czech/Slovak disunion.[53]

In broader perspective, the process that led to political divorce was hardly a model of democratic deliberation. Public opinion was not consulted through referendum. Opinion polls showed, however, that a majority of citizens in both the Czech and Slovak Republics wanted to preserve their state. Even after the division became final, polls showed that a majority in both the Czech Republic and Slovakia supported a unitary state.[54]

III. DEMOCRATIC PRINCIPLES
AND INTERNATIONAL MEDIATION

Both Canada and the former Czechoslovakia have addressed separatist challenges without the substantial involvement of third parties. At times, however, external actors have been called upon to
mediate disputed separatist claims. There can be little doubt that
international mediators will continue to play a significant role in attempting to resolve such disputes.[55] And so it is worth considering
whether insights derived from previous experiences, including
those of Canada, Czechoslovakia, and the former Yugoslavia, can
enhance the effectiveness of international responses to separatist
claims.

Among the most significant recent instances of such mediation
was the EC's attempt (later joined by the United Nations) to foster
a peaceful resolution of conflicts surrounding separatist claims in
the former Yugoslavia. Its efforts proved to be stunningly ineffec-
tual. But like any failure of this order, the European initiative merits consideration for the lessons it offers.

A. *The Badinter Commission*

The EC assumed the leading role in mediating territorial disputes
in the former Yugoslavia after the Republics of Slovenia and Croa-
tia declared their respective independence on June 25, 1991. On
August 27, 1991, the EC and its member states agreed to convene
both a Conference for Peace in Yugoslavia and an Arbitration
Commission operating within the framework of that conference.[56]
The latter, known as the Badinter Commission after its chairman,
Robert Badinter, was established to help ensure "a peaceful accommodation of the conflicting aspirations of the Yugoslav peoples."[57]
By year's end, the commission would play a central role in imple-
menting the EC's recognition policy for breakaway Yugoslav republics.

Of special interest here is the novel role that democratic principles played in the EC recognition process generally and in the work
of the Badinter Commission in particular. That process was established through two declarations adopted on December 16, 1991.

The first, "Guidelines on the Recognition of the New States in Eastern Europe and in the Soviet Union,"[58] established a common policy governing recognition by the EC and its member states of new states that might emerge from the former Soviet Union and Yugoslavia. A separate Declaration on Yugoslavia[59] added further preconditions for recognition with respect to the SFRY.

The EC policy represented a major innovation, establishing conditions for recognition of new states that went substantially beyond the traditional international legal criteria for statehood.[60] Broadly, candidates for recognition were defined as states that "have constituted themselves on a democratic basis, have accepted the appropriate international obligations and have committed themselves in good faith to a peaceful process and to negotiations."[61] As elaborated in the EC declarations, these criteria sought to ensure both that issues arising from the transitions in the former Soviet Union and Yugoslavia would be resolved through negotiations and that the states that emerged through peaceful processes would guarantee respect for the rule of law, democracy, and human rights, with special attention to the rights of minorities.

The Declaration on Yugoslavia established a process pursuant to which Yugoslav republics seeking independence had to request recognition by December 23, 1991. The Badinter Commission was to take a decision by January 15, 1992.[62] Under circumstances prevailing at that time, these requirements effectively forced Bosnia to seek independence and to hold what proved to be a provocative plebiscite. As noted earlier, Bosnia had no interest in seceding until Croatia and Slovenia withdrew from the former Yugoslavia. Once this happened, however, a majority of Bosnian citizens believed they would enjoy greater security in an independent Bosnian state than in a rump Yugoslavia.

By letter dated December 20, 1991, Bosnia requested EC recognition. In an opinion rendered on January 11, 1992,[63] the Badinter Commission noted that although Bosnian authorities had made the commitments required by the EC recognition policy, "the Serbian members of the [Bosnian] presidency did not associate themselves with those declarations and undertakings" and that Bosnian Serbs had taken a number of measures to dissociate themselves from the independent state whose recognition was sought.[64] The commission therefore concluded that "the will of the peoples of Bosnia-Hercegovina to constitute the [Socialist Republic of Bosnia-Hercegovina (SRBH)] as a sovereign and independent State cannot be held to have been fully established."[65]

The commission suggested, however, that its assessment "could be reviewed if appropriate guarantees were provided by the Republic applying for recognition, possibly by means of a referendum of all the citizens of the SRBH without distinction, carried out under international supervision."[66] Heeding this suggestion, Bosnia held a referendum on March 29 through April 1, 1992. Bosnian Serbs, who constituted 31 percent of the republic's population, boycotted the ballot. With a turnout of 63.4 percent, the vote in favor of independence exceeded 99 percent.[67]

Believing that recognition would help avert in Bosnia the kind of violence that had been triggered by Croatia's declaration of independence, the EC and United States issued a joint statement on March 10, 1992, expressing their willingness to recognize the Republic of Bosnia and Hercegovina. The EC issued a statement on April 6 indicating its intention to recognize Bosnia the following day, and on April 7 the United States issued a statement reflecting the (first) Bush administration's belief that Bosnia, Croatia, and Slovenia met "the requisite criteria for recognition."[68] Recognition by other countries quickly followed.

The results were disastrous. On April 6, 1992, in anticipation of EC recognition the next day, Bosnian Serb rebels attacked the Holiday Inn of Sarajevo, signaling the onset of the armed conflict that would ravage Bosnia for three and one-half years. Without a commitment to help defend Bosnia's borders militarily, Western recognition of Bosnia exacerbated rather than mitigated the risk of armed conflict.

In effect, the EC recognition process forced Bosnia to seek recognition under the gun. As noted, the declaration establishing that process required Yugoslav republics seeking recognition to apply within a week. The Badinter Commission precipitated another disastrous development when it suggested that Bosnia hold a referendum. The EC's ill-considered deployment of democratic processes was, proverbially, like pouring kerosene onto a fire. This is not to suggest that the EC process was the principal or even a primary cause of conflict in Bosnia. The question is whether a different strategy could have been more effective.

B. *Lessons of the Badinter Commission*

Key aspects of the EC's recognition policy, including opinions of the Badinter Commission, were deservedly controversial. It may therefore be tempting to dismiss this precedent as a manifest failure. But if the Badinter Commission was flawed,[69] the underlying model of an intergovernmental institution that can assist in resolving disputed territorial claims may serve a useful role.[70]

This is not to suggest, however, that states should create a new institution whose sole mandate is to mediate contested separatist claims. The notion of such a body would be anathema to most states confronting separatist challenges. States may be more inclined to utilize the services of an institution whose mandate is to help mediate ethnic tensions broadly defined[71] than to turn to a body established to address separatist claims as such. Also, a more broadly gauged approach would improve prospects for addressing the concerns of ethnic minorities within the framework of existing states rather than at a point when the logic of separation has become inexorable.[72]

Even so, more effective use should be made of processes in which issues relating to recognition (or its functional equivalent) *cannot* be sidestepped. Of particular relevance in this regard are processes relating to new membership in intergovernmental organizations (IOs). Some IOs, including the European Union (EU) and Council of Europe, already condition membership on applicant states' meeting basic standards relating to human rights and democracy.[73] The EU and its precursor, the EC, have at times effectively used the accession process to encourage applicant states to democratize and ensure minority rights.[74] But the EU has neither consistently used this leverage nor used it to maximum effect.[75]

Ideally, more rigorous enforcement of rights-related preconditions to membership in IOs would induce established states to improve their treatment of minorities while creating an expectation among secessionists that there would be a protracted period before their claims for recognition might even be considered.[76] This might be especially useful in volatile situations, producing a cool-ing-off period during which mediators could attempt to head off se-cession by securing effective assurances of minority rights. After all, grievances underlying separatist aspirations sometimes *can* be as-suaged through effective assurances of group autonomy and other minority rights.[77]

At the very least, intergovernmental institutions that include in their membership criteria conditions relating to democratic prin-ciples and human rights, such as the EU, should treat these criteria as seriously as other conditions of membership.[78] Insistence on such conditions is no guarantee that new member states will oper-ate in accordance with democratic principles. But a political com-munity that has already demonstrated respect for democratic val-ues and human rights is surely a better risk than one that has done no more than pledge to respect them.

If enforced wisely, this approach could make it possible to side-step the vexing questions latent in the notion of a remedial right to secede. In the view of one scholar, remedial secession is justified only when "it is clear that all attempts to achieve internal self-de-termination have failed or are destined to fail."[79] Yet this proposed test begs hard questions: How severe does a state's denial of partic-ipatory and other rights have to become before the victim group is entitled to secede? How long must the repression persist before it is "clear that all attempts to achieve internal self-determination" would be futile? Whether a government satisfies international stan-dards of political participation rarely lends itself to a straight up or down determination; forecasting the future of a nation's demo-cratic path is more perilous still.

CONCLUSION

Principles of self-government are scarcely the only considerations that should guide responses to separatist claims. But they have re-cently assumed unprecedented relevance. In some circumstances, they may weigh in favor of separatist claims. Still, international law's deepening devotion to democracy remains what it has long been— a commitment above all to full participatory rights within estab-lished states. Emerging norms recognizing a right to self-govern-ment lend support to separatist claims principally when those same norms have already been profoundly, irrevocably breached. And so it is trite but useful to remind ourselves that the most successful policy toward secessionist movements is one that dampens separatist aspirations—and that is implemented well before intrastate tensions reach the breaking point.

NOTES

1. The ranks of separatists have lately included northern Italians; Crimeans in the Ukraine; Tamils in Sri Lanka; Kashmiris in India; Abkhazians and South Ossetians in Georgia; Corsicans in France; Armenians in Nagorno-Karabakh; Hungarians in Slovakia; Tibetans; residents of Somaliland in Somalia; non-Muslims in southern Sudan; Basques in Spain; Taiwanese; residents of Irian Jaya, Aceh, and several other regions in Indonesia; Montenegrins and Albanian Kosovars in Yugoslavia; and Kurds in Turkey and Iraq. Closer to home, Quebec separatists continue to press their cause; so do secessionists in Hawaii. A 1992 study identified active movements seeking their own state or substantial autonomy in over sixty states. Timothy D. Sisk, *Power Sharing and International Mediation in Ethnic Conflict* (New York: Carnegie Corporation, 1996), 1.

2. For nearly half a century following World War II, Bangladesh stood alone as a state created by virtue of an armed separatist movement. Donald L. Horowitz, "Self-Determination: Politics, Philosophy, and Law," in *Ethnicity and Group Rights*, NOMOS XXXIX, ed. Ian Shapiro and Will Kymlicka (New York: New York University Press, 1997), 426.

3. See Timothy William Waters, "Indeterminate Claims: New Challenges to Self-Determination Doctrine in Yugoslavia," *SAIS Review Journal of International Affairs* 20 (Summer-Fall 2000): 113. For present purposes, the influence of legal principles on mediation efforts is more noteworthy than the fact that the breakup of Yugoslavia attracted international mediators. The violence surrounding the breakup of Yugoslavia made its dissolution first and foremost a matter of international security. Thus it is no surprise that a succession of intergovernmental organizations and states tried to secure a peaceful resolution of the conflict. Less predictable were the ways in which mediators addressed the dissolution of the former Yugoslavia through novel applications of international law.

4. Wilson proposed a draft provision that would commit the Contracting Powers to effect "such territorial readjustments, if any, as may in the future become necessary by reason of changes in present racial conditions and aspirations or present social and political relationships, pursuant to

the principle of self-determination." Woodrow Wilson, "Covenant (Wilson's First Draft)," in David Hunter Miller, *The Drafting of the Covenant*, vol. 2 (New York: G. P. Putnam's Sons, 1928), 12.

5. Representatives of the Aaland Islands, which were under the jurisdiction of Finland, had sought annexation to Sweden at the Versailles Peace Conference, invoking the "right of peoples to self-determination as enunciated by President Wilson." *Papers Relating to the Foreign Relations of the United States: The Paris Peace Conference 1919*, vol. 4 (Washington, D.C.: Government Printing Office, 1943), 172. The Aaland Islands had belonged to Sweden until 1809, when they were surrendered to Russia as a result of conquest. Finland, too, was incorporated into Russia in 1809, and the Aaland Islands were, in the words of a League of Nations Commission of Jurists, "undoubtedly part of Finland during the period of Russian rule." "Report of the International Committee of Jurists Entrusted by the Council of the League of Nations with the Task of Giving an Advisory Opinion upon the Legal Aspects of the Aaland Islands Question," *League of Nations Official Journal*, supp. 3 (1920): 9. With the outbreak of the Russian revolution, Finland declared its independence from Russia, and the population of the Aaland Islands expressed their desire to be separated from Russia and reattached to Sweden. See "Report of the International Committee," 7, 10. Finland took the position that the Aaland Islands had been incorporated in the state of Finland, which had attained independence in 1918. "Report of the International Committee," 10. While Sweden proposed that the islanders be allowed to determine their status through a plebiscite, Finland insisted that this would constitute interference in a matter that, under international law, was solely within its domestic jurisdiction. The League appointed a Commission of Jurists to examine whether the League was competent to consider this petition. A Commission of Rapporteurs was appointed to assess the merits of Sweden's petition.

6. In a widely cited portion of its report, the Commission of Jurists asserted that although the principle of self-determination of peoples played "an important part in modern political thought" and had been recognized in some international treaties, the latter "cannot be considered as sufficient to put it upon the same footing as a positive rule of the Law of Nations." "Report of the International Committee," 5. A report by the League-appointed Commission of Rapporteurs (see n. 5) agreed that the principle of free determination "is not, properly speaking, a rule of international law." *The Aaland Islands Question: Report Submitted to the Council of the League of Nations by the Commission of Rapporteurs*, League of Nations Doc. B7.21/68/106 (1921), 27.

7. *The Aaland Islands Question*, 28. The commission further suggested that it "should not have hesitated to consider" the solution of allowing the

Aaland Islands to separate from Finland and become part of Sweden if this were "the only means of preserving its Swedish language for Aaland" (29). The Commission of Jurists left open the possibility that "a manifest and continued abuse of sovereign power, to the detriment of a section of the population of a State, would, if such circumstances arose," bring an international dispute arising from the situation within the competence of the League. "Report of the International Committee," 5.

8. General Assembly Res. 2625, UN GAOR, 25th sess., supp. no. 28, 121, UN Doc. A/8018 (1970).

9. Ibid.

10. Ibid. The full sentence of this quotation is:

Nothing in the foregoing paragraphs shall be construed as authorizing or encouraging any action which would dismember or impair, totally or in part, the territorial integrity or political unity of sovereign and independent States conducting themselves in compliance with the principle of equal rights and self-determination of peoples as described above and thus possessed of a government representing the whole people belonging to the territory without distinction as to race, creed or colour.

11. Antonio Cassese, *Self-Determination of Peoples: A Legal Reappraisal* (New York: Cambridge University Press, 1995), 114.

12. *United Nations World Conference on Human Rights, Vienna Declaration and Programme of Action,* UN Doc. A/CONF.157/24 (part I), para. 2 (1993), 20–46; *Declaration on the Occasion of the Fiftieth Anniversary of the United Nations,* General Assembly Res. 50/6, para. 1 (1995), UN Doc. A/RES/50/6 (1995). The relevant text of the latter provides that UN member states will

[c]ontinue to reaffirm the right of self-determination of all peoples, taking into account the particular situation of peoples under colonial or other forms of alien domination or foreign occupation, and recognize the right of peoples to take legitimate action in accordance with the Charter of the United Nations to realize their inalienable right of self-determination. This shall not be construed as authorizing or encouraging any action that would dismember or impair, totally or in part, the territorial integrity or political unity of sovereign and independent States conducting themselves in compliance with the principle of equal rights and self-determination of peoples and thus possessed of a Government representing the whole people belonging to the territory without distinction of any kind.

13. *In the Matter of Section 53 of the Supreme Court Act (Reference re Secession of Quebec)*, 1998, 2 S.C.R. 217, para. 134.

14. See Gregory H. Fox, "Self-Determination in the Post-Cold War Era: A New Internal Focus?" *Michigan Journal of International Law* 16 (1995): 733; Thomas Franck, "The Emerging Right to Democratic Governance," *American Journal of International Law* 86 (1992): 46; Hurst Hannum, "Rethinking Self-Determination," *Virginia Journal of International Law* 34 (1993): 57–63.

15. International lawyers often use the term *external self-determination* to refer to the right of people inhabiting a defined territory that is subject to colonial rule or foreign occupation freely to determine their political status.

16. Dec. 16, 1966, 993 United Nations Treaty Series 171 (entered into force Mar. 23, 1976).

17. Dec. 16, 1966, 993 United Nations Treaty Series 3 (entered into force Jan. 3, 1976).

18. Of particular relevance in this regard is the third paragraph of Common Article 1, which provides: "The States Parties to the present Covenant, including those having responsibility for the administration of Non-Self-Governing and Trust Territories, shall promote the realization of the right of self-determination, and shall respect that right, in conformity with the provisions of the Charter of the United Nations."

19. On the basis of his review of the text and the *travaux préparatoires*, Judge Cassese concludes that Article 1(1) "requires that the people choose their legislators and political leaders free from any manipulation or undue influence from the *domestic* authorities themselves" (italics in original). Cassese, *Self-Determination of Peoples*, 53. He also writes: "As far as the internal self-determination of *peoples living in sovereign States* was concerned, the drafting history of Article 1 shows that self-determination was generally considered to afford a right to be free from an authoritarian regime" (59–60; italics in original).

20. Franck, "The Emerging Right," 46.

21. Ibid., 47.

22. Security Council Res. 940 (1994).

23. As I note later, the contours of this concept are ill defined.

24. My arguments in this section draw upon a previously published article. See Diane F. Orentlicher, "Separation Anxiety: International Responses to Ethno-Separatist Claims," *Yale Journal of International Law* 23 (1998): 44–60.

25. In the view of one writer, "Boundaries comprise a problem . . . that is insoluble within the framework of democratic theory." Frederick G. Whelan, "Prologue: Democratic Theory and the Boundary Problem," in

Liberal Democracy, NOMOS XXV, ed. J. Roland Pennock and John W. Chapman (New York: New York University Press, 1983), 16. Richard Briffault writes that "the concept of self-government says nothing about who is the 'self' that does the governing." Richard Briffault, "Voting Rights, Home Rule, and Metropolitan Governance: The Secession of Staten Island as a Case Study in the Dilemmas of Local Self-Determination," *Columbia Law Review* 92 (1992): 800. Robert Dahl takes a more nuanced approach. He seems to side with the views just cited when he observes that "we cannot solve the problem of the proper scope and domain of democratic units from within democratic theory." Robert A. Dahl, *Democracy and Its Critics* (New Haven, Conn.: Yale University Press, 1989), 207. But he adds that "it would be a mistake to conclude that nothing more can be said" (207). He goes on to develop criteria, rooted in democratic principles, for assessing claims as to the proper scope and domain of democratic units (207–9).

26. Jamin Raskin, "Legal Aliens, Local Citizens: The Historical, Constitutional and Theoretical Meanings of Alien Suffrage," *University of Pennsylvania Law Review* 141 (1993): 1444.

27. As Alfred Cobban explained, "The revolutionary theory that a people had the right to form its own constitution and choose its own government for itself easily passed into the claim that it had a right to decide whether to attach itself to one state or another, or constitute an independent state by itself. The effect of revolutionary ideology was to transfer the initiative in state-making from the government to the people." Alfred Cobban, *The Nation State and National Self Determination,* rev. ed. (New York: Thomas Y. Crowell, 1969), 41.

28. John Stuart Mill, "Considerations on Representative Government" (1861), in *Utilitarianism, On Liberty, Considerations on Representative Government* (London: Everyman, 1993), 392.

29. See Allen Buchanan, *Secession: The Morality of Political Divorce from Fort Sumter to Lithuania and Quebec* (Boulder, Colo.: Westview Press, 1991), 4 ("Surely a political philosophy that places a preeminent value on liberty and self-determination . . . and holds that legitimate political authority in some sense rests on the consent of the governed must either acknowledge a right to secede or supply weighty arguments to show why a presumption in favor of such a right is rebutted").

30. Robert Dahl makes much the same point—though he does not frame it in terms of a utilitarian justification—when he suggests that, all other things being equal, "one set of boundaries is better than another to the extent that it permits more persons to do what they want to do." Dahl, *Democracy and Its Critics,* 208. In Dahl's view, this approach "reasserts the value of personal freedom" (208).

31. My discussion here draws upon and reflects contemporary liberal versions of republicanism rather than more conservative traditional renderings.

32. Cass R. Sunstein, "Beyond the Republican Revival," *Yale Law Journal* 97 (1998): 1554 (footnote omitted).

33. Ibid., 1555 (footnote omitted).

34. A similar argument could be framed in terms of deliberative democracy, a close cousin of contemporary versions of civic republicanism. A core claim of deliberative democracy is that "when citizens or their representatives disagree morally, they should continue to reason together to reach mutually acceptable decisions." Amy Gutmann and Dennis Thompson, *Democracy and Disagreement* (Cambridge, Mass.: Harvard University Press, 1996), 1. In this conception of democracy, citizens deliberate by appealing to "reasons or principles that can be shared by fellow citizens" who share a basic commitment to "finding fair terms for social cooperation" (55). When these conditions do not exist, citizens may be unable to resolve their differences through persuasion.

35. Mill, "Considerations on Representative Government," 394.

36. Ibid., 391.

37. As noted earlier, other values central to international law and politics would also be imperiled by such a rule. In light of the limited focus of this essay, my discussion here focuses on concerns relating to democratic principles.

38. This risk can be mitigated somewhat by constitutional provisions that set a high bar for secession.

39. See Abraham Lincoln, "First Inaugural Address" (Mar. 4, 1861), in *A Compilation of the Messages and Papers of the Presidents 1789–1897*, vol. 6, ed. James D. Richardson (n.p.: U.S. Congress, 1898), 9.

40. Lord Acton, "Nationality," in *Essays on Freedom and Power* (1862; reprint, New York: Meridian, 1972), 165.

41. Ibid. A potential strategy for mitigating these risks is to insist that territorially bounded communities seeking independence demonstrate their commitment to human rights, including minority rights, as a precondition to their admission as members in intergovernmental organizations. See Section III.B.

42. Here I am relying on a variation of what Robert Dahl calls the Principle of Affected Interests: "Everyone who is affected by the decisions of a government should have the right to participate in that government." Robert A. Dahl, *After the Revolution?* (New Haven, Conn.: Yale University Press, 1970), 64. In the version on which I rely, the principle would be stated this way: "Everyone who is significantly affected by a decision should have the right to participate in making it." This is not to say, however, that

everyone affected by a decision is entitled to an equal vote. Elsewhere I have argued that the relative weight of different citizens' interests should be taken into account when boundary disputes are resolved. Orentlicher, "Separation Anxiety," 59–60.

43. As one writer observed, Bosnia cannot "belong to either Croatia or Serbia—it can act as a bridge between the two but its relationship with both republics must be equal." Misha Glenny, *The Fall of Yugoslavia: The Third Balkan War,* 3d ed.(New York: Penguin Books, 1996), 144.

44. My discussion here focuses on claims of groups wishing to secede from a lawfully established political authority and is not fully relevant to circumstances in which a territory is unambiguously entitled to exercise the right of external self-determination under international law. In the latter context, citizens of the imperial or invading power do not have a legitimate right to determine the political status of the territory in question.

45. *In the Matter of Section 53 of the Supreme Court Act (Reference re Secession of Quebec),* 1998, 2 S.C.R. 217.

46. Ibid., para. 88.

47. Ibid., para. 91.

48. This kind of zero-sum game not only is suboptimal in terms of democratic values but also has profound security implications. In the tense environment surrounding contested separatist claims, winner-take-all plebiscites are almost sure to inflame nationalist passions. Worse, they may provoke sweeping violence—as happened when the United Nations administered a plebiscite to determine the status of East Timor in 1999.

49. The set of negotiations that culminated in political rupture was instituted following elections in 1992 with the limited object of forming a federal government and drafting its program for approval by competent federal institutions. See Eric Stein, *Czecho/Slovakia: Ethnic Conflict, Constitutional Fissure, Negotiated Breakup* (Ann Arbor: University of Michigan Press, 1997), 197, 221.

50. Václav Klaus, the Czech prime minister, was intent on adopting a market structure. His Slovak counterpart, Vladimír Mečiar, and much of the Slovak public were reluctant to abandon the Soviet-style economy.

51. It is widely believed that Mečiar pressed a number of claims that he knew the Czech side would not accept as a bargaining ploy rather than as part of a strategy aimed at securing Slovak independence. In the view of informed observers, Mečiar did not actually want the negotiations to lead to the division of Czechoslovakia. See Stein, *Czecho/Slovakia,* 222. Once Klaus concluded that accepting the Slovak position would endanger his economic policy objectives, "he refused 'to play' further" (223).

52. Relevant constitutional provisions are described in Lloyd Cutler and Herman Schwartz, "Constitutional Reform in Czechoslovakia: E Duobus Unum?" *University of Chicago Law Review* 58 (1991): 519.

53. See Stein, *Czecho/Slovakia*, 326.

54. See "Czech Republic: Most Czechs Think Partition Was Unnecessary," Reuter News Service–CIS and Eastern Europe, Feb. 24, 1993; and "Slovakia: Most Slovaks Want to Rejoin Czechs," Reuter News Service–CIS and Eastern Europe, June 3, 1994.

55. I am using the term *international mediators* broadly to include mediators representing a state other than the one in which subunits have asserted separatist claims, as well as mediators representing an intergovernmental organization.

56. In August 1992, the EC Peace Conference on Yugoslavia was replaced by the joint UN-EC International Conference on the Former Yugoslavia. See Michla Pomerance, "The Badinter Commission: The Use and Misuse of the International Court of Justice's Jurisprudence," *Michigan Journal of International Law* 20 (1998): 35 n. 11.

57. *Extraordinary Meeting of the Foreign Ministers (Brussels, August 27, 1991), EPC Declaration on Yugoslavia.* The declaration of August 27, 1991, urged the parties to the conflict in Croatia to accept both a peace conference and the establishment of "an arbitration procedure" and provided that "[t]he relevant authorities will submit their differences to an Arbitration Commission." The commission's terms of reference were supplemented in September 1991, and the body was reconstituted under new terms of reference and with a partially new composition in January 1993. See Pomerance, "The Badinter Commission," 32 n. 3, 35, 35 n. 11.

58. European Community, "Guidelines on the Recognition of New States in Eastern Europe and in the Soviet Union," *I.L.M.* 31 (1992): 1486–87.

59. "Declaration on Yugoslavia," *I.L.M.* 31 (1992): 1485.

60. In fact, the policy entailed the application of recognition criteria that effectively supplanted the traditional criteria for statehood. Notably, recognition of both Bosnia and Hercegovina and Croatia did not depend upon their meeting all of the traditional criteria for establishing statehood, such as having a government in effective control of the country's territory. See Roland Rich, "Recognition of States: The Collapse of Yugoslavia and the Soviet Union," *European Journal of International Law* 4 (1993): 43.

61. European Community, "Guidelines on the Recognition of New States," 1487.

62. Evidently the key reason underlying this rapid timetable was that the EC hoped to maintain the facade of a common policy in the face of

Germany's announced intention to recognize Croatia and Slovenia unilaterally if the EC did not recognize them in the near future. See Laura Silber and Allan Little, *Yugoslavia: Death of a Nation,* rev. ed. (New York: TV Books, 1997), 199–200.

63. Conference on Yugoslavia, Arbitration Commission Opinion no. 4, *I.L.M.* 31 (Jan. 11, 1992): 1501.

64. Ibid., 1502–3, para. 3. These measures culminated in the proclamation by an "Assembly of the Serbian people of Bosnia-Hercegovina" of the independence of a "Serbian Republic of Bosnia-Hercegovina" on January 9, 1992 (1502–3, para. 3).

65. Ibid., 1503, para. 4.

66. Ibid.

67. See Rich, "Recognition of States," 49–50.

68. Ibid., quoting White House press release, Washington, Apr. 7, 1992.

69. While criticism has focused on the decisions taken by the Badinter Commission, some critics have also faulted the body for adopting decisions that were treated as having authority "bordering on binding" even though its competence to render binding decisions had been established neither by the consent of the relevant parties nor through the enforcement powers of the UN Security Council. See, for example, Pomerance, "The Badinter Commission," 48.

70. As Thomas Franck has observed, the notable "failure of peaceful conflict resolution" in recent years may be due in part "to the inadequacy of procedures, institutions and principles equal to the contemporary zeitgeist." Thomas M. Franck, "Friedmann Award Address," *Columbia Journal of Transnational Law* 38 (1999): 5.

71. One such mechanism already in existence is the Office of the High Commissioner on National Minorities of the Organisation for Security and Co-operation in Europe. The High Commissioner attempts to mediate disputes involving national minorities with the aim of averting conflict. See "Mandate of the CSCE High Commissioner on National Minorities," reprinted in Arie Bloed, ed., *The Conference on Security and Co-operation in Europe: Analysis and Basic Documents, 1972–1993* (Dordrecht, the Netherlands: Kluwer Academic Publishers, 1993), 715.

72. A key factor behind the EC's failure to achieve a peaceful resolution of the Yugoslav crisis was that the EC process was activated well beyond the point where mediation could have been most effective. Knowledgeable observers believe that as late as December 1990 it might have been possible to broker a new constitutional arrangement that would have accommodated the respective concerns of Slovenian, Croatian, and Serb nationalists within Yugoslavia, thereby averting its violent dismemberment. Yet the EC did not adopt its common recognition policy until six months after armed

conflict had erupted in Slovenia and seven months after one of the worst massacres in Croatia occurred.

73. In 1993 the European Council adopted the following political criteria for EU accession by central and eastern European countries: "Membership requires that the candidate country has achieved stability of institutions guaranteeing democracy, the rule of law, human rights and respect for and protection of minorities." *European Council in Copenhagen, 21–22 June 1993: Conclusions of the Presidency,* SN 180/93, 12.

74. The prospect of EC membership was a positive inducement to political liberalization in Greece, Portugal, and Spain. See Laurence Whitehead, "International Aspects of Democratization," in *Transitions from Authoritarian Rule: Comparative Perspectives,* ed. Guillermo O'Donnell, Philippe C. Schmitter, and Laurence Whitehead (Baltimore: Johns Hopkins University Press, 1986), 22–23. More recently, both the EU and the North Atlantic Treaty Organization (NATO) warned Slovakia that its accession to these two organizations would be imperiled if Vladimir Mečiar, the ultranationalist former prime minister, were elected to Parliament in elections slated for September 2002. See Peter S. Green, "Slovak Voters May Offer Ousted Leader a 4th Chance," *New York Times,* Mar. 10, 2002. Mečiar's party did not receive enough votes to participate in the new government, an outcome that may have been influenced by EU and NATO policy. See Robert G. Kaiser, "Moderate Reformers Win Slovak Election; U.S. Had Warned Loss Could Sink Bid to Join NATO, EU," *Washington Post,* Sept. 23, 2002. Recent developments also highlight more direct implications of the EU accession process for separatist claims. The EU foreign policy chief, Javier Solana, used the prospect of EU membership to broker an accord between Serbia and Montenegro that would avert Montenegro's secession from the rump Yugoslavia. See Daniel Williams, "Yugoslavia Nears End, at Least in Name; After a Decade of Disintegration, Last Two Republics Agree to Form New Entity," *New York Times,* Mar. 15, 2002; Jonathan Steele, "Montenegro to Drop Aim of Independence," *Guardian (London),* Feb. 19, 2002.

75. In recognition of this, in 2000 the Open Society Institute established an EU Accession Monitoring Program to promote effective use of the accession process to foster compliance with the EU's political criteria by candidate countries.

76. These goals should not, of course, be pursued at the expense of a population's immediate security. If recognition is withheld from a vulnerable entity such as Kosovo for a protracted period, there is heightened responsibility to ensure its security in the interim.

77. Finland's assurance of generous minority rights protections has apparently gone a long way toward quelling the Aaland Islanders' desire to separate from Finland and rejoin Sweden.

78. The EC was widely faulted for recognizing Croatian independence despite the fact that the Badinter Commission expressed reservations about whether Croatia met EC recognition conditions relating to respect for minority rights. See Orentlicher, "Separation Anxiety," 67.

79. Cassese, *Self-Determination of Peoples,* 120.

2

A RIGHT TO SECEDE?

DONALD L. HOROWITZ

How should international law treat the claims of separatists who assert a right to secede from the territorial state in which they find themselves? Is there an international-law right to secede? Should there be? Increasingly, some international lawyers seem to think so.

The newly asserted right to secede is to be held by ethnic groups and is derived from a reinterpretation of the principle of the self-determination of nations. Theorists display varying degrees of enthusiasm in their advocacy of such a right, but many of them, whether they would permit secession generously or only reluctantly after certain conditions have been fulfilled, see secession as an answer to problems of ethnic conflict and violence. The position I shall take here is that secession is almost never an answer to such problems and that it is likely to make them worse. The proposals, in short, are not informed by any serious understanding of patterns of ethnic conflict or ethnic-group political behavior, and they are not well grounded in principles of international law.

Secession, I shall argue, does not create the homogeneous successor states its proponents often assume will be created. Nor does secession reduce conflict, violence, or minority oppression once successor states are established. Guarantees of minority protection in secessionist regions are likely to be illusory; indeed, many secessionist movements have as one of their aims the expulsion or subordination of minorities in the secessionist regions. The very existence of a right to secede, moreover, is likely to dampen efforts at coexistence in the undivided state, including the adoption of federalism or regional autonomy, which might alleviate some of the grievances of putatively secessionist minorities. Since most secessionist movements will be resisted by central governments and most secessionists receive insufficient foreign military assistance to succeed, propounding a right to secede, without the means to succeed, is likely to increase ultimately fruitless secessionist warfare, at the expense of internal efforts at political accommodation and at the cost of increased human suffering. Efforts to improve the condition of minorities ought to be directed at devising institutions to increase their satisfaction in existing states, rather than encouraging them to think in terms of exit options. In those rare cases in which separation of antagonists is, at the end of the day, the best course, partition can be accomplished reluctantly, as a matter of prudence, without recognizing a right to secede. But neither partition nor secession should be viewed as a generally desirable solution to the problems of ethnic conflict.

SECESSION AND SELF-DETERMINATION: A BRIEF SKETCH

The so-called right to secede has its origins in the principle of national self-determination. As is well known, that principle formed an integral part of Woodrow Wilson's plans for post–World War I Europe. The establishment of, for example, Rumania as a state for Rumanians certainly exemplified application of the self-determination principle, but even apart from the presence of minorities in such new states, the Wilsonian policy fell far short of according national or ethnic groups their own states. Indeed, Wilson may well have envisioned autonomy rather than independence, and he did not necessarily think in terms of an ethnic fulfillment for the right to self-determination. Yugoslavia and Czechoslovakia, for example, were multinational states, and Wilson's proposal that a right of self-determination be incorporated in the Covenant of the League of Nations was rejected. By the time of the Atlantic Charter in 1941, self-determination was to be limited to peoples living under foreign domination.[1] Decolonization was thus an exercise of self-determination, and it was soon made clear by the United Nations (in 1960) and the Organization of African Unity (in 1964), among others,

that secessionist threats to the territorial integrity of states would
not be regarded as further exercises of self-determination.

With the exception of decolonization and the extraordinary
emergence of Bangladesh, territorial boundaries proved to be re-
markably stable for a half century: from just after World War II to
the end of the Cold War.[2] And then a concatenation of events—the
reunification of Germany, the dissolution of the Soviet Union (and
various subsecessions in Georgia, Moldova, and Azerbaijan), Yugoslavia, and Czechoslovakia, the secession of Eritrea from
Ethiopia and of the former Somaliland from Somalia, and finally
the de facto detachment of Kosovo from Serbia—combined in the
course of a decade to render boundaries much less stable and to
encourage territorially separate groups to consider the possibility
of secession.

As all this was happening, international lawyers and philosophers had been rethinking the meaning of self-determination and
proceeding to unsettle the former understandings that had discouraged secession and international support for it. One practical
exercise along these lines was the ill-considered decision of the
Badinter Commission that, asked to pronounce on the validity of
secessions from Yugoslavia, declared Yugoslavia to be a federation
in process of dissolution—a state of affairs that entitled its constituent republics to secede intact, taking with them their minority
areas.[3] After this decision, many fewer states than should consider
adopting a federal form of government will do so. Still, it should be
noted that the Badinter Commission declared no general right of
self-determination or secession.

Most of the work of international lawyers has been theoretical. It
proceeds along several lines.

For some, self-determination forms an integral part of the right
of people to choose their own political regime and to be free of authoritarian oppression. (For Wilson, too, self-determination was
connected to ideas of popular sovereignty.) It is a building block of
what has emerged in the thinking of a few international lawyers as
a right to live under a democratic regime.[4] That such a legal right
is at best aspirational might be suggested by the fact that more than
half of all regimes in the world are still not democratic, but the
early aftermath of the Cold War was a time of great optimism.

A more cautious version of the right to secede is espoused by those who view secession principally as a "remedial right,"[5] a last-ditch response to discrimination or oppression by a central government.[6] If interethnic accommodation fails and one portion of a population is "unalterably hostile" to a group of its fellow citizens, then, it is said, there may be a right of an oppressed minority to leave the state.

Despite important differences in scope and reasoning among these justifications for secession, there is a substratum of assumptions in all of them. Secession, it is assumed, can produce homogeneous successor states. In those cases in which heterogeneity remains, it is asserted, minority rights can nevertheless be guaranteed. Like the Badinter Commission, most writers advocating a right to secede make no provision for further secessions, except, of course, insofar as infinite regress of secessionist rights may be implied in their formulations. Secession will also, it is assumed, result in a diminution of conflict that produced the secessionist movement. Rarely are these assumptions discussed or even rendered explicit, but they are essential to the analysis.

"If you can think about something which is attached to something else without thinking about what it is attached to, then you have what is called a legal mind."[7] So pronounced the late constitutional lawyer Thomas Reed Powell three-quarters of a century ago. Most theorists of a right to secession have, in this caricatured sense, legal minds. They have generally not concerned themselves with the ethnic politics that produces secessionist claims and that will be affected by new rights to secede. It is no accident that most people who do study ethnic politics are decidedly less enthusiastic about secession than are the few international lawyers who are the main proponents of a right to secede.

Heterogeneity Before, Heterogeneity After

There are always ethnic minorities in secessionist regions. There were Efik and Ijaw, among others, in Biafra; there are Hindus in Kashmir, Muslims in Tamil areas of Sri Lanka, Javanese in Aceh and Irian Jaya, Serbs and Roma in Kosovo; and there are minorities in all the rump states as well. As a matter of fact, it is often the desire of regional majorities to deal with minorities—and not to deal with them in a democratic way—that motivates or contributes to the secessionist movement in the first instance. Proponents of rights to secession assure us that minority rights must be guaranteed in secessionist states and that secession should be less favored if minority rights are unlikely to be respected,[8] but the verbal facility of this formulation masks the difficulty of achieving any such results. If, after all, conditions on the exercise of an international-law right to secede can be enforced, why not enforce those conditions in the undivided state so as to forestall the need to secede? International law has been notoriously ineffective in insuring long-standing, internationally recognized minority rights, and proponents of secession have no new ideas to offer on this matter. If the failure to respect minority rights in the undivided state induced a regional group to consider secession, why should anyone assume that the situation will be different when that group, a minority in the undivided state, constitutes a majority in the secessionist state? If anything, the treatment of minorities in smaller states is less visible to outsiders.

The more circumscribed the asserted right to secede, ironically enough, the more dangerous conditions may become for minorities in the secessionist region. By the time it is concluded that the majority in the undivided state is unalterably hostile to minority interests, thus in some formulations permitting the minority to secede, that group may have accumulated so many grudges that, in their turn, minorities in the secessionist region may be particularly vulnerable to the expression of violent hostility or the settlement of old scores. There are many examples: the fate of Serbs and Roma in Kosovo, of Biharis in Bangladesh, of Sikhs and Hindus in Pakistan at the time of partition, of Muslims in India at the same time, and of Georgians in Abkhazia, to name just a few. If the problem of minorities is that they do not enjoy "meaningful political participation"[9] in the undivided state, there is no reason to think that minorities will enjoy it in the secessionist state either. Secession merely proliferates the arenas in which the problem of intergroup political accommodation must be faced—and often more starkly. Contrast Yugoslavia, with six or seven groups and the complex alignments they created, making it difficult for any one group to dominate, with the more dangerous situation in Bosnia, in which three groups confront each other. Secession can hardly be said to solve the problem of intergroup accommodation, except, of course, insofar as it enables the former minority, now a new majority, to cleanse the secessionist state of its minorities—which it could not do previously—and induces the rump state to do the same with members of the secessionist group who find themselves left on the wrong side of a new international boundary.

THE EFFECT OF NEW INTERNATIONAL BOUNDARIES

Recognition of a right to secede is thus likely to be, not the end of an old bitterness, but the beginning of new bitterness. It is, of course, easy to question whether a slavish devotion to territorial integrity is still appropriate. There has been a great deal of loose talk about the allegedly artificial character of many international boundaries and the part played by colonial convenience in settling them. In fact, even in Africa, where this charge is most frequently encountered, boundaries were not settled as disrespectfully of ethnic patterns as is frequently asserted.[10] In any event, patterns of settlement are such that virtually any boundaries would have a large element of arbitrariness to them. Secession would not be a way of rectifying boundaries, because there are no truly natural land boundaries.

If it does not solve boundary problems, secession does do something else. A secession or partition converts a domestic ethnic dispute into a more dangerous international one. And since states are able to procure arms with few of the restraints that periodically bedevil insurgents, the international dispute often involves escalating weapons and the prospect of international warfare. Consider the nuclear armaments possessed by India and Pakistan and the recurrent warfare between those states.

One reason for the greater danger that often follows secession is the activation of irredentist claims. For reasons explicated elsewhere,[11] the serious pursuit of irredentas—movements to retrieve kindred people and their territory across international boundaries—has been relatively rare in the post–World War II world. But successful secession or partition is likely to change this benign state of affairs. Either the rump state or the secessionist state will desire to retrieve minorities stranded on the wrong side of the border.

There are examples readily at hand: Kashmir, Serb claims in Bosnia and in the Krajina region of Croatia, warfare between Ethiopia and Eritrea. And when irredentism gets going, it usually involves ethnic cleansing, so as to eliminate troublesome minorities in the region to be retrieved. A recent quantitative study of the effects of partition finds that partition does not prevent further warfare between ethnic antagonists and that it has only a negligible (and easily reversed) positive effect on low-grade violence short of war.[12]

The recurrent temptation to create a multitude of homogeneous ministates, even if it could be realized, might well increase the sum total of warfare rather than reduce it. The right direction for international boundaries is upward, not downward, so that states are so heterogeneous that no one group can plausibly dominate others.[13] Although this degree of benign ethnic complexity is exceedingly difficult to achieve, it is still true that India, with its many groups, is a better model than Kosovo or Rwanda, with just two or three.

THE EFFECT OF RIGHTS TO SECESSION ON EFFORTS AT INTERNAL ACCOMMODATION

Articulating a right to secede will undermine attempts to achieve interethnic accommodation within states. As things now stand, the principal reason that states are reluctant to devolve power to territorially concentrated minorities, by means of either regional autonomy or federalism, is their fear that it will lead to secession. That fear is usually unfounded unless the conflict has already dragged on for a long time and the central government has been utterly ungenerous. Nevertheless, central governments are risk averse about devolution. The best way to dry up devolution as a tool of interethnic accommodation—and a promising tool it is—is to establish a right, recognized in international law, for territorially concentrated minorities to secede. If there is a recognized right to secede, the first stirrings of territorially based ethnic discontent will be likely to be met with repression. The possibility that federalism or regional autonomy can lawfully ripen into secession will make any such experiment too costly to entertain. It has been difficult to persuade central decision makers in Indonesia and Sri Lanka to devolve power to regions. A right to secession would easily dissuade them.

One reason central governments are so reluctant to countenance the possibility of secession, even for troublesome regions
that some central decision makers might wish to be free of, is that
the secession of one region upsets ethnic balances and forces
groups in other regions to think afresh about whether they wish to
remain in the truncated state with its new ethnic balances. This was
clearly visible in Yugoslavia after the Slovene and Croat decisions to
secede, when others had to decide in turn whether the relative expansion in Serb power in the rump state was in their interest.
Yoruba narrowly decided to stay in Nigeria, despite the relative increase in Hausa power when Ibo decided to leave the state in 1967,
and the departure of East Bengal (Bangladesh) from Pakistan
destabilized relations among the groups that remained in the rump
state. Quite often the fears of central authorities about secession
are derided as unsubstantiated apprehensions of domino effects.
But domino effects are usually conceived as action based merely on
a successful example in another location. That is not what these
central government fears refer to. What is involved in the first secession is action that affects directly, rather than just by example,
the relative positions of other groups remaining in the state.

The creation of a right to secede could not be more untimely.
More and more states have been designing internal political
arrangements, including devolution, to reduce the incidence of
ethnic conflict. That is where the emphasis needs to be, not on
making exit strategies more plausible. More about this shortly.

A right to secede effectively advantages militant members of
ethnic groups at the expense of conciliators. Since most central
governments will not recognize the right to secede, those who wish
to pursue such a course will need to resort to arms. Those who are
willing to resort to arms are by no means simply latter-day versions
of the politicians of their own group whom they seek to displace.
Contrast Hashim Thaci of the Kosovo Liberation Army with the
Kosovar political leader Ibrahim Rugova; Prabhakaran of the Tamil
Tigers with Amirthalingham of the Tamil United Liberation Front,
whom he had assassinated; or the Southern People's Liberation
Army in the Sudan with the old Liberal Party that preceded it. Violence disproportionately attracts people with an interest in aggression. The people willing to take up arms for secession are those who
are willing to be brutal with their ethnic enemies and with their

own rivals as well. As their advantage grows, new bouts of ethnic cleansing can be expected.

In some formulations, secession is said to be an exceptional right that arises if it "is the only means" available to a subnational group "to secure its members' right to self-government."[14] But the facts do not support the assumption that secession is ever "the only means." Are the Kurds in Iraq secessionist or autonomist? They have gone back and forth. Are Philippine Muslims? They, too, have gone back and forth. Ibo tried unsuccessfully to secede and then reintegrated into Nigerian politics. In such cases, it looks to outsiders at any given moment as if secession is "the only way" minorities can participate in determining their own future, but there is more fluidity to ethnic politics than those who write about populations that are unalterably hostile to each other have sensed.

Moreover, the seemingly moderate position of some proponents of a right to secession that secession is justified only if others are unalterably opposed or minorities have been victimized is not likely to work out moderately in practice, for it is an incentive to ethnic polarization. If independence can only be won legitimately after matters have been carried to extremes, then, by all means, there are people willing to carry them to extremes. In the 1980s and early 1990s, Sikh separatists in the Indian Punjab were willing to attack Hindus in order to precipitate attacks on Sikhs elsewhere in India, so as to convince Sikhs that secession was the only solution. There is no shortage of methods to satisfy tough standards of victimization or oppression. A right to secede could indeed contribute to the sense that secession is the only way.

There may be times when it is felt best to part peoples. The British believed such a time had come in India in 1947, and in the same year the United Nations believed such a time had come in Palestine. When it is prudent, parting can be done by consent, as in the former Soviet Union and in Czechoslovakia, or occasionally by international action. To do this requires the creation of no rights.

Consider the pernicious effect on the balance of intragroup opinion of a right to secede in a concrete case: Sri Lanka. Will the Sri Lankan Tamils return as readily as they would otherwise to a thoroughly reconstructed but undivided Sri Lanka if they discover that the secession to which they turned so reluctantly was merely an exercise of their rights under international law? It is always hard for antagonistic groups to accommodate each other in a single state. A right to secede will make it harder.

ORENTLICHER ON THE RIGHT TO SECEDE: AN ILLUSORY QUEST

A few international lawyers may have been a bit reckless in their willingness to countenance a right to secede, but international law has certainly not followed them. The support in international law for even a limited right to secede is very thin, indeed. Diane Orentlicher's contribution to this volume makes that abundantly clear. Orentlicher's essay begins with a treatment of self-determination and secession and then proceeds to deal with the relevance of democratic principles to an asserted right to secede. I shall consider her main arguments in that order, and I shall not comment at all on those parts of her chapter that do not bear on assertions about an international-law right to secede.

Orentlicher begins by pointing out that "international law and state practice remain deeply skeptical of separatist movements. . . ."[15] True enough. Then, pages later, she adds that, to the disfavor accorded to secessionists by international law, "international instruments and other relevant sources have long reserved a possible exception: implicit in international law's core commitment to basic human rights and democratic principles is recognition of a last-resort, remedial right for a subnational group to secede when these rights are denied its members."[16] This statement is not true. There has been no such reserved exception in international law, and there should not be one.

Orentlicher's reconstruction of international law begins with Versailles, where, "[t]o the extent consistent with other objectives," she asserts, "boundaries of new and reconfigured states were to be drawn along national lines."[17] We have already seen that Wilson's ideas and the proceedings at Versailles were confused and that decisions went in several directions. Most East European states were multinational or embraced substantial national minorities, in spite of Wilson's espousal of the principle of self-determination.

There follows a treatment by Orentlicher of a dispute over the Aaland Islands in 1920–21. That dispute was resolved by according the Swedish population of the islands autonomy within Finland, rather than independence, and in a footnote Orentlicher quotes reports of two commissions appointed by the League of Nations to deal with aspects of the Aaland Islands question. As Orentlicher says, both noted that self-determination was not a rule of international law,[18] but she quotes their "hints" and "suggestions" that secession might be available if guarantees of minority rights were not enforced. Unfortunately, she fails to cite the statement of the Rapporteurs that was far more definitive than any "hints" or "suggestions." Here is what they said:

> To concede to minorities, either of language or religion, or to any fraction of a population the right of withdrawing from a community to which they belong, because it is their wish or their good pleasure, would be to destroy order and stability within States and to inaugurate anarchy in international life; it would be to uphold a theory incompatible with the very idea of the State as a territorial and political unity.[19]

Antonio Cassese notes that, for the Rapporteurs, this statement "rule[d] out any right of secession."[20]

During this very period following World War I, minority rights treaties were widely adopted in eastern Europe and were widely unenforced. The experience with minority rights in this period was disastrous, but this experience—which also goes wholly unmentioned by Orentlicher—did not give rise to any right to secede. On the contrary, the association of secessionist impulses with the most dangerous interwar irredentism in the case of the Sudetenland would have inhibited the emergence of any such right, any "hints" to the contrary notwithstanding.

The decolonization that followed World War II did not give rise to a right of group self-determination. On the contrary, it was well established that, once foreign domination ended, the right of self-determination was spent. "But in the view of many commentators," states Orentlicher, "this generalization has long been subject to a key qualification: groups persistently denied meaningful participation in national political processes might be entitled to secede."[21] This revisionist understanding of self-determination, she continues, "derives above all from the [Declaration on Friendly Relations] adopted by the UN General Assembly in 1970."[22] That declaration reaffirmed the self-determination rights of colonized peoples and the rights of independent states to territorial integrity. "But," according to Orentlicher, "the declaration famously hinted that this right might be forfeited if a state's government did not represent 'the whole people belonging to the territory without distinction as to race, creed or colour.'"[23] Subsequent General Assembly declarations, Orentlicher adds, imply that states might forfeit their right to territorial integrity if their governments do not represent "'the whole people belonging to the territory without distinction of any kind. . . .'"[24] And so, carrying these declarations to their logical conclusion, the right to secede is a right of last resort, available when it is the only way a group can participate politically on an equal basis. Or it is if one reads the "hints," "suggestions," and "implications" correctly.

Since this claim rests mainly on the 1970 Declaration on Friendly Relations, it is important to understand the context in which the declaration was set, the negotiations that led to the final text, and the provisions of that text. Interpreting the declaration to allow a right to secede from a government that did not represent "the whole people" constitutes, to put it mildly, a generous reading.

First, consider the historical context, for the ahistorical quality of Orentlicher's analysis of the declaration is striking. The self-determination features of the 1970 declaration go back to proposals advanced by the United States and the United Kingdom in 1966 and 1967, respectively. Now, 1966 was the year in which Ibo suffered two serious pogroms in Nigeria, which finally convinced Ibo that they could not participate equally—indeed, could not even live— in Nigeria; 1967 marked the beginning of the attempted self-determination of Ibo in the form of the Biafra secession; and 1970 witnessed the end of the Biafra war with the defeat of the secessionists by Nigerian government forces. These were by no means obscure events but were, for months at a time, prominent, front-page events, by reason of their humanitarian implications and the threat the war posed to the territorial integrity of multiethnic states in Africa and elsewhere.

The secessionist state of Biafra did indeed represent a thoroughly victimized group, and the secessionist regime was extraordinarily sophisticated in making its case in the West. In the United

States and the United Kingdom, Biafran representatives purported to show that armed forces of the central government were perpetrating genocidal acts against Ibo in the territory claimed by Biafra. The Ibo claims were received with great sympathy by Western public opinion. Yet neither the United States nor the United Kingdom recognized Biafra. (Likewise, neither recognized Bangladesh in 1971 until its war against Pakistan resulted in the unambiguous defeat of Pakistani forces and control of the territory by the new Bangladesh government.) If the two states that were the strongest proponents of self-determination language in the declaration did not recognize a contemporaneous secession in conditions of extreme oppression, it is, to say the least, doubtful that the declaration that watered down their proposals was meant to endorse a right to secede.

The Biafran War goes unmentioned by Orentlicher. It was, of course, not the only event of the same period that made states wary of territorial separatism. The warfare in the former Belgian Congo from 1960 to 1964 and after had made African and non-African states alike fearful of ethnic secession and state disintegration. With separatist movements active elsewhere in Africa, in Canada, and in India, with such movements in the background in Indonesia, the United Kingdom, and France, and with the then-communist bloc fearful of the very disintegration that later overtook it, it is exceedingly implausible to think that the declaration could have been written in contemplation of a separatist fulfillment of the bare word *self-determination* in the text.

Second, the negotiations that preceded adoption of the Declaration on Friendly Relations make clear that objections to the mention of self-determination derived in large measure precisely from concerns about what its effect might be on the stability of state boundaries. States articulating those objections in the negotiations were convinced by the time of adoption that their objections were satisfied by the wording of the final draft. The British proposal had been particularly open-ended, for it would have accorded a right of self-determination—albeit not necessarily any right to secede—to a "geographically distinct and ethnically or culturally diverse" group if the central government of the state in which the group was located was not representative of the peoples in it. A great many governments were vociferously opposed to this proposal.[25] The Canadian government had been concerned, understandably enough, about a formulation that might justify the "dislocation" of a multiethnic state, and it worried that self-determination might imply "full independence."[26] Poland was anxious about the stability of "existing frontiers."[27] India made clear its view that "the right of self-determination did not apply to sovereign and independent States or to integral parts of their territory or to a section of a people or nation. Without such an understanding," said the Indian delegate, "the principle of self-determination would lead to fragmentation, disintegration and dismemberment of sovereign states," especially those with "multi-racial and multi-lingual populations. The Indian delegation was gratified to note that those principles found universal recognition in the draft declaration."[28]

These interpretations are consistent with state practice, as I shall note later. The whole thrust of objections to the drafts had been that they "could be invoked to legitimize secessionist movements and the disruption of sovereign countries."[29] The fact that vociferous objectors to earlier drafts acceded to the final text is at least some evidence that their apprehensions were allayed.

Third, there is the text itself. In the paragraphs on "the principle of equal rights and self-determination of peoples," variations on the term *self-determination* occur eight times. The first seven uses of the term either are innocuous general references or occur in contexts that refer to decolonization, which, by 1970, was the conventional sphere of application of the term. The eighth occurs in a proviso, on which Orentlicher relies. The proviso and the clause following it, which close the proclamations of the declaration, need to be set out in full:

> Nothing in the foregoing paragraphs shall be construed as authorizing or encouraging any action which would dismember or impair, totally or in part, the territorial integrity or political unity of sovereign and independent States conducting themselves in compliance with the principle of equal rights and self-determination of peoples as described above and thus possessed of a government representing the whole people belonging to the territory without distinction as to race, creed or colour. [As indicated above, this last phrase was later modified to read "without distinction of any kind. . . ."]

> Every State shall refrain from any action aimed at the partial or
> total disruption of the national unity and territorial integrity of any
> other State or country.[30]

The only reference to self-determination in the proviso is to
"self-determination of peoples as described above"; none of the de-
scriptions above refers to self-determination outside the context of
decolonization, and the reference to self-determination in the immediately preceding sentence is explicitly concerned with "people"
in a "colony or non-self-governing territory." This usage fits with the
purpose of the proviso, which is to restrict the application of the
language preceding it, rather than to create new rights. So, when
the proviso states that the declaration is not to be construed to impair the territorial integrity of states "conducting themselves in
compliance with the principle of equal rights and self-determination of peoples as described above," it clearly incorporates the well-
understood meaning of self-determination of peoples, rather than
of nations or ethnic groups, as embracing the multiethnic territories that become independent states with decolonization.

When the delegates meant something different, they knew how
to say so. The earlier-proposed language, put forward by the United
States, had stated: "The existence of a sovereign and independent
State possessing a representative Government, effectively functioning as such to all distinct peoples in its territory, is presumed to satisfy the principle of equal rights and self-determination as regards
these peoples."[31] This proposal might have supported a right to
democracy as well as a right of ethnic self-determination (though
not of secession) for "distinct peoples in the territory." Similarly,
the United Kingdom proposal had referred to "a territory which is
geographically distinct and ethnically or culturally diverse from the
remainder of the territory administering it."[32] These proposals met
with a storm of opposition. Neither the language of democracy nor
the language of ethnic self-determination survived.

Notwithstanding the reference in the proviso to the "self-determination of peoples as described above," linking self-determination in the proviso to the same phrase in the main clauses that precede it, Orentlicher relies on the "hint" that follows in the proviso
to find an "implicit" right to secede if racial and religious groups
(later, groups "without distinction of any kind") "are denied access

to the political decision-making process. . . ."[33] For this conclusion, she cites Antonio Cassese's interpretation of the proviso (which he calls a "saving clause").

Cassese's view is that "only in the saving clause [was] a right of internal self-determination . . . envisage[d], albeit indirectly."[34] His reasoning is unconventional. Provisos that begin with "Nothing in the foregoing shall" are written as limitations on main provisions. Cassese permits this one to create new rights not implied in the main provisions. He maintains that "since the possibility of impairment of territorial integrity *is not totally excluded*, it is logically admitted."[35] (Does it need to be explained that this sentence embodies a logical fallacy?) Cassese then cites *one* remark by a South African delegate that went unchallenged to support this view, despite multiple statements in the debates and changes in drafts to the contrary. He goes on to state that religious and racial groups might have a right to secede if central governments "grossly and systematically trample upon their fundamental rights, and deny the possibility of reaching a peaceful settlement within the framework of the State structure."[36]

I have suggested earlier that the proviso does not introduce any new right of self-determination. But even if it did, it certainly would not follow that it authorized secession, for secession is not the only way to achieve self-determination. The declaration itself says that, even for a colonized people, a variety of statuses short of independence "constitute modes of implementing the right of self-determination by that people."[37] So, even if there were a new right of self-determination, however unlikely it were to be conferred by the cryptic language embedded in the proviso, that right could be fulfilled in manifold ways short of secession, including, for example, territorial autonomy, minority vetoes, or an array of special group rights. And since, before the declaration, there was no right to secede, it makes no sense to conclude from the absence of a prohibition on secession—which would have been superfluous—that there is an implicit grant of permission, even under the limited circumstances specified.

The whole proviso, after all, is framed in terms of a prohibition on authorizing or encouraging action that would impair the unity and territorial integrity of states. Those are states that comport with certain principles. With respect to states that do not so comport themselves, the proviso says nothing, but the very next sentence states flatly: "Every State shall refrain from any action aimed at the partial or total disruption of the national unity and territorial integrity of any other State or country." Now, several paragraphs above the proviso, the second clause of the provisions dealing with equal rights and self-determination of peoples places on every state "the duty to promote, through joint and separate action, realization of the principle of equal rights and self-determination of peoples. . . ."[38] Assume for a moment that the distinction between colonized peoples and people living in sovereign states were really to be obliterated, so that groups within independent states would also possess rights of self-determination, including limited rights to secede. The duty of all states to promote self-determination, as stated in the declaration, would also apply to those cases in which a right to secede came into play. In such a case, the duty to promote self-determination would then come into direct conflict with the flat prohibition on state action that might impair the territorial integrity of any state. To read the proviso as producing such a conflict is to find one hint, suggestion, or implication too many.

Of course, the distinction between self-determination for colonized peoples and secession for groups in independent countries was not meant to be abolished by the insertion of a few words at the end of the proviso expressing general approval of government "without distinction as to race, creed or colour" (or, later, without regard to other invidious distinctions of the same general sort). Squeezing a right to secede out of these eight words is not responsible interpretation. Cassese, going very far out on a limb, maintains that, without the words *race, creed or colour*, the proviso would have had an even more sweeping scope. There would then have been a prohibition on impairing the unity or territorial integrity of "States conducting themselves in compliance with the principle of equal rights and self-determination of peoples as described above and thus possessed of a government representing the whole people belonging to the territory." He contends that, in that case, "any national, linguistic, ethnic, racial, or religious group not 'represented' in the government would have had a right to self-determination."[39] But this is to place on the word *representation* a precise meaning of democratic representation, which there is no evidence was intended. On the contrary, there is every reason to think, given the undemocratic character of most governments in the 1970 General Assembly, that such a meaning was not intended. It is, of course, far more likely, against the history of self-determination as having been fulfilled upon independence, that postcolonial states were simply assumed to "represent" the whole people residing in them and that the word *representing* is meant in that sense. The argument for the right to secede that Cassese builds on this word is, it seems to me, entirely specious.

Even if Orentlicher were right in her reading of the Declaration on Friendly Relations, that would not conclude the matter. If a General Assembly declaration articulates a particular right, that does not make it, ipso facto, part of the body of international law.[40] In a further discussion, unmentioned by Orentlicher, Cassese goes on to ask whether the right to secede that he purported to find in the proviso constitutes part of customary international law. He states that, on this, the declaration did not reflect existing customary law or crystallize any emerging rule of international law: "[A]t the time of the drafting, there was no existing consensus on the legal right to internal self-determination."[41] In particular, "States have been adamant in rejecting even the possibility that nations, groups and minorities be granted a right to secede from the territory in which they live. Territorial integrity and sovereign rights have consistently been regarded as of paramount importance; indeed, they have been considered as concluding debate on the subject."[42] Concludes Cassese: "[I]t cannot be denied that State practice and the overwhelming view of States remain opposed to secession. Indeed, it seems that this is one of the few areas on which full agreement exists among all States."[43] On the other hand, he says, internal self-determination for *racial* groups alone has become part of customary international law, but they, too, have no right to secede, even under extreme circumstances.

As we have seen, state practice coterminous with the drafting of the 1970 declaration, and in the very conditions of oppression that Cassese identifies as giving rise in the proviso to an asserted right to secede, was utterly inimical to any such right. That is also the view of leading texts on international law. Brownlie, in a brief discussion of the Declaration on Friendly Relations, makes no mention of its possible application to secession.[44] Malanczuk, in Akehurst's text, points out that the 1970 declaration has given rise to the development of no new legal right to secede, and he cites recent state practice that is overwhelmingly hostile to the development of any such right.[45] He also notes that the more recent 1992 UN Declaration on Minorities emphasizes "the territorial integrity of states,"[46] even as it fails to hint, imply, or suggest anything about a right of an oppressed minority to secede. (I shall say more about state practice in the next section.)

In short, then, any view of the 1970 declaration as providing a last-resort right to secede is unsustainable. Even if it were correct, the declaration has not created any right to secede in customary law, so Orentlicher must look elsewhere for such a right.

The evidence adduced by Orentlicher for a last-resort right to secede grounded in an asserted international-law right to be governed democratically is less specific but even less convincing. The right is said to derive, in the first instance, from plebiscite practice, but early plebiscite practice, after World War I, was limited and inconsistent. Later plebiscite practice, after World War II, was almost nonexistent, despite the decolonization of hundreds of millions of people living uneasily together within colonial boundaries. No traction can be gained for this argument.

Neither is there any support for a right to be ruled democratically deriving from the prohibition on colonization and the prohibition on forcible annexation. As we have seen, the former still requires postcolonial peoples to live together even against their will, and the latter is rather clearly a simultaneous expression of disapproval of the use of force and of approval of existing boundaries and territorial integrity. Here, too, then, Orentlicher fails to convince.

Orentlicher also suggests that democratic principles may be relevant to the resolution of secessionist disputes, as well they may be, but as a matter of internal affairs rather than international law. For international law recognizes no right to live under a democratic regime, in spite of the effort of Thomas M. Franck (on whom Orentlicher relies) to create such an international-law right. I shall comment on Franck's effort further in the following section. Here I would only emphasize that, for Franck, the "first building block" of such a right is the principle of self-determination.[47] We have already seen, however, that this is a cardboard building block for this purpose. We have also seen that adoption of the 1970 Declaration on Friendly Relations was preceded by an American proposal that might have supported a right to representative government. That proposal was opposed vigorously by developing countries and then-communist countries, and it did not find its way into the document. Nevertheless, Orentlicher pronounces the "evidence" supporting Franck's claim "impressive" when it was advanced and stronger since. All she cites is the UN Security Council intervention in Haiti in 1994 and unspecified "other developments." If there is such a right, it is very difficult to discern it in the standard sources of international law. Nevertheless, Orentlicher declares that an international-law right to democratic governance has "pride of place." Here, as in her discovery of a right to secede, a large component of wishful thinking is evident. How can a right to secede be built on a right to be governed democratically, which is to be built, in turn, on a right of self-determination, when the right of self-determination does not give rise to a right to secede?

In 1998, the British jurist James Crawford produced a long and exhaustive survey of state practice and the international law pertaining to secession.[48] Crawford's conclusion was unqualified: ". . . State practice since 1945 shows very clearly the extreme reluctance of States to recognize or accept unilateral secession outside the colonial context. That practice has not changed since 1989, despite the emergence during that period of 22 new States. On the contrary, the practice has been powerfully reinforced."[49] Bangladesh, Crawford noted, was best viewed not as an exemplar of a recognized right to secede but "rather as a *fait accompli* achieved as a result of foreign military assistance in special circumstances."[50] Other cases, such as Eritrea and the Baltic states, involved mutual consent. Where central governments oppose unilateral secession, Crawford found, the secessionists gain little or no international recognition. This certainly has been the case in northern Somalia and Transniestria, among others. Finally, there is "no recognition of a unilateral right to secede based merely on a majority vote of the population of a given subdivision or territory. In principle, self-determination for peoples or groups within the State is to be achieved by participation in its constitutional system, and on the basis of respect for its territorial integrity."[51] For excellent reasons, this remains the state of international law.

The Case for Humility in Public International Law

It is worth pursuing further the argument that international law has a commitment to democracy. In fact, international law has not had a particularly deep or long-standing commitment in this direction. Only in 1992 did Thomas Franck purport to discover an "emerging entitlement" to be governed democratically.[52] International law has always placed great emphasis on the writings of jurists, but traditionally for their syntheses of legal rules and for their influence on state practice that could then change the law, not for the direct creation of new rights by cobbling together new formulations. Such a practice is particularly doubtful when it is recalled that international law is a field in which judicial and bureaucratic institutions far outrun representative ones. It is dangerous and undemocratic to allow commentators to become legislators.

Why the connection of international law to democratic governance is so tenuous should be very clear. However much we may favor the worldwide spread of democracy, valorizing a right to democratic governance would imperil the universality of international law. Despite the developments of the post–Cold War period, there are almost as many authoritarian as democratic states. If international law is to enhance its influence on state behavior, which it needs to do in order to reduce and regulate interstate conflict and to facilitate interstate transactions, it cannot simultaneously undercut the governing arrangements of half the states that are to be subjected to the rules laid down.[53]

There is, of course, an even more obvious reason why international law ought to be exceedingly restrained in its enthusiasm for secession. Secession is an antistate movement, and an international law that forgets that states are its main subjects—albeit not its only subjects—risks its own survival.

There is always a tendency of law to preempt social complexity with rules, and there are many temptations to the promiscuous creation of rights. But law does best when it is informed by what Karl Llewellyn called "situation sense,"[54] a sound idea of the type of phenomenon it seeks to govern. If self-determination is a phrase "simply loaded with dynamite,"[55] in the words of Wilson's Secretary of

State, there are international lawyers who are playing with this dynamite. They could benefit from more situation sense.

LIVING WITH HETEROGENEITY

I said earlier that emphasis needs to be on fostering interethnic accommodation within states. The choice between secession or partition, on the one hand, and murderous conflict, on the other, is a
false choice. Institutions can mitigate conflict. This is much too
large a topic to discuss at length here, but since I have been so critical of those who have readily endorsed the right of ethnic groups
to leave states, it is incumbent on me at least to sketch briefly what
some alternatives might look like.

Most states are ethnically heterogeneous, and many are severely
divided. Many groups seek to treat the state as an ethnic patrimony,
as if it were homogeneous or as if they had a prior claim to legitimacy and others were there merely on sufferance. Why this is so is
a complicated story. Despite these depressing tendencies—which
are highly variable rather than universal—it is long past the time
when ethnic kinship could form the foundation for homogeneous
communities. Territorial proximity is now an inescapable basis for
political community.

In general terms, there are two competing prescriptions for
solving the problem of ethnic conflict in a democratic framework.
Each has its proponents and detractors, its strong and weak points.

The first prescription goes by the name of consociational
democracy: a formula for government by grand coalition of all
groups, for minority vetoes on important policy issues, for ethnic
proportionality in cabinet positions, civil service posts, and financial allocations, and for cultural autonomy for all groups as well.[56]
Many criticisms have been made of consociational theory, for its
neglect of democratic opposition (if everyone is in a grand coalition, where will opposition come from?) and its alleged propensity
for excessively limited government and immobilism. My own criticism is that grand coalitions are impossible where divisions are severe, because the very formation of such a coalition produces opposition based on the accusation that group interests have been

sold out. Moreover, consociation is essentially a system of guarantees and so is attractive to minorities but not to majorities, who prefer majority rule. As a result, there are consociational features adopted occasionally by states, but few full-blown consociational regimes. Grand coalitions and minority vetoes are particularly scarce.

My own preferred course involves the use of political incentives to encourage interethnic moderation. Various institutions, particularly electoral systems, are capable of inducing moderate behavior on the part of politicians. If election depends, at the margin, on the ability to gain some votes from members of groups other than one's own, then political leaders will behave in an ethnically conciliatory fashion for that purpose.[57] One thing we know is that politicians like being elected and reelected. If consociational theory provides no motive for compromise behavior, incentive theory, by definition, does not share that defect.

Yet there are obstacles to the adoption of incentives schemes as well. Although one can find incentive-based devices adopted by states, a full ensemble of institutions containing incentives to foster conciliation is not easy to find.[58] There is evidence that these devices work, but what are the incentives to adopt the incentives?

Often, processes of bargaining over institutions produce compromises that dilute the effect that could have been expected, had there been a more thoroughgoing and consistent set of institutional changes. Still, partial adoptions can have some positive effect on conciliation.

The upshot of the problem of adoption is that most severely divided societies will not soon become dramatically more harmonious. Over time, some have, and others will, but not necessarily wholly as a result of political engineering. Political engineering will play its part, a greater part at certain unusually propitious times (and such moments should be seized), but the difficulty of wholesale adoption means that many societies will muddle along, sometimes severely conflicted, sometimes better able to achieve compromise if their partial adoption of conciliatory devices is well considered. But, for present purposes, what needs to be emphasized is that efforts at conciliation will not be helped by providing either a liberal or a constrained right to secede. There is an inevitable trade-off between encouraging participation in the undivided state and legitimating exit from it. The former will inevitably produce imperfect results, but the latter is downright dangerous.

NOTES

Portions of this chapter are drawn from a paper presented at a conference on partition at Boston University in October 2001.

1. See the excellent entry by Michael Banton, "Self-Determination," in Athena Leoussi, ed., *Encyclopaedia of Nationalism* (New Brunswick, N.J.: Transaction, 2001), pp. 271–73.

2. The so-called secession of Singapore was actually an expulsion of the city-state from Malaysia and was portrayed in legal instruments as the product of mutual consent.

3. Opinions of the Arbitration Committee, reported by Alain Pellet, "The Opinions of the Badinter Arbitration Committee: A Second Breath for the Self-Determination of Peoples," *European Journal of International Law* 3 (1992): Appendix, 183.

4. See Thomas M. Franck, "The Emerging Right to Democratic Governance," *American Journal of International Law* 86 (1992): 46–91. Cf. Antonio Cassese, "Political Self-Determination: Old Concepts and New Developments," in Antonio Cassese, ed., *UN Law/Fundamental Rights: Two Topics in International Law* (Alphanaanden Rijn, Netherlands: Sijthoff and Noordhoff, 1979), pp. 137–65; Morton H. Halperin and Kristen Lomasney, "Towards a Global 'Guarantee Clause,'" *Journal of Democracy* 4 (July 1993): 60–69.

5. See Allen Buchanan and David Golove, "The Philosophy of International Law," in Jules Coleman and Scott Shapiro, eds., *The Oxford Handbook of the Philosophy of Law* (New York: Oxford University Press, 2002). See also Allen Buchanan, *Secession: The Morality of Political Divorce from Fort Sumter to Lithuania and Quebec* (Boulder, Colo.: Westview Press, 1991).

6. Robert McCorquodale, "Human Rights and Self-Determination," in Mortimer Sellers, ed., *The New World Order: Sovereignty, Human Rights, and the Self-Determination of Peoples* (Oxford, England: Berg, 1996), pp. 24–25; Gerry J. Simpson, "The Diffusion of Sovereignty: Self-Determination in the Post-Colonial Age," in Sellers, *New World Order,* pp. 48, 54–56.

7. Quoted by Thurman Arnold, "Criminal Attempts: The Rise and Fall of an Abstraction," *Yale Law Journal* 40 (1930): 58.

8. See, for example, David Philpott, "Self-Determination in Practice," in Margaret Moore, ed., *National Self-Determination and Secession* (New York: Oxford University Press, 1998), p. 92.

9. Hurst Hannum, "Territorial Autonomy: Permanent Solution or Step toward Secession?" forthcoming in Andreas Wimmer et al., eds., *Facing Ethnic Conflict* (2004).

10. See Saadia Touval, *The Boundary Politics of Independent Africa* (Cambridge, Mass.: Harvard University Press, 1972).

11. See Donald L. Horowitz, *Ethnic Groups in Conflict* (Berkeley: University of California Press, 2000), pp. 281–88; Donald L. Horowitz, "Irredentas and Secessions: Adjacent Phenomena, Neglected Connections," in Naomi Chazan, ed., *Irredentism and International Politics* (Boulder, Colo.: Lynne Rienner, 1991), pp. 9–22.

12. Nicholas Sambanis, "Partition as a Solution to Ethnic War: An Empirical Critique of the Theoretical Literature," *World Politics* 52 (2000): 437–83.

13. See ibid., p. 479; Horowitz, *Ethnic Groups in Conflict*, pp. 592–96.

14. Diane Orentlicher, "International Responses to Separatist Claims: Are Democratic Principles Relevant?" in this volume, p. 25.

15. Ibid., p. 19.

16. Ibid., p. 25.

17. Ibid., p. 21.

18. Ibid.

19. Quoted in Antonio Cassese, *Self-Determination of Peoples: A Legal Reappraisal* (New York: Cambridge University Press, 1995), p. 123.

20. Ibid.

21. Orentlicher, "International Responses," p. 22.

22. Ibid.

23. Ibid., quoting General Assembly Res. 2625, UN GAOR, 25th Sess., supp. no. 28, at 121, UN Doc. A/8018 (1970).

24. Ibid., p. 23, quoting General Assembly Res. 50/6, para. 1, UN Doc. A/RES/50/6 (1995) (emphasis omitted).

25. See Cassese, *Self-Determination of Peoples*, p. 116.

26. *Report of the Special Committee on Principles of International Law Concerning Friendly Relations and Co-Operation among States*, UN General Assembly, 25th Sess., supp. no. 18, pp. 99, 98, respectively, UN Doc. A/8018 (1970).

27. Ibid., p. 100.

28. Ibid., p. 110.

29. Cassese, *Self-Determination of Peoples*, p. 116.

30. General Assembly Res. 2625, p. 124.

31. Quoted in Cassese, *Self-Determination of Peoples*, p. 115.

32. Quoted in ibid.

33. Orentlicher, "International Responses," p. 22.

34. Cassese, *Self-Determination of Peoples*, p. 110.

35. Ibid., p. 119 (italics in original).

36. Ibid.

37. General Assembly Res. 2625, p. 124.

38. Ibid., pp. 123–24.

39. Cassese, *Self-Determination of Peoples*, pp. 117–18.

40. General Assembly resolutions "are recommendations creating prima facie no legal obligation." Ian Brownlie, *Principles of Public International Law*, 5th ed. (Oxford, England: Clarendon Press, 1998), p. 694 n. 79. But they may "elucidate and develop the customary law." Ibid., p. 694.

41. Cassese, *Self-Determination of Peoples*, p. 120.

42. Ibid., p. 122.

43. Ibid., pp. 123–24.

44. Brownlie, *Principles of Public International Law*, pp. 601–02.

45. Peter Malanczuk, *Akehurst's Modern Introduction to International Law*, 7th rev. ed. (New York: Routledge, 1997), pp. 334, 339–40. Malanczuk also cites pertinent literature to the same effect.

46. Ibid., p. 339.

47. Franck, "The Emerging Right to Democratic Governance," pp. 55–56.

48. James Crawford, "State Practice and International Law in Relation to Secession," *British Yearbook of International Law, 1998* (Oxford, England: Clarendon Press, 1999), pp. 85–117.

49. Ibid., p. 114.

50. Ibid., p. 115.

51. Ibid., p. 116. Crawford might have noted, but did not note, the contrary but truly exceptional position of the government of the United Kingdom, which has stated, in ways meant to be binding, that a majority of the people of Northern Ireland might vote to dissolve their union with Britain and to join the Irish Republic instead. But this has not been the position of other states, and it is not the position of the United Kingdom with respect to Scotland or Wales.

52. See Franck, "The Emerging Right to Democratic Governance." See also Cassese, "Political Self-Determination."

53. The International Court of Justice has itself recognized periodically that customary international law comprises a limited set of norms to assure coexistence and cooperation among states. See, for example, *Case Concerning Delimitation of the Maritime Boundary in the Gulf of Maine Area, 1984* I.C.J. 246.

54. Karl N. Llewellyn, *The Common Law Tradition: Deciding Appeals* (Boston: Little, Brown, 1960).

55. Robert Lansing, quoted in David Fromkin, *Kosovo Crossing: American Ideals Meet Reality on the Balkan Battlefields* (New York: Free Press, 1999), p. 127.

56. See Arend Lijphart, *Democracy in Plural Societies* (New Haven, Conn.: Yale University Press, 1977).

57. I have written about such devices in various places. See, for example, Donald L. Horowitz, *A Democratic South Africa? Constitutional Engineering in a Divided Society* (Berkeley: University of California Press, 1991), and Donald L. Horowitz, "Making Moderation Pay: The Comparative Politics of Ethnic Conflict Management," in Joseph V. Montville, ed., *Conflict and Peacemaking in Multiethnic Societies* (Lexington, Ky.: Lexington Books, 1991), pp. 451–75.

58. See Donald L. Horowitz, "Constitutional Design: An Oxymoron?" in *Designing Democratic Institutions,* NOMOS XLII (New York: New York University Press, 2000), pp. 253–84.

3

DEMOCRATIC PRINCIPLES AND SEPARATIST CLAIMS: A RESPONSE AND FURTHER INQUIRY

DIANE F. ORENTLICHER

Donald Horowitz has grounds for concern about legal innovations that may provide fresh inspiration to separatist movements. It is baffling, however, that he attributes proseparatist views to me. I will try here to clarify the principal sources of misunderstanding and hope, along the way, to deepen our consideration of issues that are well worth further exploration.

Horowitz's commentary proceeds from the basic premise that I propound a right to secede that is unfounded in law. Yet my essay argues that international law is deeply skeptical of secessionist claims—and rightly so.

This misapprehension stems in part from a misreading of the broad lines of my argument. My aim was to explore the implications of democratic principles for separatist claims. As a foundation for this inquiry, I briefly reviewed the evolution of relevant legal doctrine in order to establish several background points: the question I set out to examine—the implications of democratic principles for separatist claims—had scant grounding in international law until quite recently; despite this, diplomatic practice and scholarly opinion have at times foreshadowed views that have gained greater purchase in recent years; finally, the question I explore has become newly important in the realm of policy making (and not just academic theory) by virtue of recent developments evincing an unprecedented commitment by states to democratic principles. Horowitz apparently mistakes my discussion in this preliminary section, the only portion of my essay he addresses, to be an argument in support of the claim that international law has for some time recognized a right to secede.[1] This was far from my intent.

This initial misunderstanding carries across Horowitz's commentary, leading him to refute a succession of arguments I did not advance[2] while misconstruing those I made.[3] Rather than cite each instance, I hope a few examples will clarify my perspective.

Horowitz challenges what he apparently supposes to be my view of the Paris Peace Conference—that the postwar settlement provides some evidence of a right to secede. Citing my observation that, to the extent consistent with other objectives, the Paris peacemakers were guided by the principle that "boundaries of new and reconfigured states were to be drawn along national lines," Horowitz tries to show where I went astray: "We have already seen that Wilson's ideas and the proceedings at Versailles were confused and that decisions went in several directions." Yet I made plain that the "principle of nationalities" was one of several notions of self-determination applied at Versailles and that the principle of self-determination, however conceived, was given only qualified application there. More fundamentally, my discussion made clear that the peace conference did *not* give rise to a general right of secession or, for that matter, to any other version of a right to self-determination.

Horowitz turns next to my account of the Aaland Islands dispute taken up by the League of Nations in 1920–21. Noting that I "fail[ed] to cite the statement" of a League Commission of Rapporteurs "that was far more definitive" than passages addressing limited circumstances in which secession might be warranted, Horowitz implies that I misread the commission's conclusions. The statement Horowitz suggests I should have mentioned explains why, in the commission's view, international law did not recognize a general right of secession for minorities. Yet I stated unambiguously that this and another commission involved in the Aaland Islands dispute "concluded that international law did not recognize a right of national self-determination." In fact, I introduced my discussion of the Aaland Islands dispute with the claim that its resolution "put to rest" any possible question about whether international law supported separatist claims under the rubric of self-determination. I did note as well the Rapporteurs' observations concerning circumstances in which secession might be justified. As I have noted, one of my aims in the introductory section of my essay was to track early enunciations of views that now hold greater purchase, and the League commission's observations relating to remedial secession are especially important in this regard.[4]

Horowitz's treatment of the UN General Assembly's 1970 Declaration on Principles of International Law Concerning Friendly Relations and Co-operation among States in accordance with the Charter of the United Nations makes a useful contribution to an already rich scholarly literature on the subject. Although I disagree with some aspects of his interpretation,[5] I will resist the temptation to engage the point at length here, since I believe that Horowitz's principal argument is with Antonio Cassese, whose views my essay explores. It may, however, be useful to clarify the significance my essay attached to the declaration, since here, too, Horowitz has misunderstood the nature of my argument.

For Horowitz, two questions matter—whether Cassese's interpretation is legally correct and, if so, whether the views Cassese attributes to the declaration have binding force.[6] In assessing the first question, Horowitz is guided principally by the declaration's drafting history. My aims were different. I wanted to explore the implications of a highly influential interpretation[7] that is very much to the point of my inquiry because it explicitly connects separatist claims to democratic principles.

On one point, Horowitz and I have genuinely different views—the persuasiveness of the "democratic entitlement" thesis pioneered by Thomas Franck. Writing in 1992, Franck claimed that democracy "is on the way to becoming a global entitlement, one that increasingly will be promoted and protected by collective international processes."[8] Horowitz does not discern support for this claim in the practice of states. Yet a breathtaking range of activities backs up Franck's thesis.

In the view of two scholars who have closely studied issues relating to democratic governance and international law, "concerns for democratic legitimacy" have filtered "into virtually every aspect of international legal discourse."[9] For example, in 1993 the European

Union (EU) adopted accession criteria for central and eastern European countries that include a candidate country's having "achieved stability of institutions guaranteeing democracy."[10] In 1995, the EU decided to include in all new treaties with third parties a provision affirming respect for "democratic principles" as an "essential element" of the treaty.[11] Turning to Africa, a basic objective of the African Union (AU) is to "[p]romote democratic principles and institutions."[12] Governments that come to power through unconstitutional means are barred from participating in AU activities.[13]

While the Charter of the Organization of American States (OAS) has long affirmed "representative democracy," the organization has added teeth to this commitment in the past dozen years.[14] In 1991, the OAS General Assembly adopted the Santiago Commitment to Democracy and Renewal of the Inter-American System[15] and a resolution on representative democracy, which called for an immediate response by the Permanent Council in the event of "occurrences giving rise to the sudden or irregular interruption of the democratic political institutional process or of the legitimate exercise of power by the democratically elected government in any of the Organization's member States."[16] In December 1992, the OAS adopted a protocol to its charter that provides for suspension from participation in the organization of a state "whose democratically constituted government has been overthrown by force."[17]

Alongside these formal policies, states and intergovernmental organizations have committed unprecedented resources to democracy-promoting activities. Over seventy states received electoral assistance from the United Nations from 1992 to August 1999.[18] Between 1990 and 1995, the EU provided electoral assistance to forty-four countries.[19] Experts who have analyzed trends in electoral assistance say that similar statistics could be marshaled for the OAS and the Organisation for Security and Co-operation in Europe.[20] The same period has seen a surge in bilateral assistance aimed at promoting and consolidating democratic government. According to figures compiled by the Organisation for Economic Co-operation and Development, worldwide democracy assistance increased from $564 million in 1997 to $1.6 trillion in 2000.[21] One of the largest benefactors of such programs is the United States government. Between 1992 and 2001, its Agency for International Development provided $4.6 trillion in democracy programs.[22] Senior officials of the Clinton administration presented these and related initiatives in terms that go beyond Franck's more modest "emerging" democratic entitlement: "[I]n the twenty-first century, people . . . have a basic right to a form and structure of government that guarantee [civil and political] rights—in other words, they have a right to democracy itself."[23]

Are all countries fully democratic? Of course not, but no proponent of an emerging "democratic entitlement" makes this claim. The sole test of Franck's thesis cannot be to ask whether there are deviations from democratic ideals among some two hundred states. The well-established proposition that international law prohibits torture[24] would fail this test. In a survey of 195 countries covering 1997 to mid-2000, Amnesty International found reports of torture and ill treatment in 150 countries; in more than 70, the reports were "widespread or persistent."[25] At least as important as the number of states deviating from democratic principles are the responses of other states to deviations—thus it is noteworthy that the international community responded vigorously to coups in Haiti and Sierra Leone in the 1990s, approving military intervention to restore deposed leaders[26]—and the broad trend toward democratization in recent decades, reflected most strikingly in the collapse of communism in central and eastern Europe and of military juntas across Latin America.[27]

And so the question today is not whether international institutions and governments are devoting "unprecedented attention to the internal governing structures of states" (clearly they are) or whether this development "has significant implications for the current content and future direction of international law"[28] (surely it does). The issues that now confront us concern the meaning and implications of states' unprecedented commitment to democracy.

While Horowitz and I disagree about the persuasiveness of the "democratic entitlement" thesis, we are in basic accord about where the proper emphasis should lie when it comes to separatist claims. Horowitz says our focus needs to be on internal political arrangements, "not on making exit strategies more plausible." I argue that the international community's newly robust engagement in democracy-promoting activities reflects "a commitment above all to full participatory rights within established states."[29] I would still maintain, however, that secession may be warranted in light of democratic ideals in the exceptional case. But Horowitz and I are hardly worlds apart on this point. Horowitz concedes that there may be times when separation can prudently be effected through consent.

Perhaps the deeper issue then, is whether, as Horowitz may believe, we had best resist any inclination to identify principles that explain why, in the exceptional case, separation may be a prudent or legitimate course. I believe that scholars and policy makers should not shrink from addressing the question of whether, in light of states' deepening commitment to democratic ideals, there are exceptional circumstances in which separation is justifiable. Just as important, we must not hesitate to make clear why democratic principles generally discredit the claims of separatists. We can ill afford to be legal ostriches, hoping that if we ignore this question we will avoid adding further fuel to separatist flames. For if we do not make clear where we stand, it is certain that separatists will step in to fill the conceptual void.

NOTES

1. Horowitz at times implies that I argued for a general right to secede, while other portions of his commentary suggest that I advocated only a right of remedial secession. Only the latter interpretation has a basis in my essay, though my views on this issue are more nuanced and cautious than Horowitz's presentation of them.

2. An example is Horowitz's discussion of "evidence adduced by Orentlicher for a last-resort right to secede grounded in an asserted international-law right to be governed democratically." "The right is said to derive," he writes, "in the first instance, from plebiscite practice." I made no such claim. Instead, after summarizing early international legal responses to separatist claims, I suggested in the passage Horowitz cites that it might be useful to "highlight two possibilities latent" in the preceding overview before proceeding further. Far from claiming that a right to secede derives from plebiscite practice, I made the far more circumscribed observation that "diplomatic practice has at times affirmed the view that contested territorial claims should be resolved through . . . balloting." At this point in my essay, I did not express an opinion about the merits of this approach.

When I touched on the subject later, I expressed a skeptical view of plebiscites as the principal means of resolving contested separatist claims, though I suggested that balloting may play a legitimizing role within a broader process of negotiation. I noted, for example, that plebiscites played a disastrous role in resolving the disputed status of Bosnia and Hercegovina and provoked sweeping violence in East Timor. More generally, I observed that "[i]n the tense environment surrounding contested separatist claims, winner-take-all plebiscites are almost sure to inflame nationalist passions."

3. For example, Horowitz implies that I derived a legal right to be ruled democratically from international law's prohibition of colonization and forcible annexation. But my argument was not framed in the legalistic terms Horowitz evokes. Instead, I invoked the implied premise of international law's prohibition of colonization and forcible annexation to challenge the belief of many political theorists that democratic principles are wholly irrelevant in assessing separatist claims. My argument here was framed principally in terms of political theory rather than international law.

4. The significance of these views has been widely recognized by scholars of the interwar period. See, for instance, Nathaniel Berman, "'But the Alternative Is Despair': European Nationalism and the Modernist Renewal of International Law," *Harvard Law Review* 106 (1993): 1870–71.

5. One reason is that I believe Horowitz's analysis does not account for key language in the text of the 1970 declaration. In an analysis that Horowitz generally cites approvingly, James Crawford characterizes the relevant text (as revised somewhat by a later UN document) this way: "In accordance with this formula, a State whose government represents the whole people of its territory on a basis of equality complies with the principle of self-determination in respect of all of its people and is entitled to the protection of its territorial integrity." James Crawford, "State Practice and International Law in Relation to Secession," in *British Yearbook of International Law 1998,* ed. Ian Brownlie and James Crawford (Oxford: Clarendon Press, 1999), p. 117. In contrast to Crawford's formulation, Horowitz's approach effectively reads out of the text the qualifying language concerning the nature of governments that are "entitled to the protection of territorial integrity."

6. Horowitz implies that I believe the 1970 declaration reflects customary international law. This is implicit, for example, in Horowitz's observation that I did not mention a portion of Cassese's analysis expressing doubt about whether claims that, in Cassese's view, are implied in the declaration have the status of customary international law; in his observation that "[i]f a General Assembly declaration articulates a particular right, that does not

make it, ipso facto, part of the body of international law"; and in his assertion that the 1970 instrument "has not created any right to secede in customary law, so Orentlicher must look elsewhere for such a right." Yet far from suggesting that the implied claims in the relevant text of the 1970 declaration embodied customary law, I analogized their legal force when the instrument was adopted to that of "a resolution proclaiming a definitive determination of the number of angels who could dance on the head of a pin." I went on to explore the implications for separatist claims of more recent developments in state practice that evince a deepening commitment to democratic government. In light of those developments and my interest in their implications, it seemed worthwhile to consider the influential interpretation of the 1970 declaration, espoused by Cassese and others, linking principles of representative government and the right of states to territorial integrity. In doing so, I never suggested that the provisions of the declaration I addressed had the force of customary law.

7. When, for example, the Canadian Supreme Court addressed the question of whether Quebec was entitled to secede unilaterally, it took the view advocated by Cassese seriously enough to apply it to the question at hand. *Reference re Secession of Quebec,* 1998 S.C.J. No. 61, paras. 130, 134–38. The Canadian court observed that "it remains unclear" whether the view embodied in Cassese's interpretation "actually reflects an established international law standard" (para. 135). The Court found it unnecessary to resolve this question, since, in its view, "the current Quebec context cannot be said to approach" the relevant threshold justifying secession under the 1970/1993 proviso clause (para. 135). Even so, the Court seemed to credit the approach advanced by Cassese and other writers. The Court noted, for example, that the text of a 1993 UN declaration that affirmed (while expanding) the 1970 proviso clause "adds credence to the assertion that . . . a complete blockage [of a people from the meaningful exercise of its right to self-determination internally] may potentially give rise to a right of secession" (para. 134).

8. Thomas M. Franck, "The Emerging Right to Democratic Governance," *American Journal of International Law* 86 (1992): 46. As the title of this article makes clear, Franck framed his thesis in terms of an emerging right to democratic governance and not, as Horowitz implies, in terms of an established "right to live under a democratic regime."

9. Gregory H. Fox and Brad R. Roth, "Democracy and International Law," *Review of International Studies* 27 (2001): 331.

10. *European Council in Copenhagen, 21-22 June 1993: Conclusions of the Presidency,* SN 180/93, p. 12.

11. "On the Inclusion of Respect for Democratic Principles and Human Rights in Agreements between the Community and Third Countries," Commission Communication COM(95)216, May 23, 1995.

12. Constitutive Act of the African Union, Lome-Togo, Art. 3(g), June 12, 2000; see also Art. 4(m), which recognizes "respect for democratic principles" as one of the AU's own principles, and the preamble, which affirms the AU's determination to "consolidate democratic institutions and culture."

13. Ibid., Art. 30.

14. For a summary of various iterations of this commitment, see Stephen J. Schnably, "Constitutionalism and Democratic Government in the Inter-American System," in *Democratic Governance and International Law*, ed. Gregory H. Fox and Brad R. Roth (New York: Cambridge University Press, 2000): 156.

15. Organization of American States, Santiago Commitment to Democracy and Renewal of the Inter-American System, OAS GAOR 21st Reg. Sess., OEA/Ser. P/AG doc.2734/91 (June 4, 1991).

16. Organization of American States General Assembly Res. 1080, "Representative Democracy," June 5, 1991; AG/RES. 1080 (XXI-O/91).

17. A more extensive account of institutional and state practice in support of democracy can be found in Fox and Roth, *Democratic Governance and International Law*, and Brian D. Tittemore, "Prohibiting Serious Threats to Democratic Governance as an International 'Crime Against Democracy,'" Council on Foreign Relations, International Task Force on Immediate Threats to Democracy, Sept. 10, 2002.

18. Fox and Roth, "Democracy and International Law," p. 330.

19. Ibid.

20. Ibid.

21. Organisation for Economic Co-operation and Development Spreadsheet, 2002, retrieved from International Development Statistics Online (IDS/o) Web site: www.oecd.org/htm/M00005000/M00005347.htm.

22. United States Agency for International Development, Democracy and Governance Office, Democracy, Conflict and Humanitarian Assistance Bureau (DCHA), "USAID Democracy Assistance," unpublished spreadsheet on file with DCHA, Aug. 2001.

23. Harold Hongju Koh, "A United States Human Rights Policy for the 21st Century," *Saint Louis University Law Journal* 46 (2002): 325.

24. Judicial affirmations of this proposition include *Filartiga v. Pena-Irala*, 630 F.2d 876, 884-85 (2d Cir. 1980); *Prosecutor v. Anto Furundžija*, Case No. IT-95-17/1-T, Judgment, para. 137 (Dec. 10, 1998); *Regina v. Bartle et*

al., [1999] 2 W.L.R. 827, Mar. 24, 1999, reprinted in *I.L.M.* 38 (1999): 589 (Opinion of Lord Browne-Wilkinson).

25. Amnesty International, "Torture Worldwide: An Affront to Human Dignity," 2000, pp. 2–3, retrieved from www.amnestyusa.org/stoptorture/tortureworldwide.pdf.

26. See Gregory H. Fox and Brad R. Roth, "Introduction: The Spread of Liberal Democracy and Its Implications for International Law," in Fox and Roth, *Democratic Governance and International Law,* pp. 3, 9.

27. Writing in 1998, Robert Pastor observed that "democracy has spread to 117 countries over the last two decades." Robert A. Pastor, "Mediating Elections," *Journal of Democracy* 9 (Jan. 1998): 154. See also Joshua Muravchik, "Democracy's Quiet Victory," *New York Times,* Aug. 19, 2002.

28. See Fox and Roth, "Democracy and International Law," p. 329.

29. I also wrote that "democratic principles would be thwarted by a rule of international law generally favoring independence for state-seeking groups."

PART II

INTRASTATE AUTONOMY

4

AN HISTORICAL ARGUMENT
FOR INDIGENOUS
SELF-DETERMINATION

MARGARET MOORE

The right of self-determination is usually understood as the right of
a group of people to be collectively self-governing. This generally
has two aspects or can be disaggregated in the following way. First,
collective self-determination appeals to the democratic doctrine of
legitimacy and involves the claim that members of the group
should be able to choose their own government. This is sometimes
termed internal self-determination. The second idea is that the
community should be able to freely determine its own political status. The term *political status* is employed in international-law discussions of collective self-determination[1] and is usually at the heart
of indigenous claims to collective self-determination. This collective self-determination can take a number of institutional forms,
ranging from independence (from a colonial power) to secession
(from a larger state), confederation (of two states), or political autonomy within a state through either delegated power (devolution)
or constitutionally protected political autonomy (federation).

This essay puts forward two closely related historically based normative arguments for giving rights to political self-determination in
the second, more radical or complete sense that are employed by,
or on behalf of, indigenous peoples and then considers how this

right might be institutionalized in the state. The central cases on which these arguments for collective self-government are based are the indigenous peoples of the Americas and Australasia. The pattern of dispossession, conquest, and marginalization experienced by the indigenous peoples of the Americas, Australia, and New Zealand, and central to the argument deployed here, may apply more widely—to Greenland Inuit, to the Sami of northern Scandinavia, Malays in Malaysia, the Kannadigas of Karnataka state in India, the Bankonjo and Baamba of Western Uganda, and the Kinshasa in Zaire, to name a few.[2] That is an empirical question beyond the scope of the essay.

The history of the relationship between indigenous and nonindigenous peoples is contested terrain, which is nowhere illustrated better than in the controversy surrounding the quincentenary celebration of Columbus's "discovery" of the Americas in 1492. While there is, undoubtedly, a political element in historical interpretation, the basic facts of indigenous dispossession, marginalization, conquest, and colonization in the Americas and Australasia are undisputed.[3]

It is not necessary to paint a Golden Age picture of pre-Columbian indigenous societies in order to appreciate the multitude and variety of cultures of the first peoples of the Americas, whose communities ranged from the frigid Arctic barrens to the tropical Amazonian rainforests. Their cultures were extremely varied, from the ceremonial and hierarchical political systems of peoples inhabiting the coastal rainforests of contemporary British Columbia and Washington State to the egalitarian societies of the Iroquois, the Cree, and many indigenous peoples of the southwestern United States. There were sophisticated political empires in the Andean highlands and highly developed cities such as Tenochtitlán in the Aztec Empire, as well as hunting and gathering societies like that of the Inuit, who followed the caribou and erected shelters for themselves as they moved. The story of dispossession varies—in some cases, indigenous peoples were enslaved,[4] decimated from disease, or deliberately exterminated. There are many documented cases of deliberate destruction perpetrated on them by nonaboriginal people: the killing of hundreds of Lakota men, women, and children at Wounded Knee is perhaps the best known in American history,[5] but there are numerous instances where indigenous people were deliberately destroyed as obstacles to white settlement.[6] In many parts of the Americas, there were forced transfers of indigenous populations to "make room" for nonindigenous peoples, as with the Cherokees,[7] but also the confining of indigenous peoples, especially in Canada, the United States, and Australia, to small reservations.[8] In all cases their colonization within political systems marked indigenous peoples as inferior: they were classified as wards, incapable of agency, and found themselves in a tutelary relationship where they were subject peoples, their very identity and world (landscape) defined by nonaboriginal peoples who attempted to assimilate them.

This essay argues that these historical facts are relevant to the indigenous case for political self-determination in two ways. First, the historical story of theft and dispossession underwrites the reparative claim for additional resources and authority over territory that is implicit in most claims for indigenous self-government. Second, the fact that indigenous peoples constituted self-governing communities who were subjugated and marginalized is an important factor in assessing the legitimacy of the state to make rules over them.

In focusing on the historical basis of indigenous claims to self-determination, this essay differs in emphasis from one of the most popular arguments for indigenous self-government, at least among political theorists, which attempts to derive the right of political self-determination from more basic rights that are generally accepted and relatively uncontroversial in liberal democratic societies. This type of argument typically begins by stressing that groups that do not share in the dominant culture suffer various kinds of disadvantage from their minority status. Will Kymlicka argues that it is harder and more expensive for members of these groups to maintain their culture and so live a life they consider worthwhile. Therefore, some protection—and for national minorities and indigenous peoples this includes a measure of self-government—is necessary to offset the vulnerabilities that attach to being a member of a minority group. According to this argument, because a rich and flourishing societal culture is an essential condition of the exercise of individual autonomy, which liberals value, liberals have a good reason to adopt measures that would protect culture. Although this argument has demonstrated only that the existence of (some) flourishing cultural structure is necessary to the exercise of individual autonomy, but not a particular culture, proponents of this argument offer empirical evidence attesting to the "deep bond" that most people have to their own culture.[9] In this way, they suggest that people have a "legitimate interest" in not having their inherited culture damaged against their will and to suggest that one way, indeed sometimes the only way, to "prevent this is to use the power of the state to protect aspects that are judged to be important."[10]

The Kymlicka-type argument is useful in highlighting the threat posed when minority groups are forcibly included as equal, undifferentiated individuals in a state with a different majority (dominant) culture. Moreover, this argument goes some way toward meeting indigenous peoples' aspirations to be collectively self-governing: the rights envisioned by Kymlicka and other proponents of this argument would enable national minorities and indigenous peoples to enact policies that would protect their language and give them a measure of control over education and other aspects of their cultural and political life.

However, it is worth noting, even though not a decisive *philosophical* objection, that this type of argument is not structured in a way that reflects indigenous peoples' own understanding of their claims. This argument subsumes indigenous peoples under the broader category of national minorities and argues that they are entitled to the same kind of rights. This is manifestly not how most indigenous peoples see themselves or their claims. Every term that they use to describe themselves—indigenous, aboriginal, native, First Nations—emphasizes the fact that they were the land's original occupants, that they were once self-governing people, that they have a special attachment to the land, and that their rights are inextricably connected to their memory of being displaced from land to which they are attached. A leading expert on American native mobilization has claimed that natives' "sense of history is rooted here, in this land, in the geography of their present. Most forms of Indian political action are explicitly grounded in a consciousness of that history and . . . are articulated in explicitly historical terms."[11] The equality-culture-autonomy argument canvassed above does not broach these questions, or, when it does, it views these facts as relevant to explaining indigenous disadvantage or minority status but not as the fundamental basis for a claim to collective self-determination.

The point here is partly that this argument does not strongly connect indigenous memory with the institutions of political autonomy justified under this argument. However, there is another, more substantive, related issue: the way that indigenous peoples are described—as a subset of national minorities—has a strong bearing on the structure of the argument. The argument just described seems to apply better to the claims of national minorities than indigenous peoples. To see this, consider Kymlicka's description of a "societal culture," which is his term for the kind of cultural structure that is closely linked with the exercise of autonomy. A "societal culture" is defined as a culture "whose practices and institutions cover the full range of human activities, encompassing both public and private lives."[12] He elaborates that a societal culture "provides its members with meaningful ways of life across the full range of human activities, including social, educational, religious, recreational and economic life, encompassing both public and private space. These cultures tend to be territorially concentrated and based on a shared language . . . [and are] institutional[ly] embodied—in schools, media, economy, government, etc."[13] To create, and maintain, a societal culture is, Kymlicka correctly says, an "immensely ambitious and arduous project."[14] National minorities like the Québécois, Scots, Basques, Catalans, and others can plausibly be said to have a "societal culture," but many indigenous peoples do not have, and cannot reasonably aspire to, a full societal culture, which encompasses all aspects of life. This is because their original culture has been persecuted and degraded, mainly through the policies of the white settler societies among whom they live. They would require a major transformation in the conditions of their existence to be able to reasonably aspire to such an encompassing culture.[15]

The arguments advanced in this chapter depart from the main thrust of the Kymlicka-type autonomy argument in placing at the forefront the history of relations between indigenous and non-indigenous peoples. Part I develops an argument from rectificatory justice, which justifies political self-government in part as a measure to restore the self-governing status of indigenous peoples prior to colonization and the resources necessary for effective self-government. In Part II, the chapter advances an argument that questions the colonizing state's legitimate rule over indigenous peoples. Its legitimacy is brought into question insofar as the process itself was unjust and the rule involved massive violations of indigenous people's rights and the attempted destruction of them as a people. The third part of the chapter addresses the question of the form that self-determination should take. This raises issues connected to the context in which indigenous people find themselves, the challenges unique to this, and the kinds of institutional forms that are appropriate for indigenous peoples.

I. Prior Dispossession and the Claims of Rectificatory Justice

Indigenous peoples have the right to the restitution of the lands, territories and resources which they have traditionally owned or otherwise occupied or used, and which have been confiscated, occupied, used or damaged without their free and informed consent. Where this is not possible, they have the right to just and fair compensation. Unless otherwise freely agreed upon by the peoples concerned, compensation shall take the form of lands, territories and resources equal in quality, size and legal status.

—Article 27 of the Draft Declaration
on the Rights of Indigenous Peoples

One prominent argument deployed in the context of claims for indigenous self-determination begins by establishing a link between the historical treatment, and especially dispossession, of indigenous peoples and their ongoing disadvantaged status.

Many indigenous peoples, particularly in Australia and the Americas, are economically and socially marginalized, with lower literacy rates, lower socioeconomic status, and higher mortality rates than the population as a whole. This in itself suggests that they should, as a matter of justice, be entitled to additional resources and help from the larger society. However, concentrating on the marginalized position of indigenous peoples from a strictly distributive justice perspective fails to fully capture their claims and arguments. Like most victims of injustice, indigenous peoples tend to stress the importance of remembering what occurred, in part because the past injustice continues into the present (they are *still* without their land) but also because their own individual self-identity as a member of the group is bound up with the kinds of things that happened to the group, and this is partly constitutive of the kind of group it is. A crucial element of this argument is the point that their current poverty and marginalization are the direct result of the past injustice that they suffered at the hands of the white colonialists. The fact that indigenous peoples were defrauded and expropriated brings with it some responsibility on the part of the nonindigenous population to take steps to rectify this injustice.

The dispossession of native peoples weaves itself into native claims for additional rights and especially rights over territory in both arguments based on treaty rights and arguments based on rectificatory justice. The first kind of argument focuses on treaty rights and, specifically, on the fact that in many cases treaties were made but not honored or were eroded by later judicial action. There is a long history of broken promises in the relationship between indigenous and nonindigenous peoples: the American government has unilaterally abrogated certain treaties with Indian tribes;[16] the New Zealand treaty of Waitangi signed by Maori chiefs and British colonists was declared a "simple nullity" in 1877 (although its status has very recently been reinterpreted);[17] the language and land rights guaranteed to the Métis under the Manitoba Act of 1870 were rescinded by white anglophone settlers once they became a majority. Other treaty rights, of small communities, have never been honored.[18] Obviously, any society that is based on the principle of the rule of law has to take seriously the evidence that indigenous people have legal claims to land or resources that are currently not being honored.

In many cases, however, indigenous peoples did not sign treaties with the white settlers, or the treaties that they signed were clearly unfair. In many cases, indigenous peoples were reluctant to sign the treaties that the European colonists offered them because they did not think that these treaties adequately provided for their people. Some treaties were signed only when many members of the indigenous communities were sick or starving or otherwise reduced partners. Although implicit in the treaty-making process is recognition of the need for mutual respect and mutual consent, many of the treaties signed do not represent a fair or just basis for intercommunal relations. Because the historical treaties may not apply or may not represent a just basis for agreement, it may be necessary to move beyond the narrow issue of legal entitlement to additional land or resources and consider claims based on a conception of rectificatory justice.

This brings us to the second way in which historical arguments intersect with the claims of justice. In many cases, the disadvantaged status of indigenous peoples is a direct result of the actions of settler societies and of the state in which indigenous peoples are incorporated. Where the link between contemporary inequality and past oppression is causal in this way, dominant groups have a collective responsibility not only to dismantle the institutions and processes that marginalize native peoples but also to address the inequality that they experience (and that is the direct result of the past oppression).[19] Of course, the memory of oppression may be more vivid for its victims than for members of the dominant society, and the meaning of the oppression may also be different. This is because the experience of oppression helps to mobilize the victimized group but is not a defining experience for the dominant group and is often not conceptualized as a group-based action at all. Nevertheless, in the case of indigenous peoples, there are objective sources of evidence—law, documents, and narratives that can be corroborated—that the group had been oppressed, stolen from, and discriminated against, and this can be causally related to the group's current experience of poverty and marginalization.

In some ways, the structure of this argument for reparative claims on behalf of the community is similar to the claims for reparation made on behalf of individuals who have been dispossessed or are victims of injustice.[20] The basic moral and legal idea is that people should be recompensed for the injustices that they suffer. However, there is a question of whether it is legitimate for collective bodies or communities (tribes, nations, corporations, intergenerational associations) to make claims of this kind. The individual members of the community who actually suffered such wrongs may be quite different from the ones now seeking recompense, and of course the compensators may also be different people.

The two basic criteria for identifying when a group has a strong moral claim for group-differentiated rights, especially rights to additional resources, help to address this concern. The criteria are: (a) the group must be disadvantaged in comparison to other social groups; and (b) there must be an objective history of discrimination and oppression, which can be connected to their present disadvantaged status.[21] These criteria avoid two different kinds of problems. First, even where it is possible to establish prior possession and wrongful taking of land, for example, there are serious difficulties attached to actually tracing lines of descent. The idea that people may be entitled to differential rights because of their ancestry or line of descent sits uneasily with the idea that people can be responsible only for their own actions. The argument advanced here, however, avoids this difficulty because it does not require that we trace actual biological descent; it requires only that we are able to identify the group that suffered the injustice. The justification for this strategy is that, in many cases, the oppression or discrimination occurred on a group basis. These were not random acts committed by one individual agent against other individuals; rather, they involved actions aimed at members of a group precisely because they were members of the targeted group.[22] Second, this argument does not suggest that people should be held responsible for the decisions or actions of their ancestors. The key issue is that the nonindigenous population of the Americas and Australasia sought and gained advantages from the historic injustice done to indigenous peoples, and this explains the obligation to try to make up for it in some way and to rectify this injustice.

Moreover, the requirement that there be a demonstrated causal relationship between current disadvantage and prior discrimination and dispossession tends to rule out the most counterintuitive cases for additional resources based on prior injustice. Irish Americans who came to the United States during the nineteenth-century potato famine suffered from group-based discrimination, but it would be counterintuitive and wrong to compensate their descendants for the sufferings of their Irish great-grandparents because the recipients did not actually suffer the discrimination, nor did they suffer from the effects of that past discrimination. In fact, Irish Americans as a group have done extremely well in the United States, and there is no evidence of a lasting adverse effect of that period of discrimination on the fortunes of descendants of Irish Americans. This is clearly of a different order than that of indigenous

peoples, whose current disadvantage is directly related (caused) by
their prior dispossession. Indeed, in their case, the current unequal
state of affairs can be explained in historical terms, and the continuing failure to address the inequality or the disadvantage represents a continuing source of injustice. There is no suggestion here
of actual responsibility for the actions of ancestors but only recognition of the complex relationship between past events and unfair
starting points and of the way in which institutional structures can
continue to marginalize certain groups.

This argument feeds into arguments for self-determination by
justifying indigenous peoples' entitlement to additional resources;
and economic resources, including land, control over natural resources, and straightforward transfers of money, are an important
element in meaningful self-government. Moreover, as Allen
Buchanan has pointed out, with respect to treaty rights, it is difficult to uphold the land claims typically specified in treaties that indigenous people signed without also envisioning some form of collective self-government.[23]

Insofar as this rectificatory justice argument is framed in terms
of economic marginalization and inequality, it seems able to justify
additional economic resources fairly straightforwardly. However, it
is not the knockdown argument that some of its proponents assume. One problem is that many attempts to rectify historic injustice or move to the status quo ante will involve committing even
more injustices. This is because people build a pattern of expectations and attachment to land and goods that they are in possession
of. Restoring this land or these goods to the original owners may
create new, equally serious kinds of injustices. Waldron has con-
tended that this is one of the main arguments underlying the view
that injustice can be superseded with the passage of time.[24] This is
not an argument to do nothing: there are things that can be done
to make amends for past injustices and ensure that the poverty and
disadvantages facing indigenous peoples are addressed. The nonindigenous majority should agree to institutional structures that
recognize indigenous peoples' attachment to land and need for additional resources. But it means that there can be no return to the
original state of affairs, prior to the unjust dispossession of indigenous peoples.[25] There can only be some group-differentiated
rights, some recognition of the needs and claims of indigenous

peoples and their aspirations to collective self-government, within the limits of a fair dispensation to other peoples who now also live in these lands.[26]

II. COLONIZATION, DISPOSSESSION, AND JURISDICTIONAL AUTHORITY

In 1864, the descendants of the people who arrived here five hundred years ago took it upon themselves to forge a constitution without us. It became the British North America Act of 1867. In this Act, the federal government gave itself the power over "Indians and lands reserved for the Indians." It did not ask us if we agreed; it just assumed power over our peoples. We were not even there when the decision was made. We must ask ourselves, "By what right did they get that power and how have they used it?" These questions are critical to our future relationships with this nation.

—Ovide Mercredi, National (Canadian) Chief for the Assembly of First Nations, and Mary-Ellen Turpel, *In the Rapids*

This brings us to the second argument for self-determination rights, which questions the current state's claims to jurisdictional authority. The argument canvassed above needs to be supplemented by an argument concerning the jurisdictional authority of the state. This is so because the rectificatory justice argument is consistent with a number of different remedies, not only collective self-government. Other rights, which are typically argued for by indigenous people on some kind of culture or equity grounds, include rights of access to sacred sites, ancestral bones, cultural artifacts, or burial grounds; rights to education in a people's own language and schooling about the ways of life of their own culture; the right to hunt or fish in their traditional territory; the right to employ their own standards of evidence or acceptable argument or punishment practices in the legal system; and a right to full participation at all levels of political decision making that might affect their interests. This essay is concerned, not with all these claims to group-differentiated rights, but only with arguments that bear on the issue of political self-determination. Ideally, the argument should also show why collective self-determination for indigenous peoples is necessary, not only in the sense that it is a means to address the cultural and economic disadvantage that native peoples suffer (the other rights are also conceived of as remedies), but also in the sense of being morally necessary.

One argument for collective self-determination invokes considerations of the kind put forward by John Stuart Mill in relation to the liberty principle. Mill argued in *On Liberty* that each individual is most interested in his or her own well-being and so should be entrusted with rights to protect him or her from interference in making decisions over his or her own life.[27] Margalit and Raz, in their argument justifying political self-government for groups within the state, have extended this argument to groups: just as the individual is in the best position to decide how to arrange his or her life, so members of a group are best placed to judge the interests of the group. This may not be a conclusive argument, but it does offer good reasons for a presumption in favor of collective autonomy or self-government as a means to address group disadvantage.[28]

Of course, whether a group is able to make decisions in its best interests will depend upon the nature of group decision making. In fact, unless the decision makers represent, and are accountable to, the whole group, it is a mistake to say that self-government is really government by the group. For the Millian argument to work, we must assume that the decision makers are representative of the group and that there are institutional mechanisms to ensure their representative and accountable nature.

The basic point implicit in this argument—that groups are in the best position to judge their own interests and so should be given the requisite resources and jurisdictional authority to resolve their own problems and overcome the disadvantages that they face—presses on a very closely related argument for collective self-government for indigenous peoples. The idea is not simply that the groups themselves are in a good position to make decisions over their own lives but that the state in which they are incorporated has manifestly failed to work in their best interests.[29] This fact raises serious questions connected to the assumption that the state is entitled to make decisions over the lives of indigenous peoples.

This issue (of political legitimacy) lurked behind the previous argument concerning dispossession and injustice because, in many cases, indigenous peoples lack legal entitlement in that their claims and their holdings were not recognized by the conquering regime, which forcibly incorporated them. This suggests, first, that indigenous peoples were once self-governing communities, who governed themselves according to their own practices, and, second, that the conquering and colonizing regime often did not treat their claims fairly.[30]

From a liberal-democratic perspective, the process by which indigenous peoples were colonized and dispossessed was illegitimate. It is relevant to their claim to collective self-government that this process involved silencing and excluding indigenous peoples and stripping them of the institutions of self-government that they had enjoyed prior to colonization. Just as the history of imperial powers' relations with the nonwhite societies that they ruled was enacted without the involvement of the colonized peoples, so, in the Americas and Australia and New Zealand, the process of settlement and state creation proceeded without the consent of the indigenous peoples who lived there. From a legitimacy point of view, this is important not only because it involves a violation of fundamental principles of democratic governance but also because it involves the further wrong that it destroyed the self-governing regimes enjoyed by indigenous peoples.[31]

An understanding of the bases of state legitimacy is important to the claims of indigenous peoples who implicitly question the authority of the state to govern them. In many cases, indigenous peoples were entirely excluded from the processes of state creation, which raises the question of the basis for the state's authority over indigenous peoples.[32] If the exercise of legitimate authority is based on the principles of democratic consent and the sovereignty of the people, then the current state does not exercise legitimate authority over them. If indigenous peoples were entitled, through the same normative principle, to exercise collective self-government in the past, then how, normatively, has this right been extinguished?[33] It is counterintuitive to suppose that the continued subordination and unfair treatment of indigenous peoples has left them also with fewer (moral) rights and no longer entitled to collective self-government.

This argument regarding the jurisdictional authority of the state over indigenous peoples typically proceeds through an analogy with imperial forms of authority over societies in Africa and Asia and the relations between indigenous peoples and white elites in the Americas, Australia, and New Zealand. The tutelary relationship implicit in the relations between indigenous and nonindigenous peoples can properly be seen as a localized version of a global phenomenon in which European powers such as Britain, France, Portugal, the Netherlands, and (before 1918) Germany controlled nonwhite peoples everywhere.[34] These European empires extended throughout Asia and Africa and operated on the premise that European civilization was superior to other cultural forms and practices and that power was merited in some way—a result of the Darwinian competition in which the fittest tend to rule. Skin color was highly correlated with power and, by extension, civilization and progress.[35]

The Europeans' imperial relationship with their subject peoples was mirrored in the relationship between white settlers—extensions of the empire, fragments of European civilization—and indigenous peoples in the Americas, Australia, and New Zealand. The assumption that indigenous peoples were culturally backward and that their assimilation into the white society was both in their interests, and an inevitable result of the Darwinian competition among cultures, permeated almost all the policies made by white settler majorities over indigenous peoples. It was fundamental to the colonial nature of the relationship between the white social majority and indigenous people because it meant that indigenous peoples were not included in the discussions that led to the founding of the state in which they were incorporated. Indeed, in almost every respect, and every policy decision, indigenous peoples were described as wards and treated like children. As John A. Macdonald, Founding Father of Canada and its first prime minister, claimed in 1887: "The great aim of our civilization has been to do away with the tribal system and assimilate the Indian people in all respects with the inhabitants of the Dominion, as speedily as they are fit for the change."[36] The consequences of the policies based on the related assumptions of the cultural inferiority of indigenous peoples and the merits of assimilationist policies have been disastrous. Inuit communities in northern Canada were forcibly removed from their homes and relocated thousands of miles at the recommendation of distant bureaucrats who claimed to want to more efficiently direct services to scattered indigenous communities, but also as a method to establish sovereignty over the High Arctic by populating parts of it.[37] Indigenous children in Canada and Australia were forcibly removed from their families and sent to live with nonindigenous families or in nonindigenous residential schools, where they were sometimes physically and sexually abused and, even when they were not, were stripped of their indigenous culture and forbidden to speak their language.[38] The old culture was forgotten—because not taught—and the new white culture was perceived as foreign or alien and inconsistent with native identity. This was not surprising: it is hard to adopt the culture and identity of the group that engaged in large-scale theft and sometimes murder of your forefathers and foremothers. The result, of course, was that indigenous children were left with very few cultural resources, having been deprived of one culture and unable to adopt another. In short, white monopoly on policy over indigenous peoples, based on the assumption of white superiority and indigenous inferiority, has led to a legacy of failed programs. For indigenous peoples, it has meant social and economic depression and marginalization, high rates of alcoholism, suicide, and incarceration, and cultural anomie and despair on the part of a whole generation. This record provides empirical support for the point made in the previous section that groups themselves are usually in the best position to define policies and make decisions over their own lives.

There is, however, another normative argument implicit in the analogy between indigenous peoples and other colonized peoples in Africa and Asia. The colonization and subordination of indigenous peoples in Australia, New Zealand, and the Americas involved the same assumptions of cultural inferiority, strongly correlated with race, that underlay European imperialism and the related view of European entitlement to mastery over the world. The process differed mainly because, in Africa and Asia, the European population was frequently very tiny, and political control could be returned to the people who had been deprived of it simply through a process of making these territories independent. In Australia, New Zealand, and the Americas, the settlement of Europeans was more complete and the decimation of the original population more serious. These historical differences suggest two related points. The first is that if decolonization was right—if the process of stripping Europeans of their imperial control over nonwhite societies was morally right—then indigenous self-government must also be morally right. Indigenous peoples should control the conditions of their existence through the exercise of political self-government, just as the peoples of Africa and Asia have had their capacity for political agency restored to them through the process of decolonization.[39] However—and this is the second point—because of the numerical strength of the nonindigenous population, and the interdependent nature of the indigenous and nonindigenous communities in Australasia and the Americas, self-government cannot take the same form as with decolonization. The argument for self-government in both cases still has normative force, but the remedy must be different because the context is different.

III. THE REMEDY: THE PRACTICE OF INDIGENOUS SELF-GOVERNMENT

While the moral arguments in favor of indigenous self-government are very strong, the situation or context in which indigenous people find themselves means that the exercise of self-government for indigenous peoples will have to be within existing states. The analogy between imperial rule in Africa and Asia and the conquest and colonization of indigenous peoples in the New World breaks down once we consider the context in which indigenous people operate. It is clear that a different remedy than independence is appropriate.

The specific challenge for indigenous peoples, then, is to develop models of the kind of self-determination that it makes sense for them to pursue. In almost all cases, indigenous peoples have been concerned to argue for limited forms of self-government within the state, which typically involve maximal jurisdictional authority, consistent with numbers, especially over areas relating to language, culture, and resources but also with some increased representation at the center. In Mexico, this basic formula is embodied in the San Andres Accords of 1996, which outline a structure aimed at creating a multiethnic nation in Mexico that encompasses differences, permits decisions in the decentralized tradition of the Mayas, and ensures both broader political representation of indigenous people and fair representation within the justice system.[40] In Canada, the 1996 Royal Commission on Aboriginal Peoples, which interviewed hundreds of aboriginal peoples in many different communities, endorses a model of treaty federalism that is similar to the San Andres Accords in that it recognizes the interdependence of nonindigenous and indigenous communities through endorsing both shared rule and self-rule. It recognizes the previously self-governing nature of indigenous communities through emphasizing the voluntary nature of the federal project.[41] This section of the chapter discusses the implications of the argument presented thus far for the democratic accountability of indigenous communities and for the nation-building and representation policies of the central state, both of which must be modified in accordance with the basic principles of self-rule and shared rule.

Many indigenous groups are dispersed into small communities of only a few hundred people and so have limited governing capacities. The size of such communities raises the question of the extent to which they can be expected to deliver services to their communities. Indeed, in many cases it is not clear that they have the capacity to exercise the jurisdictional authority equivalent to American states or Canadian provinces. The size of the territory, natural resources, and population base limits their governing capacities. States or provinces are much better equipped than small indigenous communities to take on the tasks normally associated with internal self-government: they have far greater resources and greater access to expertise, not only in the administration of these services but also in public policy design, fiscal accounting, and so on. However, local indigenous governments are in a much better position to identify the needs and concerns of their communities. For this reason, in many spheres, there will have to be institutional forms of cooperation between indigenous and nonindigenous communities so that indigenous communities can coordinate with and draw on the expertise of larger governing bodies in such areas as health care delivery, health care reform, education, and provision of the services usually associated with local municipalities (clean water, garbage removal). At the same time, indigenous governments should have the ability to make decisions over their priorities to meet the needs of their local community.[42] There is no theoretical reason why there cannot be a third level or tier of government within federal states in which indigenous people are collectively self-governing, a level that could encompass a number of very small, isolated communities. This would be similar to the model, suggested by the European Union federalists, of having a federation within a federation (Spain in the European Union).[43]

The democratic thrust of the argument developed here, with its emphasis on the need for indigenous self-rule, has a number of implications for the kind of self-governing institutions that are appropriate. Insofar as the basis of the self-government argument rests, not on a static traditional cultural argument, but on an argument for collective self-rule, it follows that, while indigenous communities should have the jurisdictional authority to ensure by democratic means the extension of their culture in the public sphere (through teaching their own language, history, and culture), they are not *defined* by their distinct culture or tradition. Indeed, the problem with traditional culture-based conceptions of indigenous peoples is that they tend to define indigenous people in purely traditional terms and indeed suggest that self-government should be conferred on indigenous people to the extent that they adhere to traditional ways and maintain their old culture. This fails to recognize the dynamic and adaptable nature of both culture and identity. As Will Kymlicka has argued, it means cultural and political isolation, not cultural and political self-determination.[44] Further, it is consistent with attempts to deny self-government to indigenous communities. In Brazil, for example, the government indicated its preparedness to recognize and support indigenous communities *as long as* they were traditional. As soon as acculturation and adaptation to modern ways occurred, the people were no longer defined as indigenous and so lost their rights.[45] The arguments canvassed and supported in this chapter do not imply anything about the type of culture adopted in communities that have an indigenous identity. Presumably, some communities will seek to preserve some indigenous ways and to teach their language and history. However, the precise kind of accommodation that they may seek with the larger state and majority culture will be up to them to decide. The arguments put forward here explain only why indigenous people are justified in exercising self-rule in accordance with their aspirations and their historic status as self-governing peoples.

It follows from the emphasis on the interrelationship between indigenous self-determination and democratic governance that such rule should be consistent with the fundamental principles of democracy.[46] This has implications for any attempt to restrict membership within territorial jurisdictions to members, defined in ancestral or personalized terms. Most contemporary forms of self-government, including indigenous self-government (with the exception of voluntary self-governing organizations such as ones for urban natives, discussed below), are territorial in the sense that jurisdictional authority is divided into geographical areas or regions, everyone within the geographical area is subject to the authority of the rules of that legal/political regime, and the rules do not apply outside the geographical area.

Territorial self-government is inconsistent with political structures based on *membership* in a particular group or a particular ethnic identity.[47] It presupposes that all people resident within a particular jurisdiction, and so subject to its rules, have input or democratic voice in the making of these decisions. It is entirely legitimate to draw boundaries *around* areas of indigenous majorities and to ensure that the community has the jurisdictional authority to effectively control entry into the area (by regulating such things as housing permits) to prevent their local majority from being "swamped" by a nonindigenous majority, if that is what they desire.[48] However, it does not mean that they are entitled to disenfranchise nonindigenous people resident in their area or indeed to set rigid rules for membership that exclude or marginalize some people in the self-governing community.[49]

It is a fundamental premise of this discussion that the self-rule of indigenous peoples can be jeopardized not only by the imposition of alien cultures and rules but also by local self-interested elites who use their authority to preserve and maintain their power base. Mobutu Sese Seko's Congo, which was completely subordinated to its ruler and treated as his own personal fiefdom, is an extreme case of government that had become completely personalized. Problems of corruption and the exclusion and marginalization of elements of the community can also arise in smaller communities. This problem is particularly pertinent in the case of indigenous self-government because indigenous communities are typically economically disadvantaged and meaningful self-government must be accompanied by redistribution from the nonindigenous population. This raises the problem of accountability insofar as the people who provide the economic resources do not receive the services.

This can lead to a dynamic where the leaders of the indigenous community have an incentive to maximize the extraction of resources but not necessarily to pursue policies aimed at more efficiently providing services to their community. It also obfuscates the lines of responsibility and so makes unfair, nepotistic policies and allocation of resources more likely. The financial structure on Canadian reserves, for example, whereby wealth is distributed to chiefs and the band council, reproduces the authority and structure of the paternalist Department of Indian Affairs, which controlled indigenous people and treated them like children.[50] Following from the idea that indigenous peoples are entitled to be self-governing and make decisions over their own lives, this system needs to be reformed. What is needed is direct redistribution to indigenous people while, at the same time, conferring on indigenous governments the jurisdictional capacity to tax back what is needed to provide services to their communities.

The principles of shared rule and self-rule implicit in the self-government arrangements typically pursued by indigenous peoples challenge both the unitary discourse of equal and undifferentiated citizens and the binary discourse of indigenous versus nonindigenous people, which seems to suggest that the overarching state does not also include indigenous people. The first type of discourse is problematic because indigenous peoples have a different historic relation to the state: they precede it and were forcibly incorporated into it. The second type of discourse is problematic because the goal of establishing self-governing communities within the state is to create a truly inclusive and legitimate state, not a state *for* nonindigenous peoples. To recognize the interdependence of indigenous societies within the larger societies, it is important not only to confer political autonomy on indigenous people who are territorially concentrated and have a land base, such that they can be collectively self-governing, but also to address the exclusion of indigenous people in the central institutions and public culture of the state.[51]

This issue is inseparable from the question of the division of powers in any kind of federal or quasi-federal state that is organized to permit various forms of internal self-government. The terms of jurisdictional authority cannot be subject to unilateral (white) government interpretation and interference. The history of legal interpretation of indigenous rights has been very biased: indigenous peoples' interpretations of the treaties they agreed to have been ignored, and the white-dominated legal systems did not admit their oral understanding of these treaties as legitimate evidence. This suggests that there should be mechanisms at the center to ensure neutrality, at least in the sense of reflecting a bicommunal understanding of the meaning of the constitutional documents that affect indigenous peoples.

The idea of shared rule also suggests the need for mechanisms to ensure that indigenous voices are heard at the center. There are a number of ways to represent distinct interests in central institutions, but the most common, found in virtually all federations, is through the second chamber, which, historically, is designed to represent regional interests and is well suited to the expression of territorially concentrated indigenous interests.[52] As well, there are some examples (Belgium) of the expression of nonterritorial identities in the central legislative chamber.[53]

The principle of shared rule in an inclusive state also suggests the need to make the public culture of the state more permeable in the sense that the institutions of the public sphere are designed so that they reflect the character of indigenous identity in the state. The creation of internally self-governing units in which indigenous peoples obtain public services and run their own schools and communities goes some way toward accommodating indigenous identities, but it must be combined with the sense that the central institutions are cognizant of indigenous concerns and that the school curricula and symbols of the state are sensitive to indigenous culture and meaning. In countries like New Zealand, where the Maoris speak one language and have a single recognizable culture, it is possible to approach equality of recognition, for this type of diversity is amenable to statewide policies of bilingualism and biculturalism (and indeed Maori is a recognized, official language of New Zealand).

Making the state maximally inclusive also requires policies that meet the needs of indigenous people who do not live in areas that can be readily transformed into areas of collective territorial self-government. This is not merely a theoretical issue but an urgent practical one: in Canada, Australia, and New Zealand, for example, there has been a steady flow of indigenous people from depressed rural areas lacking resources to urban centers. Half of Canada's indigenous people live in cities.[54] Unfortunately, the main proposals advocated by indigenous organizations that are tribally or reserve based (such as, in Canada, the Assembly of First Nations) focus on the need for increased jurisdictional authority (self-government) for territorially based indigenous groups, even though many indigenous peoples live in urban areas and would be outside the scope of such reforms.[55] The concerns of urban indigenous people would not be addressed by instituting policies of indigenous self-government for reserves. For this reason, it is important to develop programs that permit indigenous people in urban areas to organize their own collectively self-governing organizations—to run their own schools and their own community organizations, in addition to reforming the justice system so that it more adequately meets their needs and reflects their problems and culture.

Conclusion

This essay has reconstructed two closely related arguments to justify political self-government for indigenous peoples, both of which concentrate on the experience of indigenous peoples in the Americas and Australasia: an argument for rectificatory justice based on prior dispossession and continued inequality and an argument questioning the legitimacy of the state's jurisdictional authority over indigenous people.

The third section of the chapter discussed some of the implications behind the chapter's focus on self-rule rather than cultural justifications for self-determination and the need to create institutional structures that reflect indigenous people's legitimate aspirations to be collectively self-determining. To the extent that some of the policies and practices suggested here seem to require sweeping constitutional changes, they are difficult to realize. Constitutional change is often quite difficult to effect, especially given the amending formulas of many contemporary constitutions.[56] For this reason, some of the policies might be more effectively pursued through gradual or incremental change. This should not, however, blind us to the moral imperatives behind indigenous self-determination and the need for governmental forms that not only are fully inclusive of diversity but have come to terms with the historic grievances and injustices committed in the course of settlement, conquest, and state formation.

NOTES

I am grateful for help and comments received from Allen Buchanan, Ciaran Cronin, Anna Drake, Avigail Eisenberg, Patti Tamara Lenard, Stephen Macedo, Marion Smiley, Jeff Spinner-Halev, and Bernie Yack. An earlier version of this chapter was given at the University of Madison at Wisconsin in November 2001 and at the European Consortium for Political Research workshop in Turin, Italy, in March 2002. I thank the participants for their helpful questions and comments.

1. The term *political status* is frequently used in connection with self-determination. The United Nations General Assembly Declaration on the Granting of Independence to Colonial Countries and Peoples (1960) states in Article 2 that "all peoples have the right to self-determination; by virtue of that right they freely determine their political status and freely pursue their economic, social and cultural development." As is typical of such documents, these rights are then limited by Article 6, which refers to the imperatives of the "national unity" and "territorial integrity" of states.

2. Donald L. Horowitz, *Ethnic Groups in Conflict* (Berkeley: University of California Press, 2000), 202.

3. One of the most hotly contested issues is the size of the pre-Columbian aboriginal population, with aboriginal sympathizers generally reporting high estimates of the size of the population, since large populations generally assume more complex societies, while pro-Europeans tend to give low estimates of the size of the aboriginal populations (since this tends to correspond to more simple societies). As well, the higher population estimates tend to suggest the devastating effects of the conquest and subsequent settlement of the Europeans, while the lower figures suggest a much less dark picture of the European arrival for aboriginal people.

4. See D. E. Stannard, *American Holocaust: Columbus and the Conquest of the New World* (New York: Oxford University Press, 1992), 71–75; William L. Sherman, *Forced Native Labor in Sixteenth Century Central America* (Lincoln: University of Nebraska Press, 1979).

5. Dee Brown, *Bury My Heart at Wounded Knee: An Indian History* (New York: Henry Holt, 1971).

6. Some of this was perpetrated by the settlers themselves, acting without political direction, but there are also many instances of political direction. One example is that of George Washington, who instructed

Major-General John Sullivan in 1779 to attack the Iroquois and "lay waste all the settlements around." Stannard, *American Holocaust*, 126.

7. James Mooney, *Historical Sketch of the Cherokee* (1900; reprint, Chicago: Aldine, 1975).

8. From 1834 to the 1920s, under the Bureau of Indian Affairs, Indian peoples in the United States were gradually dispossessed of their territory and confined to reserves of land. See Francis Paul Prucha, *Indian Policy in the United States: An Historical Essay* (Lincoln: University of Nebraska Press, 1981), 27–34. Under the Dawes Act (or General Allotment Act), passed by the United States Congress in 1887, tribal lands were broken up and allotted to individual Indians, while "surplus" land was sold to white settlers. By 1934, some 2.75 million hectares, more than 60 percent of the remaining Indian land base, had been taken from indigenous peoples. Stephen Cornell, *The Return of the Native: American Indian Political Resurgence* (New York: Oxford University Press, 1988), 42.

9. Will Kymlicka, *Multicultural Citizenship* (New York: Oxford University Press, 1995), 107.

10. David Miller, *On Nationality* (New York: Oxford University Press, 1995), 86–87. Although this argument is primarily directed at defending the state's policies aimed at cultural protection, it clearly applies to cultural minorities who are vulnerable because they lack political autonomy.

11. Cornell, *Return of the Native*, 217.

12. Kymlicka, *Multicultural Citizenship*, 75–76.

13. Ibid., 76.

14. Will Kymlicka, *Finding Our Way: Rethinking Ethnocultural Relations in Canada* (Don Mills, Ont.: Oxford University Press, 1998), 31.

15. To be fair, Kymlicka, in *Multicultural Citizenship*, does not deploy the concept of societal culture to rule indigenous people from his argument for self-government—in fact, he suggests that claims of equality dictate that self-government should be extended to them—but it is not clear why the equality argument is not deployed to grant self-governing rights to other small cultural groups (self-government does not apply to immigrant groups, for example).

16. See C. E. S. Franks, "Indian Policy: Canada and the United States Compared," in Curtis Cook and Juan Lindau, eds., *Aboriginal Rights and Self-Government: The Canadian and Mexican Experience in North American Perspective* (Montreal: McGill-Queens University Press, 2000), 227.

17. See Roger Maaka and Augie Fleras, "Engaging with Indigeneity: Tino Rangatiratanga in Aotearoa," in Duncan Ivison, Paul Patton, and Will Sanders, eds., *Political Theory and the Rights of Indigenous Peoples* (New York: Cambridge University Press, 2000), 89–109.

18. Ovide Mercredi and Mary-Ellen Turpel, *In the Rapids: Navigating the Future of Canada's First Nations* (Toronto: Viking, 1993), 59-79. See especially the moving discussion of Cree leader Big Bear's signing of Treaty 6 in 1882 and the subsequent imprisonment of Big Bear and abrogation of the treaty only six years later.

19. Melissa Williams, *Voice, Trust and Memory. Marginalized Groups and the Failings of Liberal Representation* (Princeton, N.J.: Princeton University Press, 1998), chap. 6.

20. Janna Thompson, "Historical Injustice and Reparation: Justifying Claims of Descendants," *Ethics* 112 (October 2001): 114–35.

21. Williams, *Voice, Trust, and Memory*, 177.

22. Ibid. Iris Young, *Justice and the Politics of Difference* (Princeton, N.J.: Princeton University Press, 1990), also provides a compelling argument for these types of group-based strategies for remedying injustice.

23. Allen Buchanan, *Justice, Legitimacy and Self-Determination: A Moral Philosophy of International Law* (New York: Oxford University Press, forthcoming), chap. 9.

24. See here Jeremy Waldron, "Superseding Historic Injustice," *Ethics* 103 (October 1992): 4–28.

25. One problem with the idea of reparations for historical injustices committed against a particular group, especially when the reparations must be of a limited nature, as in this case, is that it fails to address the ongoing marginalization of indigenous peoples. Reparations are insufficient because they are similar to small affirmative action programs meant to "restore" to a group some element of what is taken from them. To the extent that they are temporary and distributive, they fail to address the overall context of injustice that may continue to operate even after reparations are made. As the sole means to address injustice, they are conservative in the sense that they do not challenge the overall structure of the society, which may be paternalistic or racist in profound ways. It is important, therefore, that the redistribution of resources, conceived of as a form of reparations or justified on the grounds of rectificatory justice, must be combined with institutional reform of the political and social systems of contemporary societies. Some element of rectificatory justice is necessary because indigenous people were unfairly dispossessed. It is also an important element in an argument for indigenous self-determination because access to resources and redistribution is an important background condition for the meaningful exercise of collective self-determination.

26. This is also recognized by indigenous peoples. See James Tully, *Strange Multiplicity: Constitutionalism in an Age of Diversity* (New York:

Cambridge University Press, 1995), and the theme that runs throughout of two-row wampum.

27. John Stuart Mill, "On Liberty" in *On Liberty, Utilitarianism, On Representative Government* (London: J. M. Dent, 1993), 80.

28. Avishai Margalit and Joseph Raz, "On National Self-Determination," in *Ethics in the Public Domain*, ed. Joseph Raz (Oxford, England: Clarendon Press, 1994). Of course, this line of argument does not address the difficult questions relating to the extent of jurisdictional authority, or territory, that such groups should have. To see this problem, consider the disanalogies between John Stuart Mill's argument for individual liberty and the justification for group autonomy. If Mill's distinction between self- and other-regarding behavior in individuals is problematic, this is doubly so for groups that aspire to self-government over (diverse) territory. In the latter case, the "self" that is self-governing is composed of two elements: (1) attachment to a group or membership in the group and (2) attachment to territory or land. To the extent that government is over a territorial jurisdiction, it is inclusive of all peoples resident in that territory and so may not necessarily correspond to group membership. This is not a decisive criticism of this line of argument, but it does suggest that there are crucial ambiguities at the heart of the extension of the Millian insight to groups.

29. The issue of cultural difference also arises, though in an indirect way, in this argument. This is because one reason why indigenous peoples are in the best position to make decisions over their own lives and the institutional structure that they live in is that they understand the meanings and values internal to their culture and that nonindigenous peoples, operating within a different cultural framework, make mistakes, even while being well-meaning, because they do not share indigenous peoples' cultural understandings and values.

30. Allen Buchanan identifies a number of different grounds for recognizing indigenous self-government. The remedial rights argument that he identifies corresponds to the rights that arise as a result of the injustice suffered by indigenous peoples, and rectificatory justice considerations justify the resurrection of some form of political self-rule that indigenous peoples were denied. This corresponds roughly to my discussion of jurisdictional authority. Buchanan, *Justice, Legitimacy and Self-Determination*, chap. 9.

31. Of course, the notion of popular sovereignty typically carries with it the idea that it is all the people who are the source of the government's legitimacy. However, this is problematic in societies that are deeply divided in the sense that the laws, policies, and institutions typically reflect the culture and understanding of only one group (the nonindigenous community) on the territory, the subordinated group (indigenous people) has

been marginalized from the process of state creation, and the members of the subordinated group are rendered vulnerable by their minority status if they are included simply as equal undifferentiated individuals.

32. In his book *Politics in the Vernacular* (New York: Oxford University Press, 2001), 122, Will Kymlicka identifies the historic differences in the relationship to early state formation as one of the key differences between indigenous peoples and minority nationalists. He argues that national minorities were losers, but players, in the process of European state formation, while indigenous people were entirely outside that process. This chapter develops that argument to highlight the parallel between the process of colonization and indigenous settlement.

33. This is related to, though distinct from, the international law account of historic sovereignty. On that account, the loss of sovereignty of the three Baltic republics and their forcible incorporation into the USSR in 1940–41 meant that the sovereignty of these areas could be revived in international law and that their place in the world community of states could be restored to them. There are some parallels with the situation of indigenous peoples, but it is not necessary to engage in such retrospective invalidation (with its enormous implications) or to suppose that the self-governing indigenous communities were "sovereign" in the sense that we use the word today. It is only necessary to note that most indigenous peoples have an account or a memory of an earlier era of political independence and that the basis on which this independence was lost was often illegal and also morally suspect. For a discussion of the relationship between the international law account and the normative account, see Benedict Kingsbury, "Reconciling Five Competing Conceptual Structures of Indigenous Peoples' Claims in International and Comparative Law," in *People's Rights,* ed. Philip Alston (New York: Oxford University Press, 2001), 100.

34. Alan Cairns, *Citizens Plus: Aboriginal Peoples and the Canadian State* (Vancouver: UBC Press, 2000), 17.

35. The point is made in Cairns, *Citizens Plus,* 14–56. However, curiously, he does not connect that historical story at all with the solutions that he proposes in the bulk of the book.

36. Quoted in Cairns, *Citizens Plus,* 57.

37. Royal Commission on Aboriginal Peoples, *The High Arctic Relocation: A Report on the 1953–55 Relocation* (Ottawa, Ont.: Ministry of Supply and Services Canada, 1994), 71–77, 115–32.

38. Andrew Armitage, *Comparing the Policy of Aboriginal Assimilation: Australia, Canada and New Zealand* (Vancouver: UBC Press, 1995), 236–67, 106–13.

39. The formulation does not clarify whether self-determination of particular groups within areas of decolonization could be morally justified.

For an argument concerning the limited contexts in which this might be the best (optimal) overall result, see Margaret Moore, *The Ethics of Nationalism* (New York: Oxford University Press, 2001), chap. 7.

40. For the text of the accord, see Acuerdos de San Andrés de Larráinzar (Spanish) and San Andrés Larráinzar Agreements (English), 1996, retrieved March 22, 2003, from United States Institute of Peace Web site: www.usip.org/library/pa/index/pa_chiapas.html.

41. The San Andres Accord in Mexico was not implemented by the government. The proposals of the Royal Commission in Canada were not acted upon by the federal government.

42. This is especially important in areas such as policing, where white majority interventions are frequently seen as attempts to control indigenous peoples by incarcerating them rather than dealing with the social and economic problems that lead to antisocial behavior. Local indigenous police services are in the best position to draw up solutions and develop trust in the community.

43. Ronald Watts, "Federal Systems and Accommodation of Distinct Groups: A Comparative Survey of Institutional Arrangements for Aboriginal Peoples," Institute of Intergovernmental Relations Working Paper Series 1998, no. 3. Retrieved June 2002 from http://qsilver.queensu.ca /iigr/Working_Papers_Series/Watts_98(3).html.

44. Kymlicka, *Politics in the Vernacular,* 130.

45. Ibid., 141.

46. On the face of it, this discussion may seem to fall victim to the same criticism that I made of the first argument for indigenous self-determination, namely that it effectively hampers indigenous people in the exercise of self-determination by requiring them to meet externally imposed standards—in that case, to be fully liberal, in this case, to be fully democratic. There is, however, a difference between the externally imposed requirements of liberal justice and those of democracy, which simply stipulate that the elites be responsive to, and accountable to, their own people. The principles are designed to ensure that indigenous people are able to effectively exercise self-rule and have the capacity to make decisions over their own lives.

47. This tension between restrictive and territorial membership forms is experienced by many indigenous communities, particularly since intermarriage rates are quite high in some countries. In the United States, for example, nearly 60 percent of Native Americans are married to non-natives (figures from Cairns, *Citizens Plus*). For a discussion of the problems that restrictive membership poses for communities, see Audra Simpson, "Paths toward a Mohawk Nation: Narratives of Citizenship and Nationhood in Kahnawake," in Ivison, Patton, and Sanders, *Political Theory,* 113–36. Re-

strictive membership is consistent with a traditionalist, cultural type of argument but not with the dynamic conception of indigenous self-determination and territorial self-government argued for in this chapter.

48. I do not show that this is justifiable here, and in fact there are arguments based on global justice that question this move. However, it is certainly unjustifiable to deny this capacity to indigenous peoples and yet have an international state system premised on the equal rights of citizens combined with restrictive entry.

49. This is a flaw in the Nisga'a Treaty, negotiated by the Nisga'a Band of British Columbia, which gives some input (of an advisory nature) to the small nonindigenous population living in the Nisga'a territory but denies them equal political rights. See the section dealing with the constitution of the Nisga'a government in the Nisga'a Final Agreement. For the full text of the agreement, see "Nisga'a Final Agreement and Background Information," retrieved January 2002 from the Indian and Northern Affairs Canada Web site: www.inac.gc.nr.prs/m_a1999/991065k/html. In partial mitigation, it must be said that indigenous peoples in general have a very low capacity to assimilate outsiders, so they do seem to require protection, although I think it is preferable to employ standard boundary drawing and increased jurisdictional authority. Moreover, the nonindigenous population does have public government in the sense that there are elected Members of the Legislative Assembly at the provincial level and Members of Parliament at the federal level operating in the area, and the Charter of Rights and the criminal law applies in the territory. Because there are many areas over which the local community has no jurisdiction, it is probably inaccurate to say that the nonindigenous population is disenfranchised.

50. This diagnosis is found in Menno Boldt, *Surviving as Indians: The Challenge of Self-Government* (Toronto: University of Toronto Press, 1993), 140. It is repeated in Tom Flanagan, *First Nations? Second Thoughts* (Montreal: McGill-Queen's University Press, 2000), 94–111, but in Flanagan's book it is put forward, not as an argument for needed reform, but as an argument against indigenous self-government.

51. Implicit in this argument is the importance of creating institutional structures that reflect the culture of indigenous peoples. The argument of this chapter is that cultural integrity is preserved best, and in a nonstatic way, by creating institutions of self-government. However, it is important to supplement this by considering ways in which the state can reflect the distinctive practices and cultures of its indigenous peoples.

52. In Canada, the failed Charlottetown Accord addressed the issue of indigenous representation at the center through provisions for representation in the Senate (sec. 7), the Supreme Court (sec. 20), and the House

of Commons (sec. 22). Obviously, in countries like Mexico, where indigenous people constitute a majority in three states, representation in central institutions is potentially easier, and more could be done through favorable weighting of indigenous interests. It is also consistent with democratic inclusion to combine territorial self-government with reserved seats, along the lines of India, which reserves 15 percent of seats for scheduled castes and 6 percent of seats for scheduled indigenous tribes.

53. See Watts, "Federal Systems," 23–24.

54. Statistics on the percentage of urban indigenous population are from Cairns, *Citizens Plus*, 8.

55. This problem is admirably discussed in Cairns, *Citizens Plus*, 126–32.

56. In Canada, comprehensive constitutional change has been depressingly unsuccessful, with the last three efforts (the Aboriginal round, from 1984–87, the Meech Lake round of 1987–90, and the Charlottetown round of 1991–92) resulting in failure. In Australia, comprehensive constitutional review of fifteen years resulted in four constitutional proposals being put to referendum, but all were rejected. See Ronald Watts, "Federal Systems," 28.

5

INDIGENOUS SELF-GOVERNMENT

JACOB T. LEVY

I. Paradoxes

Institutions of indigenous self-government that are recognized by states are by now fairly widespread. From U.S. Indian reservations to Greenland to the Canadian territory of Nunavut to the northeastern states of India, indigenous peoples are living under a distinctively indigenous level of government that comes between them and the central state. These are sometimes component units of a federation like other units, as is the case for India's tribal states or for Nunavut (a territory like the Yukon Territory). But even then, they are not *entirely* like the others; the tribal states are governed by laws restricting in-migration, tourism, and land sales that do not apply to other states. Sometimes the indigenous polities are an entirely sui generis kind of government within a federation, as with U.S. reservation governments or Canadian First Nation band councils. And sometimes, as in Greenland, the self-governing indigenous area is the only anomaly in an otherwise unitary state (Denmark).

Many of these institutions pose a number of theoretical paradoxes for arguments about self-government and self-determination. Consider the following.

First, Will Kymlicka argues that national minorities have a right to self-government because they are *nations*—"historical communit[ies], more or less institutionally complete, occupying a given territory or homeland, sharing a distinct language and culture."[1] Of all minorities, it is indigenous peoples whose rights Kymlicka has been the most concerned to defend throughout the corpus of his work.[2] But of all the groups Kymlicka considers as national minorities, indigenous peoples often have the *weakest* claim to nationhood understood in this way. All too often the populations of Indian tribes in the United States and Canada or Aboriginal bands in Australia have been reduced to triple digits or below. Only a handful of indigenous communities in those states could still hope to meet the criteria of being anything like "institutionally complete"; often they have been institutionally hollowed out. Their languages have frequently fallen into near or total disuse; the land they occupy is often not their traditional homeland (because of forced population transfers); and sometimes they do not have any discrete territory or homeland at all. If the situation is not quite so dire in New Zealand or in Greenland, it is probably worse in Siberia and most of Africa and is not much better in India.

Second, remedial arguments for self-determination, up to and including secession, posit a link between the severity of injustices to which a group has been subject in the past and the strength of its current claim to order its own affairs politically. Not many ethnic minorities can match the history of warfare, massacres, expropriation, fraud, cultural suppression, and expulsion to which many indigenous peoples have been subjected; if remedial arguments are ever valid, then they are surely valid with respect to many indigenous communities. But—save for Greenland and, at a stretch, a few places in Latin America, India, and Burma—it is almost inconceivable that any indigenous groups could successfully secede and establish their own states. The relevant states (Canada, the United States, Russia, and so on) would certainly never allow it; and even if they did, most indigenous communities are smaller in population than even tiny states such as East Timor. Self-government without secession leaves indigenous peoples all too much at the mercy of the same states whose past actions generated remedial claims in the first place.

Third, and similarly, arguments for self-government that are based on the avoidance of *future* injustices (the counterpart of remedial arguments' retrospective focus) depend on the thought that institutional bulwarks can be created, giving minorities political weight to counterbalance the majority's and the state's dangerous tendencies.[3] Indigenous peoples are among the minorities most in need of such protection. But, and for the same reasons, they are among the most difficult to provide with the necessary political power to protect themselves. Control of a huge national-minority province such as Quebec can do a great deal to prevent abuses of the minority by the central state. Control of a reservation with a few hundred or a few thousand citizens can do very little.

In short, the very vulnerability that generates such moral urgency for a range of indigenous rights (including rights of self-government) often undercuts the argument in support of such rights. The institutions may not be able to perform the function that provides their justification—whether that function is the provision of a secure and stable national culture, compensation for past evils, or the prevention of future wrongs. Among those sympathetic to liberal arguments for cultural rights of any sort, there is a widespread sense that indigenous peoples offer the easiest of justificatory cases. But indigenous self-government in particular often offers the most difficult of arguments for efficacy—arguments that are very relevant to the justifications offered.

A decade ago Yael Tamir and Will Kymlicka disagreed over whether—to simplify—cultural rights grow more or less robust as a group's size increases. Kymlicka maintained that as a group becomes larger and therefore less vulnerable to the loss of its culture, special state protections for the group become more difficult to justify. Tamir replied that some rights are impossible to exercise in very small groups and that special measures that are unjustified when the group is too small may become justified when the group becomes large enough to take advantage of them. She offered the example of state support for religious congregations in an area that lacked a *minyan*, the minimum number of Jewish men (or men and women, in some Reform interpretations) to create a congregation. It would be impossible to justify giving the subsidy to nine Jews, as they could not make use of it. It would be possible to justify giving it to ten Jews, who could. A plausible intuition underlies both of these arguments, and often there is no real conflict between them. In self-government for very small indigenous communities—and for other similarly small and poor ethnic minorities, but indigenous minorities are often among the smallest, poorest, and least powerful—the tension between these intuitions becomes especially acute, and especially poignant.

One final paradox rests not on the vulnerability of indigenous minorities but rather on the strange relationship between their cultures and the kinds of institutions set over them by central states. A key pillar of the structure of indigenous rights and indigenous law is custom. The content of indigenous rights is, in large part, given by tradition. The claim to distinctiveness and to a special status within the modern state is based on a history of existence as a separate people, with its own rules and norms and institutions. But the mechanisms of self-government under discussion here are *not* customary ones. U.S. Indian reservation governments as structured and defined by the Indian Reorganization Act of 1934 and the Indian Self-Determination Act of 1975, the unified territory of Nunavut, the tribal states of India, and so on recognize authority in a community understood as preexisting or customary—that is, the legislation or treaty that creates the governing structure depends on the idea that there is already a tribe in existence. But the authority created by those instruments and exercised by those structures is *not* a traditional kind of authority; nor is it necessarily exercised in a traditional kind of way. The recognition of custom and of customary group boundaries accompanies a sometimes decisive break with customary understandings of the group, its law, its relationship to its law, and its form of government.

Not all special or group-differentiated indigenous rights are caught in this paradox. Land rights (about which more below) and the protection and recognition of customary law rest on substantially independent bases of justification. What is of particular interest is the creation of European-style territorial governing structures, the key feature of which is legislative power. The distinction does not quite correspond to that between Hart's primary and secondary rules, as Hart includes in the latter category the rules that allow persons to create legal conditions like contract, marriage, and ownership.[4] But the distinction does depend on the characteristic that Hart thought made "modern" legal systems unique: the creation of formal institutions for the deliberate change of the law. What Jeremy Webber says of Aborigines is, in a loose and general way, true for most indigenous peoples: "[L]aw for indigenous Australians has traditionally been considered not to be the product of deliberate choice, but an inheritance, determined in the Dreaming or by what has come before, not merely by the desires of those now living."[5] But mechanisms of self-government that create statelike or provincelike powers for indigenous communities or collections of indigenous communities (the self-governing mechanisms are not always of the one-tribe, one-government sort) insist on just such an understanding of law as the product of deliberate choice.

I have elsewhere argued that, partly for reasons such as these, the recognition and incorporation of indigenous law either within the common law or as an independent body of customary law are often to be preferred to formal mechanisms of self-government. But self-government remains the preferred goal for many indigenous political movements and is considered the sine qua non by some. And self-government is often epistemologically easier for states than is customary law, the content and boundaries of which may be exceedingly difficult for outsiders to understand or even forbidden for outsiders to know (creating near-hopeless conflicts with outside legal systems); self-government may therefore be the policy choice preferred by states. So in this essay, and in light of the paradoxes noted above, I consider when, how, and why such mechanisms can be justified and when, how, and why they fail the test. I am interested in particular in remedial and counterbalancing justifications for self-government—in how these justifications are affected by the considerations noted above, in whether and when they can overcome those considerations, and in whether and when other factors will limit the justifiable extent of self-government.

I should note that I proceed here on the view that there is no first-order moral right to be governed by persons of one's own ethnicity, religion, culture, or "nation." The principles that in the context of minority rights we refer to as "self-determination" and "self-government" (though the terms themselves depend on reified collective selves) are, at best, instrumentally justified. There may be a right to have some democratic say in whatever government one is subject to; but there is no right that the *demos* be demarcated in one way rather than another. This does not undercut claims for minority self-government as much as it might immediately appear, since it denies sacrosanct status to the *demos* of the larger state as well. But it does mean that there is no intrinsic right of self-determination and that mechanisms of indigenous self-government are as much in need of justification as is any other arrangement of borders and political power.

Much, but not all, of what I will say here about mechanisms of self-government also applies to the formal indigenous institutions created by states that do not concede or recognize self-government rights. For example, the Aboriginal and Torres Strait Islander Commission (ATSIC) in Australia has delegated authority to manage a variety of federal programs for Aborigines and acts as a state-funded advocacy group for Aboriginal interests. Like reservation governments and the rest, it is a creature of state legislation, not of custom. It has even greater difficulty than they do purporting to speak for a "nation," since it represents all Aboriginal peoples in all their variety as well as the quite distinct Torres Strait Islanders. But unlike them, it has nothing like legislative authority. Its Regional Councils have some adjudicative powers, but they do not govern the tribes and bands within their respective territories. ATSIC can spend but not tax, recommend but not rule, advocate but not determine. So what I say here about self-government and lawmaking authority obviously does not apply—although many Aboriginal advocates hold out "self-government" as a goal and see administrative bodies such as ATSIC as intermediate steps. I mean what I say here to help us evaluate such aspirations, as well as extant institutions. As far as ATSIC itself goes, however, many of the considerations here *are* relevant to it; and if ASTIC is free from the possibility of internal tyranny, it is especially prone to doubts about both its independence from the central state and the coherence of its relationship to its constituents' customary rights. (Even if the forms of tribal self-government in the United States are dictated by Congress, the tribes themselves existed before the congressional legislation did.)

The Saami Parliaments in Norway and Sweden offer interesting intermediate cases. Despite their names, they are not legislative bodies. Neither state has conceded to those bodies any authority to contradict or constrain the central Parliament, to raise taxes, or to exercise police powers. The Saami Parliaments have some delegated administrative authority, including some delegated spending authority over funds mostly provided by the center, and they have some power to manage intra-Saami disputes. But for the most part they are political rather than legislative bodies. They may raise issues to the attention of their respective states' governments; they may lobby; they may pass resolutions. They are creations of central legislation in both states. Unlike the members of ATSIC, their members are directly elected—and, unlike the members of the Canadian Assembly of First Nations, which is not a creation of the state,[6] the members are elected in state-funded elections, by Saami voters on state-sponsored voting rolls. (ATSIC's Regional Councils are elected in a similar fashion, but the federal Commissioners are chosen by the Regional Councils.) They therefore have distinctively authoritative positions as the public advocates of their respective constituencies; but they ultimately remain advocacy bodies rather than legislative ones. Again, self-government remains an aspiration for many activists. Again, some but not all of what I say here about mechanisms of self-government applies to them.

II. The Perils of Self-Government

Among political theorists and philosophers, two questions about the internal justice of tribal governments are very well known. One is gender discrimination, especially gender-discriminatory rules governing tribal membership.[7] The other is religious discrimination and establishment. Both are interesting because of the apparent conflict between Indians' rights as individuals and the preservation of their traditional cultures. But not all internal abuses relate to "culture" in such a way. Tribal self-government creates *governments,* not cultural protection boards; and they are perfectly capable of acting in the ways that governments do. For example, in the United States most tribes' economies are dominated by the tribal governments—because of collective land ownership or control, because federal money is channeled through those governments, and because of distortions introduced by the casino economy. As a result, the tribal governments own, publish, and fund a large majority of the newspapers published on reservations and control most advertising in many of the rest. The results are predictable and have nothing to do with cultural distinctiveness: freedom of the press is often curtailed, especially when the newspapers investigate or criticize tribal government policies or officials.[8]

Even some basic procedures of justice are jeopardized. In the late 1990s, the Cherokee Nation of Oklahoma suffered a protracted and violent constitutional crisis when its chief, Joe Byrd, shut down judicial institutions and investigative bodies because they were pursuing charges of corruption against him—including charges that he improperly commingled federal money, Cherokee Nation employees, and Democratic National Committee activities in the 1996 election. At the crisis's climax, Byrd fired the Nation's marshals who had seized his financial records pursuant to a court order, declared that he would not be bound by the ruling of the Cherokee's highest court, engineered a procedurally illegitimate impeachment of that court's members, and had both the marshals and judges locked out of their offices so that he could reclaim his financial records. At the critical moments he was assisted by armed agents of the Bureau of Indian Affairs (BIA), whose force far outmatched that of the Cherokee judicial and law enforcement officials.[9]

The connection between Byrd, the Democratic Party, and the BIA/Department of Interior suggests that sometimes the complex relationships between the leaders of self-governing bodies and the central state can develop into a dangerous kind of clientelism and that multiple levels of government may collude with each other rather than checking each other. But the early stages of the crisis and of Byrd's coup needed no BIA encouragement or assistance, despite the fact that the Cherokees have perhaps the longest experience with European-style governing structures and the separation of powers of any U.S. tribe. On other reservations, severe conflicts among the three branches of tribal governments, charges of election fraud, and violence between political opponents have become almost routine.[10] None of these, of course, is unique to tribal governments;[11] but that, in its way, is the point I am trying to make. The difficulties with creating formal indigenous governing institutions are not quite the same as the difficulties with rights of cultural preservation, land rights, and so on; and the threats such governments may pose to the freedom of their constituents are not only "cultural" threats.

That is not to say that there is nothing to worry about in the mingling of culture and government that is common in indigenous polities. Self-government as a mechanism for the preservation of customary ways and customary laws introduces hazardous sorts of communalism and conservatism. In this, indigenous governments are somewhat less like the provinces accorded to linguistic minorities in ethnic federalism, provinces like Quebec and Catalonia, than they are like the provinces that operate under distinctive religious legal codes. States in both the Nigerian and Malaysian federations have introduced harsh versions of *shari'a* or Islamic law as their public legal systems, only sometimes bothering to exclude non-Muslims from its rule. Whereas in religiously plural legal systems such as India's, religious family law attaches to persons throughout the state, this religious-legal federalism seems to encourage an identification between a particular government and the preservation of religious and cultural purity. The province of a linguistic minority may, of course, come to be identified with the language and its survival in a way that smoothes the way for violations of the rights of speakers of some other languages; but these restrictions typically seem to be less pervasive and less invasive than those associated with religious or cultural purity. Laws banning the use of English in commercial signage in Quebec are illiberal and wrong, but they can hardly compare to execution by stoning for adultery, a sentence that has been handed down in some of Nigeria's northern states.

I hasten to add that the dangers of making cultural preservation and purity the mission of a particular polity have much to do with the culture involved and that there is something distinctively pernicious about the style of Islam adopted by those states. But the mixture of political membership requirements with cultural membership requirements and the equation of dissent with inauthenticity are dangers in indigenous as in religious polities and provinces.

Moreover, a government that is especially weak with respect to outsiders, in order to do *something*—and to be seen to be doing something—to protect a culture, may well target internal dissidents, assimilators, minorities, and vulnerable groups all the more strenuously. As was noted in the beginning of this essay, indigenous governments often suffer from just such weakness. The cultures, religions, languages, and customs they are charged with protecting continue their erosion, and the governments have little ability to affect the outside polity or society in order to slow that process. The only tools at their disposal will sometimes be limitations on the freedom of members.

III. SELF-GOVERNMENT NONETHELESS

All of that said, it is hardly the case that the *primary* threats to the rights, freedoms, or interests of indigenous persons come from their institutions of self-government (even where those exist). The history of expropriation, plunder, murder, and restriction is far too severe for us to have any confidence in the states that would fill the vacuum left if indigenous self-government were to disappear.

Nor are these state actions all in the distant past. Expropriation and misappropriation, for example, are not dangers that have come and gone. For more than a century the U.S. government, acting as trustee for hundreds of thousands of individual Indian landowners as well as more than a thousand tribes, has collected royalties for the mining, logging, farming, and grazing that are done on indigenous land and has then paid the owners. In recent years it has become apparent that BIA and the Department of the Interior have mismanaged and misplaced these funds for decades. The Department of the Interior has admitted that so many documents and records are missing or have been destroyed that it has no way of accurately calculating what is owed to the landowners. A class action lawsuit claims that the amounts run toward U.S. $10 billion; the Department of the Interior claims it is far less but still admits that it is in the billions. Even during the reform efforts prompted by the lawsuits, the Department of the Interior has sometimes slowed or stopped checks for months at a time and used delaying tactics that the federal bench found so frivolous that it ordered midtrial payments of Indians' legal fees. Successive Secretaries of the Interior (from both political parties) have been charged with contempt of court for delaying the investigation, refusing to pursue court-ordered reforms, and covering up their refusal.

The coherence of the trusteeship doctrine is surely left in shambles by a record such as this. The notion articulated by Chief Justice Marshall in *Cherokee v. Georgia*[12] that the United States stood toward Indian nations as a guardian to its ward has endured in both American law and in the law of the other common-law settler states. It is firmly settled law; I do not suppose that any argument will change that. But for the idea of wardship or trusteeship to be well grounded at all, it would have to be the case that the guardian was not itself the primary threat to the ward. Moreover, even if the paternalistic language of tutelage had ever been appropriate, in a liberal society competent persons are always entitled and expected to outgrow the need for a guardian. The United States has failed as a trustee for Indian lands and interests; Indians are certainly capable of doing better for themselves; and even if they were not, it is inappropriate to make them depend on a guardian with such a proven record of having direct conflicts of interest.[13]

It therefore seems to me that remedial and counterbalancing considerations continue to offer support for indigenous self-government—even though the remediation is inadequate, even though the counterbalancing may be weak at best. A reservation government for a tribe numbering in the dozens will not be able to directly prevent state action against the rights of tribe members—not in the way that a large linguistic province's control of its education system and representation in the central government can forestall policies of language assimilation. Nonetheless, the existence of any formal institutions of minority rights—a system of religious personal law, territorial self-government, state-funded schools, and so on—can serve a number of different salutary functions. First, formal institutions tend to entrench themselves over time. They develop a class of employees and professionals attached to them, who seek both to establish the institution in society (creating functions for it as they go, if necessary) and to protect it against invasion from above. The institutional status quo not only has inertia on its side but actively protects itself. This is by no means an unmitigated blessing; indeed, for most institutions most of the time, it is fair to count it as a disadvantage. (Think of the absurd difficulty that the U.S. Congress has in eliminating even the most economically destructive subsidies and protections for even the tiniest groups of beneficiaries—peanut farmers, mohair farmers, honey producers.) But in the realm of minority rights it has substantial benefits—if we think the central state is likely to underprotect or actively threaten the rights and legitimate interests of minorities.

Second, a formal institution can serve as a canary in the mine. Even if institutions like tribal governments lack the institutional heft to protect themselves, even if they lack the power to effectively counterbalance the state, they can provide useful information about prevailing political trends. Attacks on or the elimination of such institutions can help to highlight political moods that may later lead to injustices committed directly against members of minority groups.

Caution is necessary when evaluating such signals. A political attempt to limit mechanisms of self-government may stem from a wide range of causes. Members of the majority may believe that the institutions have arrogated so much power to themselves that they now exceed the bounds of justice. They may believe that the institutions are genuinely harmful to the interests of those they represent. They may believe that appropriate balances have been upset and need to be restored. And any or all of these beliefs may be correct and justified. The fact that an institution is intended to serve the interests of a minority and (which is different) to serve justice is no guarantee that it will always do either. Thus attacks on the institution need not indicate any malice or any desire to invade the rights of the institution's constituents. On the other hand, when there *is* malice or ill intent, it may well manifest first by an assault on formal institutions. There are good reasons in principle to be opposed to India's system of religious personal law, for example. But when Hindu nationalist parties and organizations seek the elimination of that system, Indian Muslims have probably been right to perceive further threats in the background.

Third, and related to the first two, a formal institution can be a rallying point. It can ease the difficulties associated with coordinating minority political action and can bring into politics more group members than only those affiliated with the institution. By providing organizational training and experience, by offering logistical support, and by providing a single public symbol for minority rights, formal institutions can facilitate and encourage political activism on the part of a group's general population. Again, this does *not* mean that either justice or the minority's genuine interests will necessarily be well served. Activism assisted by and centering on the defense of a particular institution can sometimes distract from issues of greater importance. And such activism can worsen the problem of the entrenchment of the status quo; if the institution ever does need reform or abolition, the political patterns it has established may make such changes impossible. But if, on balance and more often than not, we expect a minority without such institutional protection and political power to be vulnerable to injustice, then these prices may be worth paying.

If self-government is justified only in such instrumental terms, of course, then whenever self-governing institutions threaten the freedom of their constituents the justification is undermined. If the task of indigenous levels of government is to protect their members' freedoms and rights against the central state by acting as advocates and counterbalances, if they are to be polities in a federation, then they are subject to the moral constraints that bind polities; they must not operate as if they were churches or cultural associations. Abuses they commit will typically not be grounds to eliminate them; but they must be understood as abuses and, one hopes, ameliorated.

Self-government rights are constitutional fundamentals—but *not* first-order moral principles, not constitutional fundamentals in the Rawlsian sense. They are institutionally fundamental without being morally fundamental. They are morally part of the realm of the second-best—but they are best possible if we take the underlying social facts seriously. Central states cannot be trusted with the rights, freedoms, or lands of indigenous minorities, and they must be constrained as best as we can manage—even if it seems unlikely that they can be sufficiently constrained purely by institutional design, as they may be when faced with larger and more powerful minorities.[14]

With such difficult cases of counterbalancing, mechanisms besides self-government may be needed—and these may be mechanisms that are unjustifiable except as second-best measures. I have elsewhere argued against the various burdens that are placed on the alienation of indigenous land in North America, Australia, and India. These rules—either forbidding indigenous landowners from selling their land at all or allowing them to sell it only to the state and/or indigenous buyers—grow out of a combination of paternalism and state interest in having monopsony power. (In Australia, the Crown was not so much interested in monopsony power as in preventing the idea that Aborigines had any land title *at all*; if private persons could purchase land from Aborigines, that implied that the land was the Aborigines' to sell.) Today they restrict the freedom of indigenous owners; they make indigenous title into a kind of second-class ownership; they involve the state in enforcing a fixed understanding of indigenous culture (insofar as the rules are justified with reference to cultural connections with the land); and they greatly complicate and slow economic growth and poverty reduction in indigenous areas.

All of these arguments still seem to me valid; but in light of the arguments presented here, there is one important factor pushing the other way. Inalienability may slow or prevent the transfer of majority populations into indigenous areas—a transfer that has often been part of deliberate state attempts to suppress indigenous communities and to seize their lands altogether. The restrictions on alienation of tribal land in the northeastern states of India have no doubt contributed to the terrible poverty there; but they may also have helped to prevent the kind of "development" policies that have taken place across the Himalayas in Tibet, policies that have had the intent and effect of making Han Chinese a majority in the province. It is a terrible trade-off to contemplate—a policy that keeps indigenous persons poor and/or dependent might be necessary in order to keep the state from taking their lands and suppressing their culture altogether.

But inalienability, to have any credible ability to counterbalance state projects aimed at weakening indigenous communities, would have to include inalienability to the state as well, or at a bare minimum the elimination of "takings" or eminent domain authority. When the state has both monopsony power and "takings" or eminent domain power, then other restrictions on alienability do not tie its hands at all.

In the United States and Canada inalienability has sometimes meant that only the federation, not the states or provinces, could buy or seize indigenous lands; and when this rule has been observed, it has helped to preserve land rights. Indigenous peoples have often faced their greatest dangers from settlers' governments on the periphery or the frontier, and the center has sometimes been an ally. This is in any event good reason to allow indigenous levels of government to interact directly with the federal government, rather than being subordinate to state or provincial governments.[15] Denying the states or provinces the ability to acquire indigenous lands directly seems like the minimum that prudence demands; perhaps it would be sufficient as well, leaving no need for private inalienability. But to prohibit private alienation while leaving all levels of the settler state free to acquire lands compulsorily only harms indigenous landowners.

Finally, it is worth saying a word or two about the tacit view that has run through this essay concerning the rights of indigenous persons and peoples that *are* first-order rights, the rights that we ought to construct institutions to defend. The justice of indigenous claims to particular pieces of land, where these are not based only on treaties or other instruments of positive law, necessarily suppose that there are something like prepolitical rights of property. If, as Sunstein and Holmes famously argue, property rights are entirely the creature of the positive law of a state and may morally be arranged in any way convenient, then Aborigines lacked a claim in justice against the Australian state for the protection of their pre-settlement land rights.[16] (Sunstein and Holmes could admit of claims in purely *distributive* justice, but these would not justify rights to *particular* pieces of land. Indeed, such distributive arguments might well serve to *limit* the share of the Australian landmass, or its mineral wealth, that Aborigines could claim.) If we think that Aborigines (and other indigenous peoples) had rights to their land before colonization, rights that the colonists and colonial states were wrong to violate, then we are committed to the idea that justice and injustice in property relations are in some sense pre- or extrapolitical.[17]

Similarly, if liberty is understood purely as a civic and political phenomenon—as a relationship that obtains among citizens of the same state and due to the protections of that state—and if the idea of "natural liberty" is discarded, as it is in the work of Philip Pettit and other republicans, then we lose much of our ability to describe the actions of colonial regimes as restrictions of the liberty of indigenous persons, who have often been understood by colonists and have often understood themselves as nonmembers of the colonial state.[18]

Given that much, however—given a view that indigenous peoples had and have rights to their own land, and that they had and have rights of freedom to practice and maintain their own ways—indigenous self-government is justifiable, flaws and paradoxes notwithstanding.

NOTES

1. Will Kymlicka, *Multicultural Citizenship* (New York: Oxford University Press, 1995), p. 11.

2. I don't mean anything about the substance of Kymlicka's argument; indeed, it is only fairly recently that he has begun to treat indigenous peoples as an analytically distinct set of minorities—see his *Politics in the Vernacular* (New York: Oxford University Press, 2001), p. 122. Rather, I mean something about the moral concerns and intuitions that seem to have animated his project from *Liberalism, Community, and Culture* (New York: Oxford University Press, 1989) onward.

3. I explore and develop the idea of such counterbalancing in "Language, Literacy, and the Modern State," in Will Kymlicka and Alan Patten, eds., *Political Theory and Language Rights* (New York: Oxford University Press, 2003), and in "National Minorities without Nationalism," in Alain Deickhoff, ed., *Nationalism, Liberalism, and Pluralism* (Lanham, Md.: Lexington Books, forthcoming).

4. See H. L. A. Hart, *The Concept of Law* (New York: Oxford University Press, 1961).

5. Jeremy Webber, "Mabo and Australian Constitutionalism," in Duncan Ivison, Paul Patton, and Will Sanders, eds., *Political Theory and the Rights of Indigenous Peoples* (New York: Cambridge University Press, 2000), 81.

6. The Assembly of First Nations is a creation of preexisting First Nation organizations and exercises no powers delegated from Canada. Instead, "All delegated power, mandates or responsibility derive from the sovereignty of First Nations." Charter of the Assembly of First Nations, Art. 2, sec. 3. The charter is a careful and thoughtful document, showing a determination not to allow the assembly to become too great a force in its own right: "The Assembly of First Nations shall remain at all times an instrument to advance the aspirations of First Nations and shall not become greater in strength, power, resources or jurisdiction than the First Nations for which it was established to serve" (Art. 2, sec. 5).

7. See, of course, *Santa Clara Pueblo v. Martinez*, 436 U.S. 49 1978, though the issue raised there is not unique to the Pueblo. See also Kymlicka, *Liberalism, Community, and Culture*, p. 195.

8. Charlie LeDuff, "American Indian Newspapers Seek to Assert Independence," *New York Times*, November 4, 1996, p. A15; Karen Lincoln Michel, "Repression on the Reservation," *Columbia Journalism Review* 37 (November/December 1998): 48.

9. For more complete details, see Denette A. Mouser, "A Nation in Crisis: The Government of the Cherokee Nation Struggles to Survive," *Ameri-*

can Indian Law Review 23 (1998/1999): 359; Anthony M. Massad, Robert A. Layden, and Daniel G. Gibbens, "The Massad Commission Report to the Tribal Council of the Cherokee Nation," *American Indian Law Review* 23 (1998/1999): 375; Lois Ramano, "A Nation Divided," *Washington Post,* July 17, 1997, p. B1.

10. Robert B. Porter, "Strengthening Tribal Sovereignty through Government Reform: What Are the Issues?" *Kansas Journal of Law and Public Policy* 7 (1997): 72.

11. Such crises seem to me to have been relatively much more common in reservation governments than in state or city governments in the last ten years or so; but this is an impression, not an empirical finding.

12. *Cherokee Nation v. State of Georgia,* 30 U.S. 1 (1831).

13. See Billee Elliott McAuliffe, "Forcing Action: Seeking to 'Clean Up' the Indian Trust Fund," *Southern Illinois University Law Journal* 25 (2001): 647.

14. I will not even begin to try to solve here the problem noted by Donald Horowitz with such "must" statements—that the state or majority that requires such constitutional restraint is unlikely to simply voluntarily bind itself. Donald Horowitz, "Constitutional Design: An Oxymoron?" in Ian Shapiro and Stephen Macedo, eds., *Designing Democratic Institutions,* NOMOS XLII (New York: New York University Press, 2000).

15. It is also good reason to distrust the recent Eleventh Amendment jurisprudence in the United States that has effectively immunized the states against Indian tribes' suing them in federal courts for violations of treaties or of federal laws. See Jacob T. Levy, "Indians in Madison's Constitutional Order," in John Samples, ed., *James Madison and the Future of Limited Government* (Washington, D.C.: Cato Institute, 2002).

16. Cass Sunstein and Stephen Holmes, *The Cost of Rights* (New York: W. W. Norton, 1999).

17. See Richard Epstein, "Property Rights Claims of Indigenous Populations," *Toledo Law Review* 31 (1999): 1–15; David Lyons, "The New Indian Claims and Original Rights to Land," in Jeffrey Paul, ed., *Reading Nozick: Essays on Anarchy, State, and Utopia* (Totowa, N.J.: Rowman and Littlefield, 1981); Robert Nozick, *Anarchy, State, and Utopia* (New York: Basic Books, 1974); Jacob T. Levy, *The Multiculturalism of Fear* (New York: Oxford University Press, 2000), chaps. 6–7. Kymlicka defends a distributive interpretation of indigenous land rights in *Multicultural Citizenship,* pp. 219–21.

18. See Philip Pettit, *Republicanism* (New York: Oxford University Press, 1997).

6

EXPLORING THE BOUNDARIES OF LANGUAGE RIGHTS: INSIDERS, NEWCOMERS, AND NATIVES

RUTH RUBIO-MARÍN

I. INTRODUCTION

There is a growing literature on language rights as moral and legal categories.[1] This literature is flourishing in the midst of debates on multiculturalism that respond to the challenge of accommodating ethnocultural diversity within liberal democracies. These debates frequently turn on the notion of toleration. However, whatever its virtue as applied to religious pluralism, tolerance as nonintervention is simply a paradigm that fails when it comes to the accommodation of linguistic diversity. Even those who would like to see the liberal state making more progress toward disestablishing the cultural preferences of the dominant majorities recognize the limits of this approach as applied to language.[2] After all, the state has to function in some language. Language neutrality, strictly speaking, is not an option.[3] The state uses a language to educate, draft statutes, make judicial decisions, organize elections, and provide social services. It expects citizens to communicate with each other to organize themselves and act politically. As an economic venture too, the collective pursuit of material well-being rests on the possibility of multiple economic transactions and economic activities that require the use of a common language.

136

On the other hand, this linguistic dimension of the state does not comprehensively explain why people value their language. People seem to be bound to their language by more than an instrumental relationship. They do not value the skills in their mother tongue just because of the opportunities that become available through those skills as tools of communication.[4] People like the comfort of using their own language and the richness of the nuances and emotional meanings they can convey in it; they cherish the experience of living in a linguistic community without being looked down upon because of their language; they enjoy the sense of intimacy, trust, and shared identity that ties them to their citizen peers through the use of a common language, and they long for the feeling of cultural continuity they get from receiving a language from their ancestors and passing it on to the next generations. Indeed, because this is so important, most people would rather stay within their language communities than go somewhere else, even if by doing so they could improve their economic and professional opportunities. It is therefore not surprising that, historically, language minorities have fiercely resisted linguistic assimilation even when this meant forgoing the possibility of maximizing their economic or political agency within the larger state. Most national minorities have been more willing to put up a fight to gain a public sphere of their own and hence to reproduce economic and political options *in their language* (whether by claiming their own public institutions within the state or their own state) than to be assimilated. And indeed, in most cases of state disintegration over the last decade, "the rallying point of divergent identity has been language."[5]

In this context, the notion of language rights appears as a promise of cultural defense of language minorities within the state. Such rights can be thought of as protections for the minorities against the threat posed by the assimilationist force of the majority, which generally sees its culture and language embraced by the state institutions. The object of protection is people's linguistic and cultural identity. Language rights rest on the recognition of people's right to live in their language and to enjoy a secure linguistic environment and are best explained by claiming that the protection of cultural membership is necessary for the fulfillment of individual autonomy and as a basis for self-respect.[6]

Many of the scholars who have explored minority rights from this perspective have asserted a basic distinction between autochthonous ethnocultural minorities[7] and more recent immigrant groups. In this chapter I argue that this distinction is too simplistic and that a wide set of generalizable criteria should be identified to help us decide what groups should have what language rights within a given state. I identify several criteria. Although we will see that many of them are as a matter of fact more frequently met by national minorities than by more recent immigrant groups, that does not have to be the case, or at least not always. This is an empirical question. The main point is that meeting the criteria—and not the nature, or more precisely the origin, of the group—should be the determining factor in the recognition of language rights.

II. CALLING THE NATIONAL MINORITY/IMMIGRANT DISTINCTION INTO QUESTION

Starting the inquiry of which language groups should be accommodated by the state by calling on arguments of political wisdom or opportunity will probably not take us very far. It has been argued that states, most of which already show great resistance to publicly accommodating their autochthonous cultures, would rather halt immigration than let immigrants come with the expectation of reproducing the conditions that allow them to live and function in their culture and language.[8] This is probably true and is why, as a matter of political prudence, we should be cautious with our recommendations. However, the task of deciding whether this is normatively sound remains relevant. After all, many states have been and still are hesitant to grant their autochthonous minorities the rights they need to be able to preserve their culture or even to grant them a minority status,[9] yet we do not necessarily accept such hesitation as the ultimate defeat of our normative claims.

Often a dividing line is drawn between immigrants and autochthonous national minorities both in scholarly debates and in legal practice.[10] The general understanding is that the state has a limited capacity to accommodate ethnolinguistic groups. Intuitively right as this sounds, that in itself does not tell us how many or which groups should be accommodated. Commentators who have thus far upheld the dividing line have often relied on the moral relevance of consent.[11] Their claim is that autochthonous groups generally have a minority status as a result of having been conquered or voluntarily or involuntarily incorporated nations. Thus they have not waived the right to cultural self-definition that every nation has. In contrast, immigration is the result of individual decisions to freely leave behind one's country, generally for the sake of better life opportunities. The process of cultural integration in the receiving society may be harsh, but it is still the expression of free will. However important the goods of linguistic and cultural security and hence the rights to which they give birth, these are not inalienable rights.

This tidy distinction and the assumption of the voluntary cultural immersion of immigrants on which it rests are increasingly being challenged,[12] if not plainly rejected.[13] Relying on consent poses difficulties for later generations: children born into a cultural minority household have not expressed consent to cultural uprooting; only their parents have.[14] In reality, nobody expresses consent to the culture in which he or she is born, but that is beside the point. What is relevant is that although immigrant adults may well decide to leave their countries and place themselves in the position of a linguistic minority and accept the liabilities that go with it, this is not true of their children. On the other hand, even for first generations, some have argued that it is questionable whether individuals ought to be free to waive their rights to primary goods.[15] Moreover, for consent to be morally relevant, it needs to be free and informed. In other words, consensual cultural uprooting is morally relevant, but only if it is free and informed. Because that is often not the case with the kind of consent that we can assume immigrants to be expressing, we cannot draw a line that neatly separates the claims of autochthonous linguistic minorities and immigrants based on consent. Let me elaborate why I think this is the case.

A. *Freedom*

In a world with huge economic disparities and very politically unstable geographical areas, it is more and more difficult to generalize and describe migration movements as reflecting people's free choice of cultural uprooting.[16] Certainly, the floods of refugees and displaced persons would not qualify. Neither would those people who leave to escape sheer poverty. Indeed, although some people freely relinquish their cultural environment for the sake of better professional or social opportunities, or for personal reasons such as falling in love, and although this is probably an increasingly common trend in a globalized world, most people are not willing to do so. Even transnational projects, such as the European Union, that encourage people to perceive themselves as economic agents acting freely within a geographical and political space larger than that of their states have not been very successful in this respect.[17] This is hardly surprising. After all, the argument in favor of conceptualizing cultural membership as a primary good on the basis of liberal premises should at the same time ground the presumption that people are not easily prone to relinquish the language and culture of their primary socialization, at least not for good.

It may be said that more and more people emigrate not only to escape sheer deprivation or threats to their lives but because they want to achieve what they perceive to be a better life. It is a well-known fact that sometimes people who emigrate are not among the poorest in their countries, though they usually are extremely poor compared to the average in the receiving society. Immigration often requires information and resources, as well as a certain personal disposition, and this usually implies that those who, in relative terms, are the worst off remain behind. However, it is increasingly the case that the cherished project of "the good life" is a cultural product shaped in the image of life in developed capitalist societies—that is, with culturally constructed feelings of desire and satisfaction around consumption goods. It is a project that the wealthiest countries have an interest in selling abroad to expand their markets and fuel their economies. It is an expression of economic and cultural forces acting jointly. Hegemony in the mass media makes exporting the cultural product a feasible enterprise. The cultural impact in the receiving societies is undeniable. A certain way of life is displayed as the good life, and that in itself exerts a draw that affects migration patterns. Countries that export an image of a certain way of life that benefits them economically but at the same time contribute, for example, through unfair trading patterns, to the impossibility of reproducing in the sending countries the lifestyles that they export should acknowledge some responsibility for the migration patterns and the processes of cultural uprooting that they thereby stimulate. And then they, as receiving societies, have to face the question of how to accommodate within their borders, at least in part, some of the demands of cultural reproduction of the newcomers they have attracted. That some of the sending societies also deploy cultural and other constructs that limit choice may be objectionable too, but by itself this does not cancel out the responsibility of receiving countries for their own actions.[18]

In summary, choice is freely expressed when, of two viable options, one is forsaken in favor of the other in the absence of all coercion. When receiving societies render the option of remaining in one's native country less viable, either because of the grossly unfair distribution of resources and its impact on the possibilities to enjoy the minimal conditions for a dignified life or because of the constant degradation of the ways of life expressed in the cultures of such societies when they come to compete with other forms of life that are constantly publicized, they undermine the freedom that the choice of departure would otherwise express.

B. Information

To be morally relevant, consent also needs to be informed. Thus we need to assume that when immigrants leave their countries and cultures behind, they do so reasonably aware of what it means to uproot oneself culturally as well as of the fact that this is what the receiving society is expecting them to do. But we know that, at least in some cases, immigrants count on returning to their countries of origin as soon as they gather enough resources to carry out a project that makes them economically self-sufficient there and that this expectation may inhibit their willingness to give up their culture and language. Also, it is not uncommon for immigrants to take cultural factors into account when choosing a specific destination. Indeed, immigrants often pick countries and areas within those countries where they know they can be embraced by a cultural community formed by prior immigrants who have not fully uprooted themselves. The comfort of cultural familiarity and the solidarity ties that a shared language and culture often entail is precisely what they are looking for.

We may argue about the value that should be attached to what immigrants actually do or seem to do, as this largely rests on what they perceive their options at any given point in time to be. In reality, there is an inherent difficulty to freely and knowingly uprooting oneself culturally, especially for people who, before emigrating, have spent their entire lives within a secure cultural environment. Because of the situational dimension of ethnocultural identity, it is simply hard for people to anticipate the effects that cultural isolation and/or cultural degradation over an extended period of time can have on their identity and self-esteem. Indeed, such difficulty may account for much of the well-known gap between the number of immigrants who ever return to their countries of origin and those who expressly give up the dream or desire of an eventual return. The people who return are many less than those who say they are planning to eventually.

Clearly, one could say that the option to return still remains legally open, so that if immigrants do not avail themselves of it, it is because they happily accept their reality, including its cultural dimension. But in practice, in many cases the kinds of investments that most immigrants make to establish themselves in a new country are far too large, and the process of integration they undergo is far too painful, for them to experience that they have a real option of return after any minimally significant period of time has passed. Also, with time, immigrants are likely to consolidate all kinds of ties in the society in which they and their children live in manifold ways.[19] Still, none of this is theoretically incompatible with the fact that they may never fully give up their culture and language and that they may always miss the foregone security that cultural membership provided them or at least deplore the practical effects of such loss.

In view of what has been said, we could state a general principle that unless and until the state order is one in which gross disparities in the distribution of basic goods disappear, and to the extent that we recognize cultural membership as one of such primary goods, none of the better-off states (those that are generally targeted as immigration destinations) can fully discharge its responsibility for the cultural accommodation of newcomers. However, saying something more concrete about the kind of duty of cultural accommodation that derives simply *because* of the unfair redistribution of resources globally is more difficult. This is so partly because, by definition, cultural reaccommodation is, at most, a second-best option. Ideally, people should not have to leave their countries in the first place.[20] The other reasons that explain why it is so difficult to further specify the responsibilities of destination states are of a different nature. Immigration is not caused solely by the wealthiest countries. Corrupt governments are an internal evil. Some natural disasters are an evil nobody can specifically be blamed for, although their effects are clearly more severe in poor countries with weak infrastructures. Also, because cultural reaccommodation is a second-best option, it may be argued that there are better ways for states to discharge their redistributive obligations than through cultural reaccommodation. Foreign aid comes to mind. Moreover, establishing a direct connection between a country's relative resources and its duty to accommodate immigrants culturally is also difficult because more compelling needs than those of cultural reaccommodation can presumably be identified. In the end, more criteria need to come into play. However, from what has been said, one thing is clear: in today's world, prosperous countries cannot discharge their obligations to accommodate the cultural demands of those immigrants they benefit from economically by simply assuming the consensual nature of immigration.

Finally, a general assumption can be set forth whereby the responsibility of a given state increases when either in the past or in the present it bears a concrete responsibility for undermining the sending countries' economic and/or cultural resources. For example, it would seem that a colonial power that actively contributed to both the undermining of a colonized people's culture and its economic oppression throughout history ought to bear a larger responsibility when it comes to accepting immigrants from those regions and accommodating their cultural claims. The preferential treatment that some colonial powers recognize to immigrants coming from those states that were former colonies in either their immigration or integration policies seems to be a concession of this kind, and, in my view, a perfectly valid one. At the end of the day, there may still be limits to how many of such claims can be accommodated without constraining current generations in the receiving society with more diffuse responsibility for past injustices committed by their forebears.[21] Still, the general presumption holds.

III. IDENTIFYING A WIDER SET OF GENERALIZABLE CRITERIA FOR THE RECOGNITION OF RIGHTS TO LANGUAGE MINORITIES

Once we give up the aspiration of identifying a single feature to guide us in the process of recognition of language rights, we can start the search for a wider set of generalizable criteria. Also, we can imagine placing them on a sliding scale. The concrete set of language rights that any given member of a language group should enjoy in a specific state will depend on the circumstances of each case.[22] In general terms, though, we will be able to affirm that the more criteria are met, the stronger the claim for linguistic accommodation.[23] So, in my view, consensual cultural uprooting does not lose its moral relevance. It still constitutes probably one of the most important distinguishing grounds that autochthonous groups, conquered or annexed into a larger state, can call upon.[24] The point here is that it cannot be taken as the only relevant factor. Nor can it be assumed that we should treat autochthonous groups and immigrants differently because the kind of consent to cultural uprooting that immigrants express is often, though not always, insufficiently free or informed. Thus additional considerations will have to be taken into account. Here are some of them.

A. Numbers and Geographical Concentration

Ought implies *can*. As participatory goods, language and culture cannot be enjoyed in isolation.[25] That means that unless there is a certain number of language speakers and unless a certain degree of geographical concentration allows those speakers to form a community of linguistic interaction, the good underlying language rights cannot even be generated. What exact number of speakers and what degree of geographical concentration is required depends, of course, on which language right is at stake.[26] Clearly, the right to have institutions of self-government that use a specific language as *the* or at least *one of the* public languages will require larger numbers and greater geographical concentration than the right to education in one's language as a vernacular. And the latter, in general, will be more demanding than the freedom to individually address public authorities in one's language. All of these rights allow people to enjoy participatory cultural experiences, but by their very nature some simply require more participants to be able to generate the activity that produces the good that is collectively enjoyed. The sense of identity and belonging formed around a shared culture and language rests on a sum of individual acts of linguistic interaction allowing for reciprocal recognition with regard to a larger cultural group, the imagined community.[27]

Numbers are also relevant because the recognition of language rights relies on the spending of public resources.[28] Cost considerations may be decisive in recognizing limits to the kinds of rights, to the number of groups, and to the institutional designs to accommodate such rights. Also, because of cost considerations, number and geographical concentration should be considered jointly. A language might be spoken by a relatively small number of people, but if they happen to be very geographically concentrated it may become unreasonable not to grant such a group some language rights, such as the right to use its language in state services and activities, among other reasons, because such conditions do not favor the learning of the majority language.[29] Even though cost or efficiency considerations are generally not recognized as sufficient to determine the nonrecognition of rights, the recognition and enforcement of the whole system of social, civil, and political rights require the spending of limited public resources. It is not possible to determine the reach of any such right and of any additional cultural rights that may be recognized without considering the impact that this recognition may have on other, no less fundamental rights.[30]

This is why the idea of a certain numerical threshold—which will, of course, vary depending on what language right we are talking about—makes sense. In some countries with constitutionally sanctioned language rights, like Canada, this numerical threshold has been explicitly embraced in the configuration of the right.[31] This does not mean that the smallest groups or even single individuals have to be denied *all* language rights. People and groups should still be able to freely use their language in the private domain. Moreover, concerning interactions with public authorities, people can still make valid language claims in order to be able to use their language in these interactions in a minimally effective manner. For that, they need not claim a right to have their language and culture protected as such. Think of the right to translation in court or the right to have one's children receive some education in their own language, at least in the early stages, to make sure that they can effectively enjoy their right to an education in general.[32] Furthermore, the state should actively engage in eradicating social patterns of linguistic discrimination through public policies that may, for instance, require dedicating special resources to facilitating the presence of minority languages in the public media so as to enhance the public acceptance of minority cultures and languages.

We should also take into account that, whatever language rights are recognized, however minimal they may seem, such rights can always help increase the numbers of speakers and their future linguistic demands.[33] As soon as a sufficiently large group can use its language in the private and economic domain without discrimination, market forces will start catering to that group, and this will also enhance the market value of the language skill and the status of the linguistic group. Moreover, although the smaller minority groups could resent the privileged position of the larger minority groups, it is hard to see how accommodating only the majority can help in any way either the interests of the smaller minority groups or those of justice.[34] Indeed, arguably, even smaller groups are better off in a system that recognizes language rights of a set of viable minority cultural and language groups than in one that offers no guarantees of protection for any minorities at all.[35] The provision of protections against the assimilating force of the majority offers the best circumstances under which the smallest groups can eventually achieve the numerical threshold to become one of the minorities with public accommodation.

All of this explains why in most countries autochthonous linguistic minorities are in the condition to claim and enjoy language rights that more dispersed and/or smaller immigrant communities are not. It also accounts for our intuition that there is something objectionable in situations in which very small autochthonous communities are linguistically accommodated (think, for instance, of the Rhaeto Romansch in Switzerland) while very large and geographically concentrated immigrant communities are not. For instance, some objections have been raised in the Canadian debate about French language rights in areas where there are relatively few francophones and comparatively larger immigrant populations, such as Ukrainian or Chinese.[36] Finally, these considerations would raise interesting legitimacy concerns were the state to allege lack of numbers or insufficient geographical concentration as a justification for not recognizing language rights after a deliberate policy of linguistic dispersion of immigrants or of extermination or discrimination of autochthonous minorities. In my view, the majority should not be able to benefit from its own wrongdoing. We should avoid creating incentives for the oppression and discrimination of autochthonous groups.[37] As far as immigrants are concerned, unless it can be shown that migration is the result of fully free decisions, a policy of forced dispersion to prevent the upsurge of cultural claims would not be legitimate either.

B. *Expression of Individual and Collective Choice*

In most multilingual societies, the knowledge of different languages or the belonging to different language communities[38] does not open up the same opportunities in terms of social mobility. Some languages have a greater communicative value than others because they allow for interactions with more people and in a larger variety of settings. Some are more empowering than others because they enjoy social prestige or allow for interactions with economic and political elites. Languages or accents can be a source of liability even when they have an objectively large communicative value if they are associated with a certain social status or class. Think of Spanish in the United States. Given all of this, it is important that there are ways to ensure that language maintenance rests really on free individual and collective choices, and it is understandable that some people have shown a rather skeptical attitude toward language and cultural maintenance rights that may end up cloistering people in ghettos.[39]

The maintenance of a linguistic minority should not be the result of a majority policy that draws instrumental benefits from it. Linguistic traits can be used as markers to stigmatize, and linguistic exclusion can be a tool upon which to build a caste society. De Varennes recalls how English literacy requirements for voting as practiced at one time in the United States and former Rhodesia were aimed at disenfranchising black or Spanish-speaking citizens.[40] Environmentalist arguments for language survival and the way in which linguistic diversity enriches all of us may also be motivated by the right intentions but may raise similar concerns if the price of such celebrated diversity is that some groups will see their options severely curtailed because of the range of options their language makes available to them. Necessary protections have to be taken against the will of the majority but also to prevent attempts at manipulation by ethnic elites. Such elites may have obvious interests in the maintenance of the language to preserve the distinctiveness of the group, and thus the group itself and their own privileged position within it, especially if at the same time they can provide their own children with the greatest range of options, including those offered by the mainstream society. Finally, plausible as the interests of parents in the passing on of their culture to the next generations may be, a legitimate concern arises when parents' choice vastly limits their descendants' options of economic well-being, professional success, and social recognition in a given society. Compulsory education in modern democracies limits parental authority partly because of this reason.

In a multilingual state, liberal democracies committed in principle to ensuring citizens' equal opportunities have to grant everyone, whether originally an immigrant or not, a right to effectively learn the language(s) that offer the largest realm of options. But this is different from a right to receive their education in such language. Given the adequate means, people can grow up learning several languages so as to become reasonably functional in all of them, even if they use only one in their ordinary lives. Because of the inevitable linguistic dimension of the state, the majority language is one of the languages people should have a right to learn. But not the only one. So, for instance, to the extent that English becomes more and more a dominant language throughout the world, there should be a right assisting members of both the linguistic majority and minorities within the state to learn it. Similarly, within the framework of the European Union, to the extent that certain languages become de facto linguae francae in European institutions, the state should ensure everyone's right to learn them so that everybody can benefit from the opportunities, including employment options, that such knowledge provides and can follow and participate in debates of political relevance that are held within those institutions in those languages.

This does pose some problems, however. If I say that immigrants in Canada and in Spain who live in Quebec or Catalonia should have a right to learn English or Castilian and not only French or Catalan, this right may work against the efforts to preserve Catalan and French as minority languages. In my view, what this means is that, when recognized, such a right should come along with the possibility that the linguistic minority establishes the duty of those living within its geographical domain to learn the minority language or even to have it be the language in which education is conducted. After all, when public education is conducted in the majority language, a duty to learn it is also de facto being recognized. In other words, we should be concerned about creating incentives for secession by not accepting policies within provincial boundaries that would be perfectly legitimate if conducted within state boundaries.[41]

The degree to which the right to learn the most widely spoken or economically powerful languages is effectively ensured will be one of the relevant indices that language maintenance, as a minority claim, is really the result of free individual and collective choice and not of internal oppression by group leaders or perceived lack of options by the minorities. It has been argued that the most secure path to cultural maintenance is social exclusion and marginalization.[42] Ethnocultural identity, as a locus of secure belonging, becomes crucial when other sources of self-esteem fail. When the receiving society does not provide newcomers a meaningful option to effectively learn the majority language, they will be more likely to claim the right to retain their prior languages and to reproduce public spaces that function in them. When the triggering feature of aspirations of culture maintenance is frustration with the inability to climb the social ladder and enjoy full equality, we cannot assume those aspirations to be a true expression of free will.

What this means is that linguistic assimilation policies, presumably the least costly and least potentially divisive ones for the receiving society, should be accompanied by other policies that allow immigrants to ultimately express their cultural preferences as well and their prioritization of cultural versus economic or professional interests. Thus, to give an example, bilingual education could be justified on two grounds: first, because and to the extent that studies show that it enhances the general cognitive capacities of students and hence the better learning of the majority language and the curricula in general, given the emotional elements that are involved in the process of language learning and the subsequent implications for people's self-esteem;[43] and second, because it allows immigrants to gain mastery of the majority language while not losing relevant knowledge of their mother language. They need this to be able to assert and articulate their cultural preferences, something that I claim they have a right to.

Because upward mobility is clearly one of the encouraging factors of migration and because of the difficulty of having languages coexist in terms of equal power, immigrants will perceive mastery of the majority language as essential for ensuring mobility and avoiding discrimination. This means that when the right to learn the majority language is effectively granted, and not only formally recognized, we can expect, as a general rule, that a process of cultural uprooting and integration into the mainstream culture will take place. This again, may account for some differences in the claims of national minorities as opposed to those of immigrants. However, this does not have to be the case. If immigrants look for or find at arrival the possibility to live in a community where they can still achieve the meaningful existence they were hoping for while not fully giving up their culture and language, they may choose to maintain both. To say that immigration, as a mass phenomenon, is largely driven by the attraction of the promise of economic prosperity and social mobility is an obvious truth. But that does not imply that immigrants will always take the path that maximizes their economic prospects regardless of other considerations. Were they to find their culture or a culture with which they could better identify flourishing in the receiving society, they might settle for less social mobility. The overall balance, when compared to their situation in the sending society, might still be positive.

Although the numbers of those willing to settle for less mobility and more cultural protection may initially be small, presumably, the more people opt for cultural reproduction, the stronger their cultures will become, and the more options of social mobility they will grant to their members. We can see this happening in some areas in the United States, such as Florida with Spanish.[44] Presumably, a flourishing minority culture could create incentives both for the members of the minority to remain within it and for the members of the majority society to reach toward it, and this would become crucial in the process of recognition and the elimination of stigma that generally underlies cultural oppression in immigrant societies.

That, if given the choice, immigrants would choose the option of living in their language and within their cultural communities, provided they were generally respected and not looked down upon, while enjoying meaningful professional and social opportunities, should not surprise us. Once again, we know that most people would not emigrate and leave their culture behind in spite of the promise of greater prosperity. Granted, there is allegedly a process of natural self-selection at play, and we can assume that immigrants may be more economically driven or motivated than other people. Still, this does not mean that the maximization of economic prosperity will always guide their options, especially when the reality of cultural isolation suddenly strikes them. That so many commentators assume that maximizing economic prosperity will be the absolute priority of immigrants often reveals their own cultural bias. How to prioritize human ends is a matter not only of human nature but of cultural patterns. Indeed, the differences in patterns of integration that we can sometimes observe among different immigrant groups may at least in part reflect the priorities set by their own cultures. Be that as it may, empirical evidence of whatever kind would be of limited use in drawing normative conclusions because, as discussed above, such evidence is once again based at most on subjective and not always well-informed perceptions.

Many immigrants simply do not perceive that they have an option of cultural reproduction and security in the receiving societies to start with. Instead, they become aware of the difficulty of their full integration in societies that treat them and their cultures as second class. They thus stop the most natural practice of linguistic reproduction and quit speaking in their mother tongue to their children in the household to encourage them to learn the majority language, even when their own knowledge of it is precarious. They do this to spare their children from the stigma that they think they would otherwise encounter, in a belief that too often proves to be well founded. But when stigma and discrimination are the underlying threats, it is also difficult to talk of a genuinely free expression of interests. Clearly, this is not only a matter of prejudice. Even without past or present stigma, numbers are relevant. The majority language will always provide more options, and as long as this is the case, newcomers will have a large incentive to learn it. My argument is that they have a right to do so and that, in principle, they also have a right to retain their language, something we can assume most people would like to do. And because the two are not incompatible, the reasons why immigrants would freely choose to fully forgo the latter are not clear, especially if they gradually come to perceive that through their language they can also have meaningful options in the receiving society.

In summary, whether a minority language community survives should not be simply assumed to be the result of free individual or collective choice, at least not as long as the social, professional, economic, and prestige opportunities offered by that language are significantly different from those offered by competing languages within the same society. The inequality between languages is not always an expression of injustice. Size alone or the time that a community has been established can determine its dominant position. As long as those extreme differences in opportunities persist, there is an obligation to strengthen the mechanisms for and the option of assimilation into the mainstream society while at the same time keeping those of language and cultural maintenance minimally open. Language minorities should have an exit option that allows them to abandon the realm of secluded and protected equal recognition within their bounded cultural group for the sake of what they perceive to be a better life.[45]

On the other hand, until such exit option is meaningfully guaranteed, undermining the basis of cohesion of such groups by denying their cultural maintenance claims (for instance, the claim to have their languages taught at school) can only result in their further oppression and discrimination. Their individual members will find that they can neither integrate into the mainstream society nor strengthen their own communities. Hence creating the conditions for the expression of free will regarding language maintenance requires strengthening both the exit and the nonexit option by supporting the efforts of those members of the group who are still fighting for its survival. It would be perverse for the majority culture to deny oppressed groups cultural maintenance claims by alleging the weakness of their cultures as contexts of meaningful life options when it is itself partly responsible for such decay. This is why, although the existence of a viable and flourishing culture is one of the most telling signs of cultural assertion as a fully free option, it cannot be set as an unqualified condition for the recognition of a valid claim to cultural preservation.

These considerations are important for understanding why we tend to interpret the collective claims of autochthonous ethnocultural groups that enjoy indices of economic prosperity similar to those of the majority society (think of francophones in Canada or Catalans in Spain) as more free and less suspicious assertions of collective cultural self-definition than those of immigrant groups. But again, this is an empirical matter. There are cases in which autochthonous minorities no longer constitute flourishing societies whereas immigrant groups may be on the route to becoming such. The United States offers interesting examples in this regard. On the one hand, we have a growing Hispanic community, based on a linguistic common denominator, enriched through different elements from many separate cultures that are then incorporated into a common culture. This distinctive culture is strengthened in the process of interaction with the mainstream Anglo culture, from which it borrows elements that distinguish it from its cultures of origin and that also serve as a background against which relevant differences can be asserted. It is not inconceivable that, with time, the social stigma of the use of Spanish or Spanish/Hispanic accents will be so reduced that immigrants from Spanish-speaking countries may conceive of ways of living meaningful options mostly in Spanish or, more likely, in both Spanish and English for them and their children. And my claim is that they should have a right to do so and that there would be no reason for us to suspect that, under those circumstances, they were not expressing a fully free choice even if it did not open to them exactly the same kind of opportunities that the choice to live in English exclusively would have.

On the other hand, we have autochthonous groups such as some Native American tribes that are clearly in decline as a result of past systematic oppression and ongoing discrimination. Because in many cases the options that these eroded cultures can offer to their members are so few, the fact that they still exist, or the fact that they are autochthonous groups, should not in and of itself be taken to express that what explains their survival is a free choice of cultural maintenance, no matter what. Often it is the awareness that discrimination awaits them in the mainstream society that discourages people from leaving the tribe. Under those circumstances, for the reasons mentioned before, strong exit *and* nonexit options should be guaranteed. So, for instance, the right to be taught the majority language may not be a sufficient exit guarantee, and a right to a perfectly bilingual education may be called for, as well as a right to measures that facilitate the integration of those who decide to leave the group to join the mainstream society (think, for instance, of education quotas within mainstream educational institutions). On the other hand, the group, because of its particularly vulnerable position and the fact that this is the result of past oppression, may claim that those who nevertheless decide to stay or to come have to function in the minority language and have it be the language of exclusive use in their self-governing institutions.

The need to ensure minimally effective exit options would also undermine the legitimacy of some linguistic policies. Forcing immigrants to concentrate geographically in an area in which they can add to the numbers needed to make the project of cultural reproduction viable at the expense of limiting their access to opportunities offered otherwise by the mainstream society and culture would not be an option. This would be especially so if the project entailed reallocating immigrants that had already invested their energies in the effort of integrating into the mainstream society and its language. It might be different, however, if those minority societies that welcomed immigrants became with time flourishing societies.

A different but related question is whether it is legitimate to limit the range of linguistic options of immigrants so as to lessen the cultural impact of such options on already existing minority language groups, even if the limits require immigrants to forgo some social and economic progress. Take the example of Quebec, where, according to the Quebec Clause originally defined in the province's education code, only the children of parents who had been educated in English in Quebec, and thus neither immigrants nor Canadians educated in English outside Quebec, had a right to education in English inside Quebec. The Canadian Charter explicitly invalidated this option by ensuring, in the so-called Canada Clause, that every Canadian whose parents had been educated in English in Canada, whether inside or outside Quebec, had the right to educate his or her children in English inside and outside Quebec. However, the limitation still applies to immigrants or francophones, who may not have the right to have their children educated in English in Quebec, something that inevitably limits their mobility options within a prevailingly English-speaking Canada and, for that matter, North America.

In my view, there are at least two relevant considerations for judging the moral validity of such practices. The first has to do with the extent of the limitation of the exit option that the restriction implies. Limitation is one thing; total denial a different one. Thus even if the education of francophones or newcomers in Quebec, whether they were immigrants or Canadians, could be legitimately expected to be in French, we could still argue that people should in principle have a right to move anywhere in the country, as well as the right to learn good English anywhere they decide to settle. Again, learning English and learning *in* English are two different things. Given the linguistic dimension of the state, making sure that people have a right to learn the majority language is required by a minimal commitment to the ideal of the state as a bounded sphere of equality that requires some commitment to the notion of equal opportunities. This is very different from holding a right to be educated mostly or exclusively in English, as such a right would allow for collective cultural experiences in English that would probably interfere much more seriously with Quebec's legitimate end to comprehensively function in French.

Another relevant consideration would be the extent to which the minority language that is being protected already offers opportunities for a flourishing existence, as is obviously the case of French in Quebec. In judging this, however, we should once again be aware of the danger of cultural bias and stay away from the temptation of relying exclusively on economic indicators. The importance given to economic prosperity, accumulation of wealth, or professional achievement may differ in the two cultures that are being compared. The best sign of health would therefore be the existence of a significant group of people freely committed to its preservation.

If what has been said is right, we can see why some other well-extended state practices have been uncontroversially accepted. Currently, English is consolidating a hegemonic role in the international arena as the language of international trade that makes international mobility and opens up transnational opportunities. While in their commitment to ensure equal opportunities many states are trying to allow every citizen, and not just a social elite, to learn second languages and especially English, they do not feel obliged to do so at the expense of undermining their national languages. Thus, in spite of the growing importance of English, states are not deciding to give up their national languages as those in which public education or public deliberation takes place. They simply try to teach English as part of the curriculum, as part of what allows people to function in the modern world, as I think they should. In my view, at least as long as the options that citizens can have in such languages are reasonable, there is no need to give up the national language, even if it could be shown that, for the maximization of citizens' economic or professional opportunities, this would be advisable in the mid- or long term. With time, in a globalized world, people may still collectively and freely decide to go for that trade-off. But this is an unlikely scenario if the starting assumption, the deep attachment of people to their languages, is correct and if this kind of attachment justifies taking measures to protect the group trying to preserve its culture, language, and way of life from extraordinary external pressures.

C. The Threat to Autochthonous or Consolidated Linguistic Groups

The thesis that links the recognition of cultural rights to individual autonomy rests on the assumption that the rights of a given generation cannot be sacrificed for the sake of the coming generations. The concern is not with preserving languages or cultures that are intrinsically worth protecting or for the sake of enhancing overall cultural diversity. Neither are we simply trying to ensure people's right to live in a culture and language, for if we did, there would be nothing wrong in simply adopting assimilationist policies. All that would matter would be for people to be offered some cultural framework. Rather, the central idea is that, to lead a fully autonomous life, most people cherish the possibility to live within their language and culture.[46] This means that we cannot design language rights to protect the cultural and identity needs of new groups without taking into account the effects that this may have on other groups that are already established in the state community. In other words, the protection of the groups already present can limit the cultural aspirations of newcomers.

What this means in each case and how this principle should be institutionally articulated depends, once again, on many different circumstances. Claims of self-government by new groups would probably be more threatening to existing minorities with self-government powers than other types of language maintenance claims, such as, for instance, the right to learn one's heritage language in a way that allows it to flourish at home and in civil society. Furthermore, the number of existing groups will need to be taken into account. It may make a difference whether the claims of newcomers are received in societies living with a delicate balance to accommodate already existing and consolidated minorities or in relatively homogenous societies. Also, if self-government rights are claimed (at either the municipal or the regional level), where they are asserted will matter. The claims of immigrants to have some geopolitical space to publicly reproduce their cultures would threaten the existing minority cultures and their institutional autonomy in a way that they would not threaten the majority. This would be even more so when there was a certain cultural affinity between those immigrant groups and the state majority culture that threatened to outnumber existing minorities. In Canada, the concern of the francophone speakers in Quebec has not been so much with the anglophone minority that has traditionally lived inside the province as with the threat posed by new immigrants who have traditionally had more incentives to embrace English than French, and presumably the same would have applied regardless of whether English was the native language of immigrants. Once again, the underlying assumption is that when it comes to the public recognition of different language groups there are limits: only a limited number of languages and the cultures they represent can be fully accommodated without exercising excessive pressure on the weaker ones, and hence without violating their group right to protection against such external pressures. Just like the limitations posed by cost considerations that we mentioned above, the limitations to the recognition of cultural and language rights of immigrants that derive from this may leave us without a fully satisfying answer. Again, part of the problem is that, ideally, immigrants should have been able to enjoy the whole range of civil, social, political, and cultural rights to begin with in their society of origin.

An interesting question to explore is to what extent the existing majority, and not only autochthonous or consolidated minorities, can limit the cultural claims of newcomers. Can the limitations be justified on the basis of an alleged need to preserve the cultural distinctiveness of the majority nation? Because we take the respect for individual autonomy and its connection with a secure cultural and linguistic environment to be the guiding concern, the starting assumption is that the state cannot impose an official culture on its citizens. There has to be a free civil society where cultural options are expressed and can interact dynamically. The democratic process of "cultural appropriation" (i.e., the allocation of a geographical and political space to a certain culture) is a bottom-to-top process, not vice versa. Whatever protections may be required by ethnocultural minorities, it is illegitimate for an ethnocultural group that at any given moment is in power to perpetuate its privileged position over other groups, whether immigrant or autochthonous minority groups, and to do so in the name of an official culture that allegedly represents the cultural essence of the nation-state, or the basis of its shared cultural identity projected not only into the past but also into the future. So, for instance, the preference for one official language can never represent the effort of a group to reserve power for itself.[47] The identity of the political community may change over time, even dramatically so. Thus the initiative to sanction English as the official language in the U.S. Constitution and, more broadly, the English Only movement represent in my view the illegitimate attempt of the English-speaking majority in the United States, which, as of today, is far from being culturally threatened, to use its current political power to avoid any degree of sharing of the public culture with the Spanish-speaking population.[48] Similarly, individual members of linguistic majorities cannot be under an obligation to preserve the purity of their culture. They are free to reject it for the sake of other options that may come to be socially available if they perceive them as more freedom enhancing altogether. There is nothing objectionable about cultural shifts, including linguistic ones, when they result from truly free choices.

In my view, the only legitimate scenario for the state to take active measures to preserve its language(s) as "the language(s) of the country," even if this entails restricting some of the claims of linguistic reproduction of newcomers, comes when, in spite of the numerical majority of language speakers of a given national language, that language is seriously threatened by other internationally hegemonic languages, such as English, or when, generally as a result of prior linguistic domination, there is a disconnection between the numerical representation of a language and its social and political power. The attempts to recover the Estonian and Latvian languages in Latvia and Estonia come to mind here. Needless to say, the restriction of language claims of immigrants on such grounds would be especially justified if their language coincided with the one occupying an internationally hegemonic position. There is no doubt that autochthonous and consolidated language minorities, such as the Catalans or the Basques in Spain, would always regard with suspicion the use of majority power to protect the majority language from alleged external threats. The reasons for this are, to a large extent, symbolic, but they cannot be set aside just because of that. More and more publications in Catalonia adopt the policy of Catalan as a first language and English as a second language. Even if we have reasons to think that English poses at least as important a threat to the long-term survival of Catalan as Spanish, there is no equivalent history of cultural oppression of the Catalan people by the English, and this reality and its symbolic implications cannot be forgotten.

On the other hand, if cultural reproduction is really a leading concern, we should be aware that protecting the state's majority culture and language may be, under certain circumstances, the best guarantee against the assimilation of both national minorities and majorities by an internationally hegemonic culture with perhaps more subtle but no less imperialistic ways. Maybe thinking of ways to compensate for the unintended cultural effects of the measures of protection of the majority language on linguistic minorities would be a way out of the conundrum. So, in the Spanish case, measures to protect Spanish from the assimilating force of English should presumably be accompanied by measures that counteract the effects of this policy on Catalan, Basque, or Galician. Forcing foreign companies to write the labels of the products they want to put in the market in Spain in Spanish, or making public funds available to encourage the production of software in Spanish to counteract the always wider use of English in computer technology, should be accompanied by measures that provide an equivalent duty to write the labels in Basque when the products are to be distributed in the Basque Country or to provide funds for the production of software in Catalan.

In the end, any assessment of a given situation will have to ponder the rights that come into play, namely the rights of the state majority, which, seen from an international perspective, becomes a minority to be protected, and the rights of the minorities within the state, as well as the individual rights and freedoms of the state's both majority and minority members. Once again, for the measures to be legitimate, they have to be guided by a concern to protect the majority culture from external assimilation forces and not to assimilate internal minorities, whether autochthonous or not. Serious threats, and not mere weakening of the degree of the hegemony of the national majority language, may be required. Chauvinism is not protected.

The main thrust of the argument remains that, in principle, the use of majority power to perpetuate one group's privileged cultural position over that of other groups coexisting within the state, or to "freeze its cultural essence," is illegitimate. This is not to say that the majority language cannot receive symbolic recognition or that any specific action that *produces* the result of strengthening such language is by definition illegitimate. As we will see, other legitimate interests may be at stake, and they do not necessarily have to be related to the protection of cultural goods. Just to mention an example, teaching the majority language in public schools clearly has the effect of strengthening the language and the culture it represents. However, it can also be justified in terms of the integrative potential that it serves. For one thing, it allows every citizen to function responsibly and autonomously as a citizen when that is the language ordinarily used by public institutions and in society. On the other hand, as mentioned above, if that language is the one that opens up more possibilities for social mobility in civil society, ensuring that every citizen can learn it becomes part of a commitment to the notion of equal opportunities. What is not legitimate is to take measures to perpetuate the majority's cultural hegemony per se, repressing the natural expansion of other languages in civil society. This is consistent with the fact that in a liberal framework, the concern expressed for the protection of languages and cultures is linked with the recognition of individual autonomy and of the ways in which cultural and linguistic security furthers it, not primarily with the survival of any given language or culture in and of itself.

D. *Limits of the Receiving Society: General Divisiveness*

Sometimes the concerns about the limits of the receiving society are expressed in terms of divisiveness and not so much in terms of cultural hegemony. Here the problem is not so much with the cultural threat that the recognition of new groups as holders of cultural rights poses to other existing cultures and their languages. Rather, the concern is with the fact that some degree of both shared culture and communicative transparency is needed for solidarity, mutual trust, and other related civic virtues—all of them essential for the good functioning of liberal democratic institutions—that would arguably be difficult to achieve without a common language. These fears are especially raised in countries that draw a significant percentage of their population from immigration flows. Because these countries already have to cope with a large degree of cultural pluralism, they may be keener than others to identify at least some shared cultural elements to feed the notion of a common citizenship.

In my view, this is a plausible concern. How it ought to be addressed in practical terms will once again depend on the circumstances, such as the kinds of rights claimed (rights of self-government clearly having a larger divisive potential than other rights), the number of languages and cultural groups with aspirations of permanence, and the degree of intelligibility between them. Interesting, however, is the fact that the cost and efficiency considerations that we mentioned above may not necessarily point in the same direction as the limits imposed by concerns about divisiveness or about threats to preexisting national or consolidated minorities. Thus, while rights to self-government may be more divisive, rights to accommodate different languages in shared public institutions may actually be more costly, at least when the number of speakers of a language is very small and their degree of geographical concentration very high. Just think of the costs involved in having institutions that have to function in several languages simultaneously. So whereas someone concerned about divisiveness would probably advocate a personal system of accommodation of language diversity, someone concerned about cost would probably recommend a territorial arrangement, at least in some cases. Also, although it may be less costly to accommodate new speakers of a given language when that language is already accommodated as a minority language within that society, the addition of new members may alter the balance of existing forces between majority and minorities in a way that threatens the survival of minorities. Think, for instance, about English-speaking immigrants in Quebec who could benefit from already existing institutions, such as English schools, but whose use of such institutions would end up strengthening the anglophone majority in the country at the expense of the francophone minority.

In any event, certain considerations need to be generally taken into account. Maybe the most important one is that, as far as the dream of a shared identity goes, it is precisely the awareness of a distinct cultural identity that usually underlies claims of cultural preservation, wherever they come from. It is the perception of a sufficiently distinctive identity that generally feeds the claims of self-government and secession of historically oppressed ethnocultural minorities. This dooms the attempt to use a certain language and culture, generally those of the majority, as an element of cohesion because it excludes from the parameters of "commonness" those elements that minorities identify most strongly with, language generally being one of them.

As for more recent immigrant groups, although they may claim some rights of cultural reproduction, the state may also take some integrationist measures, such as ensuring that they become perfectly functional in the majority language and build a new identity around it, that they can share with the rest of the citizenry and that supplements, more than replaces, their old identities. Because of the reasons stated above, these attempts are bound to be more successful with recent immigrants than with consolidated national minorities. But if and when immigrant groups put forward culture and language claims, whether this is the result of deficient mechanisms of integration or simply of the gradual consolidation of a distinctive cultural identity that claims public recognition, it may be too late to think of a common language as a straightforward and undisputed element of shared identity. It is not clear that the sheer celebration of linguistic pluralism itself can generate that necessary degree of shared identity either, but denying the political relevance of such pluralism will clearly have counterproductive consequences.

In other words, there are limits to the use of a language policy as a tool of nation building in societies where language minorities set the recognition of their cultural distinctiveness as a condition for expressing their loyalty to the state. One could still argue that a common language may be required at least as a tool of interaction or lingua franca. This too would be important to avoid divisiveness. And it may make sense for that language to be that of the majority. The alternative of relying on translation would be very expensive and, more importantly, would not sufficiently serve the interest in direct communication and hence the goals of transparency and trust that democracies need, especially when the number of languages claiming public accommodation is great and the languages are diverse. Moreover, because the claim is not one of privileging a single ethnocultural identity as the official one but, more pragmatically, recognizing the need of a common language of interaction, such a goal can more easily coexist with identity claims of language minorities.

Clearly, the duty for every citizen of the state to learn a lingua franca when that language is the majority language will inevitably have a symbolic effect and a practical impact on the strengthening of such culture to the detriment of minority cultures. This may raise legitimate claims of cultural compensation. We could think, for instance, of the possibility for minorities to have their own institutions of self-government in which their language is used as the dominant language. We could also think of an equivalent duty of

the native speakers of the majority language to learn at least one of
the other national or consolidated languages as part of a manda-
tory school curriculum for the sake of ensuring the cultural recognition of minority groups and thus civic harmony. Abandoning the
aim of a lingua franca in linguistically diverse societies because of
the imperfect achievement of cultural neutrality that such an option implies, instead of trying to identify ways of compensating for
the differential impact, would be a doubtful strategy. Ultimately,
the need for intelligible communication, not only in the common
political institutions but also in civil society with a market economy,
will impose a de facto lingua franca, and its cultural impact will not
be any less significant just because it is less expressly recognized.[49]

IV. Conclusion

Liberal democracies have to take the challenge posed by multilin-
gualism seriously. The inevitable linguistic dimension of the state
and hence the impossibility of linguistic state neutrality is a source
of valid concern if we are willing to recognize that language security or the option for people to live in their language is something
that most people cherish as important for the possibility of living a
fully meaningful life. Because in the past secure belonging to a national community with a national language has often been taken
for granted as a shared experience, and because the assumption
has generally been false, multicultural theorists are now struggling
to create a space for the explicit recognition of language rights.

Once this is acknowledged, the question becomes how to identify which groups should be linguistically accommodated and in
which state. In a world divided by states encompassing both autochthonous majorities and minorities, it could make sense to recognize that the cultural needs of autochthonous minorities have to
be accommodated within the larger state unit so that the state can
claim authority over the people and the territory (i.e., so that it can
legitimately claim to be "their" state), especially since cultural and
linguistic neutrality is not an option. Because each state contains a
limited number of ethnocultural groups with historically grounded
claims to cultural self-preservation linked to a past of annexation or
conquest, the accommodation of their cultural maintenance claims
would be much less divisive than is often assumed by critics of every

form of multiculturalism, especially when one compares it to the alternative of nonrecognition and the costs and strains that it implies.

Gross unfairness in the distribution of the most cherished assets among states (wealth, peace, democracy, public health, etc.) and the failure of the international society to face even minimal obligations of redistribution bring in additional considerations. Large flows of immigrants, refugees, and displaced persons are forced to abandon the secure cultural context that their national cultures offer them. Also, more and more, an integral element of the definition of the "better life" that immigrants strive for is a certain lifestyle interestedly exported by the wealthiest countries in unfair conditions of power over trade and the media. In this scenario, the question as to the responsibility of each individual state that receives and benefits from immigration from less affluent countries to allow for possible claims of cultural reproduction becomes salient.

For the reasons I mentioned, deciding how to concretize this generic international responsibility of the well off versus the least well off and of the cultural imbalances it generates is not an easy task. On the other hand, once the full disclaimer underlying the argument of the free nature of migration is given up, there is a need to find a set of normatively sound criteria to decide which linguistic groups should be granted accommodation rights. Here I have suggested that numbers and geographical concentration matter as feasibility conditions. I have also argued for the importance of ascertaining that whatever claims of cultural reproduction language minorities put forward are the result of free expression of individual and collective choice. Finally, the limits of the receiving society, in terms of costs, divisiveness, and threats to those language groups already consolidated within the state, should also be considered in deciding which groups should be linguistically accommodated and what forms of accommodation are adequate.

Much more needs to be done. Presumably, even more generalizable criteria can be identified. Another challenge that must be faced is how to prioritize the different criteria or to solve the tensions that may come up if these happen to point in different directions. Much more could also be said about which language rights, out of the whole array, should be specifically recognized. I would hesitate to do this at this level of argumentative abstraction, as I believe that, in most cases, it requires greater sensitivity toward the richness of the phenomenology of real cases than can be captured in an essay such as this one. Some problems are easier to solve in practice than in theory (especially if theory is done in the traditional, sociologically naive way), for on the ground, decisions are never made within institutional, sociological, or historical vacuums. Reality often imposes useful constraints. In the end, this is only the start of a conversation whose primary purpose is to introduce complexity into the debate and unsettle some of the tidy yet oversimplified distinctions that have become commonplace within it, while at the same time offering tools and categories that allow us to make progress in defining normatively sound principles for the fair allocation of language rights in multilingual societies.

NOTES

My thanks to Joseph Carens, Will Kymlicka, Allen Patten, Stephen Macedo, and Pablo de Greiff for very useful suggestions on earlier drafts.

1. F. De Varennes, *Language Minorities and Human Rights* (The Hague: Kluwer Law International, 1996); Snezana Trifunovska, *Minority Rights in Europe: European Minorities and Languages* (The Hague: T.M.C. Asser Press, 2001); and Will Kymlicka and Alan Patten, *Language Rights and Political Theory* (New York: Oxford University Press, 2003).

2. Brian Walker, "Nationalism and Modernity," in *Theorizing Nationalism*, ed. R. Beinder (New York: State University of New York Press, 1999), 219–45.

3. Will Kymlicka, *Multicultural Citizenship* (Oxford, England: Clarendon Press, 1995), 111; Joseph H. Carens, *Culture, Citizenship, and Community* (New York: Oxford University Press, 2000), 77–78; Rainer Bauböck, "Cultural Citizenship, Minority Rights, and Self-Government," in *Citizenship Today: Global Perspectives and Practices,* ed. Alex Aleinikoff and Doug Klusmeyer (Washington, D.C.: Carnegie Endowment for International Peace, 2001), 319–21.

4. Leslie Green, "Are Language Rights Fundamental?" *Osgoode Hall Law Journal* 25, no. 4 (1987): 639–69.

5. Pierre Coulombe, *Language Rights in French Canada* (New York: Peter Lang, 1996), 71.

6. Charles Taylor, "The Politics of Recognition," in *Multiculturalism and the Politics of Recognition,* ed. Amy Gutmann (Princeton, N.J.: Princeton University Press, 1993), 25–73; Kymlicka, *Multicultural Citizenship;* Yael Tamir, *Liberal Nationalism* (Princeton, N.J.: Princeton University Press, 1993); Avishai Margalit and Joseph Raz, "National Self Determination," in *Rights of Minority Cultures,* ed. Will Kymlicka (New York: Oxford University Press, 1995), 79–92.

7. We could define ethnocultural minorities as more or less territorially concentrated groups, holding a distinct culture, a common sign of which is often a distinct language as well as claims of nationhood that are generally linked to a past of conquest or annexation by the state.

8. Kymlicka, *Multicultural Citizenship,* 99.

9. For instance, the 1995 Council of Europe's Framework Convention for the Protection of National Minorities, which represents significant progress for minority rights in international law, in order to overcome the resistance of signatory states, leaves it to each of them to specify whether there are minority groups in its territory that are protected under the convention. Article 27 of the 1966 International Covenant on Civil and Political Rights provides that "[i]n those States in which ethnic, religious or linguistic minorities exist, persons belonging to such minorities shall not be denied the right, in community with the other members of their group, to enjoy their own culture, to profess and practice their own religion, or to use their own language," but again, it does not offer any criteria as to which groups qualify as linguistic minorities deserving state recognition.

10. The European Charter for Regional or Minority Languages, of June 26, 1992, which entered into force on March 1, 1998, and is the first international treaty of general application dealing comprehensively with the issue of linguistic diversity in Europe, defines in Article 1 the "regional or minority languages" that fall under its scope of protection as those "traditionally used within a given territory of a State by nationals of that State who form a group numerically smaller than the State's population." It expressly excludes the languages of migrants, and the Explanatory Report of the Charter dwells on this point by indicating that the purpose of the charter is not to resolve the problems arising out of recent immigration.

11. Kymlicka, *Multicultural Citizenship,* 95–98; Nathan Glazer, *Ethnic Dilemmas: 1964–1982* (Cambridge, Mass.: Harvard University Press, 1983), 149; and Michael Walzer, "Pluralism in Political Perspective," in *The Politics of Ethnicity,* ed. Michael Walzer (Cambridge, Mass.: Harvard University Press, 1982), 6–7.

12. Joseph H. Carens, "Liberalism and Culture," *Constellations* 4, no. 1 (1997): 43–45; Iris Marion Young, "A Multicultural Continuum: A Critique of Will Kymlicka's Ethnic-Nation Dichotomy," *Constellations* 4, no. 1 (1997): 48; Dénise Réaume, "The Constitutional Protection of Language: Survival or Security," in *Language and the State*, ed. David Schneiderman (Montreal: Editions Yvon Blais, 1991), 37; and Thomas Pogge, "Accommodation Rights for Hispanics in the United States," in *Hispanics/Latinos in the United States: Ethnicity, Race and Rights*, ed. J. Gracia and P. de Greiff (New York: Routledge, 2000).

13. Bikhu Parekh, "Dilemmas of a Multicultural Theory of Citizenship," *Constellations* 4, no. 1 (1997): 54.

14. Pogge, "Accommodation Rights," 182.

15. Bauböck, "Cultural Citizenship," 337.

16. Kymlicka, *Multicultural Citizenship*, 98–99; Bauböck, "Cultural Citizenship," 337.

17. In its document "New European Labour Markets, Open to All, with Access for All," COM (2001), 28.02.2001, the European Commission complains about low mobility inside European Union: only 2 percent of European nationals are resident in another member state. On an annual basis EU mobility is less than 0.4 percent.

18. Special thanks to Pablo de Greiff for clarification on this point.

19. Ruth Rubio-Marín, *Immigration as a Democratic Challenge: Citizenship and Inclusion in Germany and the United States* (New York: Cambridge University Press, 2000), 31–34.

20. Kymlicka, *Multicultural Citizenship*, 98.

21. In the case of multilingual societies, when the majority language was the one historically used as the instrument of conquest, the impact of the preferential treatment granted to immigrants from former colonies who speak the state's majority language and to their cultural claims has to be pondered against the interest of autochthonous language minorities in not being outnumbered. Imagine, for instance, a scenario where Latin American immigrants who settled in Catalonia would claim a right to have their children educated mostly in Spanish, something that would contradict Catalonia's education policy, which encourages Catalan as the main vernacular.

22. For a powerful defense of contextualization as the best methodological approach to multicultural questions, see Carens, *Culture, Citizenship, and Community*.

23. Elsewhere, I have distinguished between three types of language rights as cultural protections. Ruth Rubio-Marín, "Language Rights: Exploring Competing Rationales," in Kymlicka and Patten, *Language Rights and Political Theory*. One type satisfies the demands that

the state and its institutions accommodate language minorities in both practical and symbolic ways (such as by recognizing their official status or by allowing the speakers of such language to use it in their interactions with public authorities); the second type consists of powers of self-government recognized to language minority groups to enact their own measures to protect their linguistic environment (for instance, by designing their own language policies, including educational policies, or having their own set of public institutions use their language predominantly). Finally, a third type of language rights are promotional rights, or rights of the minorities to be assisted by the state in their effort to protect themselves against the assimilationist forces they encounter in civil society (for instance, qualified access to public funding to promote the use of minority languages in the media, in technology, or in the arts).

24. In my view, a past of conquest, annexation, or, more generally, oppression not only strengthens the moral grounds upon which the claim of accommodation can be made but will also have an effect on the kind of rights that can be claimed. So ways of symbolic recognition may be especially called for in order to restore the collective self-esteem and identity of a historically oppressed or conquered people. Finally, it will also have an impact on the way in which other considerations may or may not legitimately restrict accommodation claims. So, for instance, numerical considerations that, as shown below, deserve to be taken into account should not be as decisive when the loss numbers of group members or the relatively low percentage of the overall population that the group represents are precisely a consequence of the injustices committed in the past by the majority.

25. Réaume, "The Constitutional Protection," 48.

26. As a general criteria, Réaume argues that it is those linguistic communities with a significant size that deserve protection because they are "viable language communities able to sustain for their members a reasonably full cultural life." Réaume, "The Constitutional Protection," 52. Instead of defining a priori which communities deserve protection, I think that we should decide not only which groups but also which language rights make sense for each group to enjoy. The size and concentration of a group may be sufficient for it to enjoy some "cultural experiences" but not others.

27. Notice that population size is indeed one of the criteria more commonly accepted in national and international legal instruments recognizing language rights. See, for instance, the European Charter for Regional or Minority Languages, Articles 8–11, or the Draft of an International Convention on the Protection of National or Ethnic Groups or

Minorities, Articles 20–24, both cited in De Varennes, *Language Minorities and Human Rights*, 93 n. 102.

28. Ibid., 95.

29. See De Varennes, *Language Minorities and Human Rights*, 94, where he mentions the possibility that in spite of the overall low numbers of Breton speakers in France, some government services may be provided in that language in Brittany, and where he gives the example of Switzerland and its level of cantonal autonomy, which has allowed access to public services and job opportunities to individuals who speak Italian even if they represent only 3 percent of the total population.

30. Carens, "Liberalism and Culture," 37.

31. See Article 20 of the Canadian Charter of Rights and Freedoms, recognizing that people have the right to communicate with and to receive available services from any head or central governmental office in English or French and with respect to any other office where "there is a significant demand for communication with and services from that office in such language." Thus language rights are sometimes shaped or interpreted by a sliding-scale approach whereby the larger the numbers, the greater also the prerogative that the right supports. Such approach is the one we find in Article 23 of the Canadian Charter of Rights and Freedoms, which recognizes that the right to have one's children receive primary and secondary school instruction in the language of the English or French linguistic minority population of a province "a) applies wherever in the province the number of children of citizens who have such a right is sufficient to warrant the provision to them out of public funds . . . and b) includes, where the number of those children so warrants, the right to have them receive that instruction in minority language educational facilities provided out of public funds." See also Article 8 of the European Charter for Regional or Minority Languages, endorsing the sliding-scale approach to decide the type and level of language use in the area of state education.

32. See Rubio-Marín, "Language Rights." In that piece I claim that there are two types of language rights. The first type includes those language rights whose object is to protect people's cultural identity. The second type is what I call instrumental language rights. By that I mean linguistic rights whose primary purpose is to ensure the effective enjoyment of other rights that are not directly concerned with people's cultural identity. The argument I defend in that piece is that whatever position we take on whether immigrants should enjoy the same cultural protections as autochthonous national minorities, no distinction should be made as far as instrumental language rights are concerned. And although I argue that numbers may make a difference in the

recognition of instrumental rights too, that will be the case only with some and not with most of them because cost considerations here are of a different nature, since instrumental language rights have more modest (and arguably less expensive) aims than the protection of cultural identities.

33. Rubio-Marín, "Language Rights."

34. According to Réaume, full justice would be achieved if all qualified entities received the benefit in question, but each claim should be judged independently of all others. Réaume, "The Constitutional Protection of Language," 55.

35. A somewhat less demanding version of this point is articulated by Green, who claims that "the marking off of some groups is democratically defensible as long as it leaves speakers of other languages not worse off than they would have been without it and language tolerance is respected." Green, "Are Language Rights Fundamental?" 665–66.

36. Clearly, if one takes the country as a whole, francophones are the largest minority language community. As Carens pointed out to me, this point raises the question of whether there are moral reasons for choosing one geographical area rather than another for purposes of determining language rights.

37. Kymlicka, *Multicultural Citizenship*, 100.

38. Notice that the two are not the same. Using language as a marker of belonging reaches much further than just proving some sort of linguistic competence. Even though somebody may be perfectly capable of mastering a foreign language, a foreign accent is almost impossible to remove completely and may be sufficient to cause one's options to be curtailed by discrimination forces.

39. Pogge, "Accommodation Rights."

40. De Varennes, *Language Minorities and Human Rights*, 102–3.

41. Carens, *Culture, Citizenship, and Community*, 130.

42. J. Spinner, *The Boundaries of Citizenship: Race, Ethnicity and Nationality in the Liberal State* (Baltimore, Md.: John Hopkins University Press, 1994), 63.

43. Obviously this raises the question of what would happen if those studies showed that bilingual education was less effective in teaching the majority language or the curricula. In my view, because the evidence in the field is bound to be disputed and, given the underlying economic interests, of questionable objectivity, parents should have a right to decide whether they want to give their children a bilingual education. The option ought to exist. Part of the problem of gathering conclusive evidence in spite of the experience that some countries are already accumulating in bilingual education is that in many cases the programs are

largely underfunded so that, in reality, the choice is between sink-or-swim and poor education in general.

44. Granted, we cannot generalize on the basis of the experience in Florida, which is very much shaped by the special circumstances of the Cuban community in Miami. But what cannot be generalized is the expectation that immigrants can easily recreate a flourishing society in their language. From this it does not follow that they would not do so, were they given the option and were they to find the right environment. The idea is that in all these cases, a chain phenomenon could take place following a similar pattern of other cases of language revival. See, in this regard, Stephen May's description of the process of language revival of the Maori language in Aoteroa/New Zealand. Stephen May, *Language and Minority Rights: Ethnicity, Nationalism, and the Politics of Language* (New York: Longman Group, 2001), 273–306.

45. Children in those groups, for instance, should have a right (which could presumably be enforced even against their parents' will) to learn properly the majority language at school, and measures should be taken to prevent the discrimination of members of the linguistic minority within the majority society.

46. Young, "A Multicultural Continuum." On people's attachment to their culture as opposed to simply their need to have some culture, see Kymlicka, *Multicultural Citizenship,* defending the former (84–94), and Jeremy Waldron, "Minority Cultures and the Cosmopolitan Alternative," *University of Michigan Journal of Law Reform* 25 (1992): 751–93, defending the latter.

47. Gerald Neuman, "Justifying U.S. Naturalization Policies," *Virginia Journal of International Law* 35 (1994): 267.

48. This is not to say that it is morally wrong for states to declare that a certain language has official character. In my view, that largely depends on the context and on the actions that such declaration is supposed to legitimate. There is nothing wrong, for instance, with having an open clause such as that of Article 7 of the Constitutional Law of Croatia, which provides that where a minority represents more than 50 percent of the population the relevant minority language becomes the official language in the concerned area. There is nothing in principle objectionable about the Spanish Constitution recognizing the official status of Spanish, as the majority language and making other languages, such as Catalan, Basque, and Galician, co-official as a recognition of their historical nature. We may still debate whether the rights and duties that the Spanish Constitutional Court has derived from such official and co-official status are legitimate. Finally, there is nothing wrong either about Estonia establishing Estonian as the official language of the state despite

and because of the presence of a large Russian-speaking minority and as a way of symbolically restoring a past injustice. What is illegitimate about the movement in the United States is that it comes as a reaction against the use of other languages, mostly Spanish, both in civil society and by the public administration, that would be perfectly legitimate otherwise under both freedom of speech and equality considerations.

49. Alternatively, we could think of the possibility of creating a sort of Esperanto as a neutral common language that would serve as a lingua franca. In assessing this option we should be aware that the fact that such language is not the original language of any of the national or consolidated groups does not necessarily make it culturally neutral. Thus, in linguistically diverse postcolonial states, the language of the former colony is often kept as a lingua franca. Think of the role of English in India. However, that does not make it culturally neutral. Also when such a language is one that enjoys international hegemony, which is often one of the reasons why it gets chosen, legitimate questions come about as to the cultural impact of such a policy on both majority and minority local cultures and languages. The option of a sort of Esperanto is unsatisfactory as well. It may ensure impartiality, but it does so by denying everyone's claim to recognition through the public accommodation of their language and culture. Carens 1997a, 81; cf. Bauböck, "Cultural Citizenship," 327 n. 9. This is probably why it was abandoned so soon in the European context despite its many apparent practical advantages.

7

CAN THE IMMIGRANT/NATIONAL MINORITY DICHOTOMY BE DEFENDED?: COMMENT ON RUTH RUBIO-MARÍN

ALAN PATTEN

I. THE PROBLEM

Language diversity is a fact of life in societies around the world. In the United States as many as forty-five million people speak a language other than English at home, and in many other countries—including Canada, India, Nigeria, South Africa, Switzerland, Belgium, and Spain—more than a quarter of the population have as their mother tongue a language that is different from the majority's. This fact of language diversity presents a difficult and perplexing problem for policy makers and institutional designers. When, they must consider, should people be regarded as having a right to enjoy the benefits and services of public institutions in their own languages, and when can people be legitimately asked to accommodate themselves to the language of the majority instead?

In the United States, and in many other places, this problem is addressed through what might be termed a "norm-and-accommodation" policy. A normal language of public communication is designated—either explicitly in the constitution or implicitly through the de facto operations of government offices and institutions—

and then various special accommodations are made for people with limited proficiency in this language. In the United States, English is the usual language of the courts, of the federal and state legislatures, of government offices and agencies receiving public funds, and of the public school system. But people with limited English proficiency enjoy a range of different rights and entitlements that help them to communicate in the public domain and thus to secure the protections and benefits of the law. They can demand an interpreter in a court of law and, where numbers warrant, that bilingual ballots be made available at polling stations. Federal offices and agencies are required, where demand is high enough, to arrange for interpreters or bilingual staff to serve people who lack fluency in English. And since the 1974 Supreme Court decision in *Lau v. Nichols*,[1] states have been required to provide some form of accommodation in their education systems for children with limited English, either in the form of a transitional bilingual education program or through some kind of English as a Second Language program.

In other jurisdictions, the fact of language diversity is addressed quite differently. Certain selected languages are designated as "official," and then a series of rights are accorded to all speakers of those languages. In contrast with the norm-and-accommodation approach, this approach typically involves a degree of equality between the different languages that are selected for official status. In a situation of perfect equality, any public service that can be received in one official language can also be received in the other; any piece of public business can be transacted in any of the official languages; laws, judgments, and records are kept in all the official languages; and so on. Unlike the special accommodations offered under the norm-and-accommodation approach, the enjoyment of official-language rights is not contingent on a lack of proficiency in the majority language. A person is free to exercise his or her official-language rights in a minority language even if he or she is fluent in the majority language. In contrast with a norm-and-accommodation model, then, an official-languages regime is not just instrumental. There is a further "identity" or "intrinsic" value at stake with official languages that is not reducible to facilitating the communication necessary to access the protections and benefits of public institutions.

Canada and the European Union (EU) are good examples of jurisdictions that have adopted an official-languages approach to language diversity. In Canada, English and French speakers have (with some qualifications) rights to government services and public education in their own languages, wherever they live in the country and quite independently of whether they are proficient in the other official language. In the EU, speakers of the eleven "national" languages of the member states have an unqualified right to correspond with the European Commission in their own language and can expect that all official EU documents will be translated into their own language.

The Canadian and European examples point, however, to a further feature of jurisdictions that adopt some form of official-languages regime. Invariably, those jurisdictions award official-language status to some languages spoken by people that they cover but not to others. English and French are official languages in Canada, but the one hundred–plus languages spoken by recent immigrants are not, even though the numbers of people speaking these nonofficial languages in some places may far exceed the numbers speaking one or the other of the two official languages. In British Columbia, for instance, Chinese speakers outnumber French speakers by a ratio of nearly six to one, but the latter and not the former enjoy official-language rights.[2] The same pattern is discernible in the EU. Official status is enjoyed by the eleven majority or "national" languages of the member states but not by languages spoken by national minorities (e.g., Catalan, Welsh) or by immigrant languages (Arabic, Turkish, etc.).

A division of language groups into those that are included and those that are excluded seems impossible to avoid for any jurisdiction that decides to adopt an official-languages regime. With the great migrations of people characteristic of the world today, many countries are host to dozens—sometimes hundreds—of different language groups. There is simply no way that such countries could extend official-language status to each and every one of these languages. At most, members of many of these language groups could hope to enjoy the sorts of special transitional accommodations offered under a norm-and-accommodation regime.

For some critics, the inclusion/exclusion associated with official-languages regimes is a decisive problem with such schemes. Official-language status is awarded to languages in recognition of the identity and cultural interests of speakers of those languages. To say that official-language status cannot be extended to every language seems to concede that these interests cannot possibly be satisfied for everyone. But it is arbitrary, say the critics, to seek to satisfy these interests for some people and not for others. It is far less arbitrary, they claim, simply to designate some widely spoken language as a convenient lingua franca and then to ask people to use this language in public situations, perhaps with the help of transitional accommodations. This way language is regarded merely as a tool of communication, and the link with identity, to which it is ultimately impossible to do justice, is severed. The inclusion/exclusion problem is overcome by refusing to open up a Pandora's box full of identity claims and instead settling for a more modest form of inclusion—one in which everyone is expected to integrate into a common language of citizenship and is offered only transitional assistance along the way.[3]

Defenders of official-language regimes respond to this criticism by charging that it rests on a naive premise. Designating a single language of public communication is not a way to avoid taking a stand on heavily freighted questions of identity and culture, nor does it succeed at dissolving the line between inclusion and exclusion. Rather, it means *moving* this line to create a smaller class of languages that are included—a class of one—and a larger class of those that are excluded. Native speakers of the majority language enjoy the symbolic recognition, and the assistance with their identity and culture, that comes with having their language designated for public usage. Native speakers of all other languages, by contrast, are offered no comparable recognition or assistance. For defenders of the official-languages approach this is a step backwards in terms of inclusion/exclusion, not forwards.

Although more could be said on both sides of this debate, let us suppose that an official-languages approach is at least a *permissible* way for public institutions to respond to linguistic diversity. A jurisdiction that adopts this approach is still left with the inclusion/exclusion problem. It must still face the difficult decision about which languages will be accorded official status and which languages will be refused it. Is there any principled way of making this decision, or is any such decision necessarily arbitrary, as the critics charge?

A standard answer is that a principled way of settling the inclusion/exclusion problem would center on the distinction between national groups and immigrants. National groups—be they the majority group or a national minority—can reasonably demand that their languages be given official status. Immigrant groups, by contrast, can be reasonably expected to settle for norm-and-accommodation rights.

The best-known defense of the view that this is a *principled* solution to the problem is associated with the work of Will Kymlicka. In his 1995 book *Multicultural Citizenship*, Kymlicka maintains that the contrasting ways in which national and immigrant groups come to find themselves under the jurisdiction of a state provides a morally relevant basis for treating their cultural-linguistic claims differently. National groups, he argues, were typically involuntarily incorporated into the state through conquest or annexation or voluntarily joined the state at some moment of confederation but with the implicit or explicit guarantee that their cultural and linguistic claims would be respected. The members of such groups thus never gave up the rights that they can claim to cultural-linguistic protection and recognition.[4]

Immigrants, by contrast, at least in the ideal case, "choose to leave their own culture" and thus can be regarded as "waiving" their rights to live and work in their own culture.[5] The expectation that immigrants integrate into the host society is not unjust "so long as immigrants had the option to stay in their original culture."[6] Kymlicka admits that refugees, including "economic refugees," cannot really be thought of as voluntarily leaving their home society.[7] But he does not think that treating such refugees as though they were national minorities is the best way to address their predicament. The injustices that force them to flee their country "must ultimately be solved in the original homeland."[8]

II. BEYOND KYMLICKA'S CONSENT THEORY

In her contribution to the present volume, Ruth Rubio-Marín takes up the issue of how different kinds of language rights should be allocated to different groups. The first part of the chapter develops a critique of Kymlicka's view to argue that the national minority/immigrant dichotomy is too simplistic. The remainder of the chapter goes on to propose an alternative account involving a set of "generalizable criteria" that should be used in assigning different kinds of language rights to different groups. According to Rubio-Marín, these criteria will, in some contexts, and as a contingent empirical matter, support a differential treatment of immigrants and national minorities. The key point for her is that a theory of language rights should not start out from an a priori distinction between these kinds of groups but should let itself be guided by a broader set of contextual considerations.

In what follows, I will offer a brief exposition of Rubio-Marín's critique of Kymlicka and of her alternative "generalizable criteria" approach (Section II). After drawing attention to what I regard as some counterintuitive implications of Rubio-Marín's own approach (Section III), I return to Kymlicka's consent-based theory (Section IV). This theory is almost universally regarded as flawed, but I shall argue that it can be resuscitated if several key sections of Kymlicka's original argument are repaired.

Rubio-Marín's main reason for thinking that Kymlicka's approach is flawed is fairly standard in the literature. Like a number of recent critics, she doubts that immigrants can, in general, be regarded as having voluntarily waived their language rights.[9] Certainly, we cannot regard the children of immigrants as having consented to waive their rights: they may not even have been born yet at the moment of immigration. Moreover, according to Rubio-Marín, "[F]or consent to be morally relevant, it needs to be free and informed." There are reasons to think that neither the freedom condition nor the informational one is satisfied for many immigrants.

A choice, to be called "free," must have at least two viable options and an absence of coercion. Very often, Rubio-Marín argues, the political, economic, and cultural circumstances faced by people in developing and/or war-torn countries are such as to make emigration the only eligible option and to introduce an element of necessity into the "choice" to leave. There are also reasons, she thinks, for questioning whether the decision to emigrate is generally an informed one. Immigrants may not realize the scale of the cultural adaptation that the receiving society is expecting of them, and they may find it difficult to anticipate the cultural isolation they will experience. "In today's world," Rubio-Marín concludes, "prosperous countries cannot discharge their obligations to accommodate the cultural demands of those immigrants they benefit from economically by simply assuming the consensual nature of immigration."

As an alternative to the consent-based approach to assigning language rights, Rubio-Marín proposes a set of four criteria that can be employed to determine the concrete set of language rights that members of different language groups can reasonably claim. Her first criterion focuses on numbers and geographic concentration. All else being equal, more numerous groups, and those with a greater degree of territorial concentration, should be able to claim a stronger set of language rights.

A second factor to be considered is whether the extension of some set of language rights to a particular group thwarts or facilitates what Rubio-Marín calls the "expression of individual and collective choice." A frequently voiced concern about minority language rights is that they may have the effect of ghettoizing the very minorities they are intended to assist. In the United States, for instance, critics of bilingual education charge that it has discouraged language minorities from learning English and handicapped their ability to participate fully in the larger society. Without necessarily accepting the empirical claims being made by these critics, Rubio-Marín at least partly accepts their underlying normative principle. She thinks that one way in which different language rights claims should be sorted out is according to whether those rights would discourage acquisition of the majority language.

Rubio-Marín's third and fourth criteria both focus on the impact of language rights on the receiving society. According to her third criterion, rights claims by new groups should be examined for their possible impact on the culture and language of the groups that are already established in the society. "Only a limited number of languages . . . can be fully accommodated without exercising excessive pressure on the weaker ones, and hence without violating their group right to protection against such external pressures." "The protection of the groups already present can limit the cultural aspirations of newcomers." Whereas the third criterion emphasizes the cultural integrity of existing vulnerable groups in the receiving society, Rubio-Marín's fourth and final criterion emphasizes the interest that everyone in the receiving society has in the presence of some overall shared culture and framework of "communicative transparency." This will mean that language rights claims should be assessed, in part, according to their tendency to encourage or discourage divisiveness.

III. IMPLICATIONS OF THE NEW THEORY

As I mentioned earlier, Rubio-Marín believes that the policy implications of her account may end up coinciding with those associated with standard, consent-based theories. A careful, contextual application of her four criteria may show that immigrants should be refused certain language rights that national minorities can legitimately claim. Her key objective is not to reject the immigrant/national minority dichotomy altogether but to establish that it is, at best, a contingent, empirically arrived at way of sorting out language claims that may not hold for every case.

Since the immigrant/national minority dichotomy is one that many people find intuitive, it is worth exploring just how far the policy implications of Rubio-Marín's account would converge with those of the consent-based theory. If we focus for the moment on her first criterion, it is not clear that the convergence would be very great. The countries of North America and Europe are host to a number of immigrant groups that are very significant in size and whose members often live clustered together in major cities and towns. At the same time, some of the national and indigenous groups present in these societies are very small and/or quite territorially dispersed.

Consider again the comparison between French and Chinese speakers in Canada. Outside Quebec, French speakers are both less numerous and less territorially concentrated than Chinese speakers, yet it is the former, not the latter, who are considered a "national" group and who enjoy official-language rights. If we followed Rubio-Marín's criterion, however, it would be the Chinese speakers who had the stronger claim for official-language rights. Of course, the presence of a French-language-majority province in Canada—Quebec—may be relevant to the strength of the claim that French speakers elsewhere in the country can make to language rights. But this rejoinder is not available for the case of indigenous languages (nor is it for some of Europe's national minorities). On Rubio-Marín's criterion, Cree speakers would have a much weaker claim

to significant language rights than Chinese speakers, whereas on
Kymlicka's view the opposite would be true.

Nor do the policy implications of Rubio-Marín's account change
in any obvious way if the focus is shifted to her second criterion. In
her view, both the members of a national minority and immigrants
would have an interest in learning the majority language. It is clear
how, in general, the granting of significant language rights to linguistic minorities might impede the realization of this interest. But
it is less clear why this is likely to be more of a worry for immigrants
than for national minorities and thus how an application of this criterion could give special support to the view that national minorities are likely, as a contingent empirical matter, to have stronger
rights claims than immigrants. If anything, immigrants are, as
Rubio-Marín observes, likely to be more open to cultural-linguistic
adaptation than national minorities. Thus there would seem to be
less of a trade-off between granting immigrants language rights and
encouraging them to learn the majority language than there would
be for national minorities.

Rubio-Marín's third and fourth criteria do support something
like the immigrant/national minority dichotomy because they re-
volve around a contrast between the rights and interests of established members of the receiving society and the rights and interests
of newcomers. As I will suggest in the next section, I think that this
contrast is an important one for thinking about the issue that
Rubio-Marín is exploring. But it is puzzling to me how Rubio-Marín
can deploy it without begging the very question she has set out to
answer. For what she is looking for, in effect, is some reason for
thinking that it is legitimate to privilege the interests of established
members over newcomers. Since the idea that newcomers "waive"
certain rights has been dismissed, it is not clear what could justify
assigning this kind of priority to established members in her view.

Perhaps the third and fourth criteria could be revised in such a
way as to weaken their reliance on the established member/new-
comer contrast. But then, once again, it would no longer be clear
that Rubio-Marín's theory would support—even as a general empirical tendency—anything like the immigrant/national minority
dichotomy.

None of this is necessarily an objection to Rubio-Marín's strategy
of articulating certain general criteria rather than relying on a the-

ory of consent.[10] It is perfectly open to her to argue that we should go wherever the general criteria lead us, even if they point away from the immigrant/national minority dichotomy. This would give her theory a radical edge, insofar as most countries in the world do operate with a rough-and-ready dichotomy between immigrants and national minorities and the theory would be condemning such a practice. But of course the mere fact that a theory has radical implications is not a reason to think that it is mistaken.

Still, I think that many people would find the policy implications of Rubio-Marín's view counterintuitive in comparison with those of Kymlicka's theory. It is thus worth at least considering whether Kymlicka's theory might be resuscitated. In the remainder of this chapter, I offer a brief sketch of a few of the claims that would have to be established to repair the consent-based theory.

IV. The Consent Theory Reconsidered and Defended

In my view, there are two significant weaknesses in Kymlicka's original presentation of the consent-based argument. If these sections of the argument can be shored up, then the claim that immigrants waive certain cultural and linguistic rights starts to seem more plausible.

The first weakness is connected with the broader argumentative context in which the claims he makes about consent appear. Kymlicka claims that access to a secure societal culture is a necessary precondition of individual autonomy and to this extent represents a kind of Rawlsian "primary good." He also argues, on a variety of grounds, that people have interests in being able to access, not just any secure societal culture, but, in particular, their *own* societal culture—the one in which they were born and raised. Encouraged by some of Kymlicka's statements, readers have tended to put these two different claims together to reach the conclusion that access to one's own societal culture is, for Kymlicka, a primary good.

But if access to one's own societal culture is such an important and fundamental good, then it is puzzling how immigrants could ever be thought to have waived their rights to re-create their own societal culture in the receiving society.[11] It looks, on Kymlicka's theory, as if they would be renouncing their own freedom. And we might legitimately question whether this is something that people could give up or indeed whether it is something that a liberal receiving society could ask anyone to give up.

The solution to this problem, however, is not to jettison the consent theory. A better response is to be more careful in describing the way in which access to their own culture is a good for immigrants. We should be careful to disentangle the claim that "access to *a* societal culture is a primary good" from the claim that "people *have interests* in accessing their *own* societal culture." It is quite possible to accept both of these claims without mushing them together into the single proposition that "access to one's own societal culture is a primary good." One's own societal culture is a potential source of comfort, familiarity, identity, and pride and a way of talking about, and being in, the world that is to some extent unique. These all point to reasons for thinking that people have interests in being able to access their own societal culture. But they are not reasons for thinking that a person's very freedom would be fatally compromised if he or she were cut off from his or her own societal culture. It is possible for immigrants (and others) to find the range of meanings and options they need to be free in a new societal culture if they can manage to learn that culture's language and master the rudiments of its way of life and if the receiving society is willing to accept them with toleration and openness.

So one weakness in Kymlicka's presentation of the consent theory is that it is offered in the context of what seems to be an overheated account of one's own societal culture as a primary good.[12] This makes it hard to see how anyone could be asked to waive away any cultural-linguistic rights. If we substitute for this account a more nuanced and toned-down view of the interests that people have in accessing their own culture, then it becomes more reasonable to believe that certain cultural-linguistic rights are the kinds of things that people could sometimes legitimately be asked to give up.

A second weakness in Kymlicka's original discussion of the consent theory is that it focuses too much attention on the situation of the immigrant and not enough on the rights and interests of members of the receiving society. This gap in the argument can be seen from two different angles. On the one hand, even if there are immigrants who really would consent to give up certain rights, it would still be necessary to determine whether it is legitimate for a (liberal) receiving society to ask them to do so. Most readers would agree with Kymlicka that an American emigrating to Sweden could be asked to waive his rights to English-language public services. But readers would probably look at the case differently if Sweden were asking the American to give up the freedom to practice his own religion. However voluntary the American's acceptance of such a condition might be, there are some things a liberal society should not ask of anyone.[13]

It is the inverse case that is more relevant for the attempt to shore up Kymlicka's argument, however. Just as it may not be legitimate for a territorially based group to attach certain conditions to voluntary immigration, it *may* be legitimate for such a group to attach certain conditions to immigration that is not fully voluntary. The members of a group may have certain important interests of their own in being able to control a particular territory—interests that are weighty enough to ground rights to control access to the territory and to attach conditions to admission to the territory. Having these rights may, for instance, help members of the group to ensure their own security, to protect the conditions necessary for democracy, and to maintain their own cultures and languages.

From the fact that some immigrants have arrived involuntarily, then, it does not necessarily follow that they should enjoy *all* the same rights and entitlements as established members of the receiving society. To establish this conclusion, it would also need to be shown that the situation of the immigrants in question is such as to completely nullify any right that existing members of the society would otherwise have to control access to their territory or attach conditions to admission. The established members may have an extensive set of duties to badly off people in other countries, including duties to assist them in the development of the economic and political systems of their original societies, and duties to admit a certain number of them every year as immigrants or refugees. But the interests the established members have in the flourishing of their own society may mean that these duties stop short of a duty to admit such people without any special conditions at all.

Consider an analogy with the problem of homelessness. The homeless are almost invariably very badly off, and, as a result of their situation, some of their actions—such as taking refuge in a mall on a cold day—might not be classifiable as fully voluntary. In my view, the plight of the homeless places more privileged citizens under a significant set of obligations to do something, in the way of both providing temporary shelter and addressing the underlying social causes of homelessness.

Although the duties of more privileged citizens to the homeless are extensive, they arguably do not go so far as to require those citizens to billet homeless people in their own homes (even if they have the space). People have an interest in a degree of household privacy, and it is arguable that this interest is weighty enough to make it permissible for them to exclude others from being billeted in their homes and to do their best to fulfill their duties to the homeless in some different way. And even if someone were convincingly to argue that alternative ways of addressing homelessness were all likely to be ineffective, it would still seem reasonable for families to demand of their billets that they follow various preestablished house rules.

It would be a mistake, then, to jump immediately from the plight of the homeless to the conclusion that the homeless have a right to be accommodated in the homes of more privileged people with no special rules or conditions attached. Even the privileged may have certain rights and interests that are relevant to assessing what an ethically defensible solution to the problem of homelessness might be. In the same way, it is also a mistake to move directly from the premise that a migrant is badly off, or lacks the conditions conducive to fully voluntary decision making, to the conclusion that people in better-off countries have a duty to admit him (or a certain number of people like him) without any special rules or conditions attached. In both cases, the mistake is to assume that the situation of the less privileged completely nullifies any right or interest that the more privileged might have in the conditions of their own flourishing.

Now admittedly, for people committed to a strongly impartialist and cosmopolitan ethic, this may not seem like a mistake at all. The more privileged have no claims at all, on this view, until the situation of the less privileged has been raised to the point at which there is perfect equality. I have some sympathies with this form of argument and suspect that the obligations of the more privileged toward the less privileged may be *very* demanding. Still, I think there should be at least some prerogative left in a reasonable political morality for a set of self-regarding choices. And I suspect that asking newcomers to waive certain cultural-linguistic rights may be a good example of just the sort of demand made by the more privileged that falls into this zone of reasonable partiality. Or, to put this more cautiously, I think that establishing a claim of this kind would go a good part of the way toward shoring up Kymlicka's consent-based theory.

V. Policy Implications

Regarding the policy implications of this account, several qualifications and reminders are worth emphasizing. One is that only the immigrants themselves can waive away cultural-linguistic rights. As Rubio-Marín points out, the children of immigrants cannot possibly be deemed to have consented to anything, nor can subsequent generations. Strictly speaking, then, the morally relevant distinction is not between immigrant groups and national minorities but between (as Rubio-Marín perceives but does not account for) newcomers and established members of the receiving society. The immigrants may be asked to waive their rights to choose for their children a public education in which their home language is the medium of instruction. But if those children reach adulthood after they have moved to the receiving society, then, for the purposes of the argument I have been sketching, they should, as adult citizens, no more be considered as "newcomers" than those whose families have been there for centuries. They should thus have the same chance as any established members of the society to demand official-language rights for eligible members of their language group.

The second qualification is concerned with the right that established members have to attach conditions to the admission of immigrants into their society. This right, I suggested, is grounded in the morally legitimate interests that established members have in things like security, protecting the conditions of democracy, and maintaining their own languages and cultures. Many cultural-linguistic claims that immigrants might make, however, do not conflict in any way with these interests. Imagine, for instance, that a significant group of immigrants demand that their local school board offer second-language teaching in the language that they use at home. It is hard to see how meeting this demand could possibly conflict with any of the legitimate interests of the receiving population. This sort of cultural-linguistic claim, then, is not something that immigrants can be reasonably asked to waive.

Finally, I should emphasize that the consent theory I have reconstructed is not intended to apply to what I called earlier "norm-and-accommodation" rights. Immigrants may need significant transitional accommodations—in the form of temporary government services in their own language, and help learning the majority language—if they are to receive the equal protection and benefit of the law. Since it would not be reasonable for the receiving society to ask immigrants to give up their entitlement to the equal protection and benefit of the law, it would not be reasonable for it to ask immigrants to waive their norm-and-accommodation rights. The consent theory, as I have sought to revive and defend it, is addressed only to the problem of how official-language rights should be assigned.

Notes

1. 414 U.S. 563.

2. Statistics Canada, "2001 Census: Population by Mother Tongue, Provinces and Territories," retrieved May 12, 2003, from www.statcan .ca/english/Pgdb/demo18c.htm.

3. The Pandora's box image and several other ideas referred to in this paragraph are suggested by Daniel Weinstock in a series of recent articles. See especially "Le problème de la boîte de Pandore," in *Nationalité, citoyenneté, et solidarité,* ed. Michel Seymour (Montréal: Liber, 1999), 17–40, and "The Antinomy of Language Policy," in *Language Rights and Political Theory,* ed. Will Kymlicka and Alan Patten (New York: Oxford University Press, 2003), 250–70.

4. Will Kymlicka, *Multicultural Citizenship* (New York: Oxford University Press, 1995).

5. Ibid., 95.

6. Ibid., 96.

7. Ibid., 98.

8. Ibid., 100.

9. See, for example, Weinstock, "Le problème," p. 29; Joseph Carens, *Culture, Citizenship, and Community* (New York: Oxford University Press, 2000), 81; Sujit Choudhry, "National Minorities and Ethnic Immigrants: Liberalism's Political Sociology," *Journal of Political Philosophy* 10, no. 1 (2002): 61–65.

10. Another theorist who has proposed a "general criteria" strategy is Carens, *Culture, Citizenship, and Community*, 77–87. I gesture at such a strategy in the closing paragraphs of Alan Patten, "Political Theory and Language Policy," *Political Theory* 29 (2001): 691–715.

11. Weinstock, "Le problème," 30; Choudhry, "National Minorities and Ethnic Immigrants," 61–63; Rainer Bauböck, "Cultural Citizenship, Minority Rights and Self-Government," in *Citizenship Today: Global Perspectives and Practices*, ed. Alex Aleinikoff and Doug Klusmeyer (Washington, D.C.: Carnegie Endowment for International Peace, 2001).

12. I say "seems" because I am not certain that the account in question is in fact Kymlicka's. I was not able to find in *Multicultural Citizenship* an explicit statement that access to one's own societal culture is a primary good. Kymlicka does say that "we should treat access to one's culture as something that people can be expected to want, whatever their more particular conception of the good" (86).

13. Carens, *Culture, Citizenship, and Community*, 81.

PART III

CONSTITUTIONALISM
AND SECESSION

8

DOMESTICATING SECESSION

WAYNE NORMAN

I. Introduction

It is a curious fact that the most enthusiastic case for constitution-alizing a right of secession has been made by theorists with little sympathy for secessionists (at least for those in reasonably just democratic states). They recommend making secession legally possible but also hope that the groups entitled to secede will not want to take advantage of this opportunity. At first glance, this looks like stereotypical liberal evenhandedness of the sort mildly ridiculed in John Dewey's famous definition of the liberal as someone refusing to take his own side of the argument.

But first glances can be misleading. Part of the argument for a constitutional secession clause is that this can make secession and the disruption of secessionist politics *less*, not more, likely. So while these liberal theorists are hoping that national minorities will not vote to secede, they are also actively encouraging a policy that should make it less likely that minorities will even mobilize to demand a referendum. We will discuss later several reasons why a fair and legitimate secession clause might make secession, as well as secessionist mobilization, less likely. But for now it is worth noting that such a clause could require, for example, a higher level of support in a secessionist referendum than secessionist leaders would insist upon in its absence. Hence the twofold metaphor of "domes-ticating" secession: bringing it within the realm of domestic law and thereby, given the right conditions, declawing it.

The full case for constitutionalizing secession is a complex blend of normative arguments about justice, democracy, recognition, and the right to self-determination, along with conjectures about the political sociology of multiethnic societies and nationalism, as well as views about constitutionalism and statecraft in federal democracies. It is an understatement that this case has yet to be made in a systematic fashion. Much of it consists of almost bullet-point–like considerations intended to show that one is not necessarily crazy to think that constitutionalizing secession will have numerous benefits, including the possible benefit of making secession less likely in the democratic multinational state.[1] The reason for the ragged state of this case is (I believe) relatively easy to identify but difficult to rectify. So far we have tended to treat the issue of whether (and if so, how) to constitutionalize secession as an application of a moral theory of secession. In other words, we find out under what conditions territorially concentrated groups have a moral right to secede, and then we ask whether this right should be constitutionalized. Instead, we really have to treat this issue as part of a much broader discussion (or theory) of multinational federal justice and constitutionalism: What forms of recognition and political autonomy are appropriate for territorially concentrated minority groups, and how do we balance these forms of minority self-determination with the need for some kind of common identity and equal citizenship across the larger state?[2]

I want to argue that we should treat the issue of constitutionalizing secession as one part of a possible answer to this complex latter question, rather than as a kind of institutional application of a normative theory of secession per se. In other words, to use the more-often-than-not misleading metaphor, it has more to do with how we think about the terms of marriage than divorce in the multinational state.[3] If I am right about this, we are probably going to have to wait awhile before we can expect a rigorous, systematic justification for a constitutional secession clause (or for not having one, or for having any particular formulation of such a clause). For while great advances have been made on the moral theory of secession since the discussion began in earnest with Allen Buchanan's 1991 book,[4] relatively little work has been done by political philosophers on minority rights to self-determination *within* the state or on the evaluation of federal constitutional arrangements more generally.

Before proceeding, I should clarify my focus on "multinational states": What are they, and why do they figure so prominently in discussions of secession? The short answer to the first question is that they are states in which there is more than one group with a national self-consciousness, more than one group that considers itself to be a "people." It has been estimated that over 90 percent of states contain significant, historically rooted minority groups (about a third do not even have a majority group).[5] Most states in Europe, for example, are multinational in this way; and most, at least in western Europe, grant some form of autonomy, recognition, or special status to their national minorities.[6] Multinational states are of central relevance for discussions of secession because virtually every serious secessionist movement in the past century has involved a historically rooted ethnocultural minority group with a national self-conception (i.e., most of its members have considered it to be a nation or considered themselves to be a people).[7] Serious secessionist movements do not arise, for example, among groups of recent immigrants or within regions (say, wealthier regions) whose inhabitants identify with the larger nation. They arise among territorially concentrated national minorities, usually living in an historic homeland, more often than not within administrative boundaries (like a federal province) in which members of the group form a majority. Moreover, secessionist movements in Western democracies—be they violent or not—are always characterized by nationalist mobilization within the relevant minority group. While such movements may raise various concrete and material grievances, they also typically think of themselves as "stateless nations" hoping to rectify their unfortunate historical situation by acceding to the status of states themselves.

In this chapter I am concerned only with the constitutional options for multinational states of the sort just described. There may possibly be some reason for "uninational" states to contemplate having a secession clause in their constitutions, but I will not be searching for it here. More specifically, I am concerned in the first instance with the constitutional options for states that exhibit most or all of the following characteristics:

- An advanced, reasonably stable, democratic system with a history of peaceful transitions of power following elections
- At least one territorially concentrated ethnocultural minority group with (1) a national or quasi-national identity and (2) a political-territorial jurisdiction in which this minority forms a majority
- A dominant secessionist movement within this group and this jurisdiction that is committed to the peaceful, democratic pursuit of independence
- A level of support for secession within the minority group, or within the minority group's region, that fluctuates somewhere between 20 and 60 percent

In short, I shall be concerned in the first instance with the options for political and constitutional reform in countries like Belgium, Canada, France (with respect to its overseas *Départements*, and perhaps to Corsica), Spain, Switzerland (potentially), and the United Kingdom. Of course, any recommendations for states in this sort of situation *might* apply by extension to a tremendous number of states that face actual or potential secessionist threats but that fail at this time to satisfy one or more of the above conditions.[8] A more systematic theoretical approach to federalism and secession should also be relevant for constitutional engineers in international mediating authorities (including the United States and the European Union) that are called upon from time to time to broker federal or confederal arrangements in deeply divided multinational states like Ethiopia, Bosnia, Yugoslavia, Macedonia, and possibly Afghanistan and Iraq.

Over the next three sections we will look at three different patterns of arguments for recognizing some kind of legalized secession procedure in the constitution or basic law of a multinational state:

1. Arguments that propose to institutionalize more or less directly the prescriptions of a moral theory of when secession is justified (*applied moral reasons*)[9]
2. Arguments that are concerned with ensuring that secessionist politics, and any actual secession attempt, are car-

ried out within the rule of law according to fair democratic norms (*democratic rule-of-law reasons*)

3. Arguments that a secession clause can enhance the quality and strength of the federal union (*democratic federal-union reasons*)

II. Applied Moral Reasons

Most readers would not bat an eyelash at the opening paragraph of Chapter 4, "A Constitutional Right to Secede," in Buchanan's groundbreaking 1991 book:

> Preceding chapters clarified the concept of secession, identified different types of secession and conditions under which secession can be attempted, and offered a moral framework that provides substantial (though admittedly incomplete) guidance for resolving disputes about secession. But a moral framework without an appropriate institutional embodiment is merely a moral vision; and vision, though necessary for right action, is far from sufficient. This chapter begins building the bridge from vision to action, from theory to practice, by exploring how a right to secession might be included in one exceptionally powerful institution: the constitution of the modern state.[10]

There is nothing wrong with Buchanan's general advice about the need to move from theory to practice here. What is interesting about his argument in the ensuing chapter, however, is how little of it follows or builds out from his moral theory of secession per se. In fact, he argues explicitly against what he calls a "substantial approach" that would try to apply his preferred theory of secession directly. Among other things, this approach raises the problem of the "biased referee," which I will rehearse in a moment. As an alternative to directly applying his moral theory of secession, Buchanan relies on contractualist, "veil of ignorance" reasoning that, by the very nature of such reasoning, forbids contracting parties to make use of controversial moral theorizing. I will return to this contractualist argument in Section IV below, since I believe that it belongs in the category of "democratic federal-union reasons."

The applied-moral-reasons approach argues for a constitutional clause that will, as nearly as is practicable, facilitate secessions when and only when they are justified by the best moral theory of secession. But what is the best moral theory of secession? This question has been the primary focus of most of the normative literature on secession over the past decade. It is now common to distinguish three rival candidates (there are also a few hybrid theories mixing elements of these three theories):

1. *Nationalist theories of secession,* which hold that a territorially concentrated group may secede if and only if it is a nation and the majority of members of the nation (or inhabitants on the territory it proposes to take with it) want to secede[11]
2. *Choice theories of secession,* which hold that (with certain caveats) *any* geographically defined group may secede if and only if the majority of its members choose to[12]
3. *Just-cause theories of secession,* which hold that a group has a right to secede only if it has "just cause": for example, if it has been the victim of systematic and continuing discrimination or exploitation, or if its territory had been illegally incorporated into the larger state against its will (within recent memory)[13]

Each of these types of theories springs from important insights about the phenomenon and morality of secession: secessionist movements arise almost exclusively among national minorities mobilized on nationalist lines; we cannot envisage a legitimate secession that does not have substantial popular support, at least within the seceding region; and the international community has only ever generated much sympathy for secessionist movements by peoples who have clear just cause.[14]

Of course, actual theories of these three types are loaded with details, including caveats and compromises that try to meet some of the challenges of institutionalizing the theory in the real world. This is not the place to explore or evaluate these theories at length.[15] For my purposes it is sufficient to focus on the third category, just-cause theories. There are two reasons for this: first, this seems to be the preferred kind of theory for most political theorists who have examined this topic; and second, my arguments are addressed primarily to theorists who are inclined *not* to recommend constitutionalizing secession—and these theorists are very unlikely to be sympathetic with either nationalist or choice theories. There is reason to think that critics of constitutionalizing secession do in fact think that systematic injustice is a sufficient (and probably necessary) ground for a moral right to secede.[16] Presumably for nationalist and choice theorists, favoring constitutionalizing secession is a no-brainer; the only questions concern the details and wording of the clause itself.

On its own, the just-cause theory of secession tells us little about whether a given state should include a secession clause in its constitution or what such a clause should look like. The theory does help us decide when groups would have a moral right to secede, but of course there are many moral rights that need not and often *should* not be constitutionally entrenched. Similarly, there are many injustices that do not have specific remedies (let alone radical remedies) laid out in constitutional law. And of course there are many different constitutional traditions, and it is very difficult to generalize across these traditions.

Still, in the next two sections, III and IV, I will argue that there is a strong case for domesticating secession in certain kinds of states—reasons that go beyond simply entrenching a moral right to secede. And if this case is compelling, then we might begin with the assumption that the precise form of the secession clause should mirror, to some extent, the moral considerations that justify secession. In other words, the just-cause moral theory of secession does not imply that there should be a constitutional secession clause; but if there is reason to think that there should be such a clause, then the just-cause theory may help us decide what it should look like. Presumably, just-cause theorists will prefer a clause that makes it most likely that groups that have just cause will be able to secede and that those without just cause will not be able to secede.

But it is not at all clear how this insight should be institutionalized. I have already alluded to Buchanan's argument against any direct attempt to codify this principle. Buchanan is himself the "father" of the just-cause theory in the recent literature; but he also underscores the problem of the "biased referee."[17] In secession disputes it is unlikely that a neutral party can be found within the state to judge whether the minority has suffered a sufficient degree or kind of injustice to justify its seceding. Even (perhaps *especially*) in democratic settings—such as those found in multinational states like Canada, Belgium, and Spain—the question of whether national minorities have been unjustly treated is a deeply contested one among politicians, lawyers, academics, and ordinary citizens. Secessionists and unionists are likely to disagree about what kinds of incidents or events can give just cause to secede, about whether such events have occurred, about whether they have been or could be rectified by measures short of secession, about whether any particular violations were significant enough, and so on.[18]

For this reason, just-cause theorists in favor of constitutionalizing secession have tended to recommend *procedural* mechanisms that would make it possible for oppressed groups to secede, while discouraging what I have elsewhere called "vanity secessions," defined as "secessions by groups lacking just cause."[19] Such mechanisms include rules that would make it difficult for secessionist politicians to capitalize on fleeting sentiments in favor of secession (e.g., requirements to hold a series of referendums over a period of years, or conversely a requirement that no more than one referendum on secession can be called within a twenty-year period).[20] They also typically include qualified or supermajority requirements for secessionist votes, in part to use very strong support for secession as a kind of proxy for whether the group has just cause. In democratic states with relatively strong secessionist movements (e.g., in Quebec, Flanders, Scotland, Catalonia, and the Spanish Basque Country), core support for secession within the minority's territory often hovers in the 20 to 30 percent range and rarely exceeds 50 percent.[21] At least in this sort of country it is assumed that it would take considerable outrage, caused presumably by at least the perception of ongoing injustice, to create a sustained level of support for secession well above the 50 percent level. For this reason, some just-cause theorists have recommended a secession clause that would call for, say, two-thirds support from voters in the seceding region: real injustice could generate such support, but mere nationalist rabble-rousing could not. (For the sake of brevity, I shall sometimes call an entrenched right to secede that includes qualifications and conditions that make secession more difficult to achieve a *rigorous* secession clause.)

As part of a sustained critique against just-cause theories of secession, Margaret Moore has recently called into question procedural institutions that rely on a correlation between popular support for secession and the justice of a group's cause. As she notes,

"This is an empirical relationship, which is intuitively plausible, but unsupported."[22] Of course, correlated variables do not march in lockstep. We can think of many possible or historical situations of groups falling outside the generalization: for example, groups that have clear just cause to secede but will not be able to mobilize even bare majority support for secession, perhaps because of a large population of non–group members on their territory. Or consider groups that are mobilized along minority-nationalist lines to support secession even in the absence of just cause: "It may even be because of past injustice or exclusion by the majority group in the state, [rather than] any current injustice committed by that group or the state."[23] As Moore notes, these facts do not "impugn [the] just-cause theory in itself, conceived in non-institutional terms,"[24] but, to put it in the terms I am using here, they do suggest that some just-cause theorists have expected too much of the theory when it comes to grounding a constitutional secession clause.[25]

So even if the just-cause theory is the most plausible account of the morality of secession, it does not seem to imply that there should be a constitutionalized secession procedure, nor can it point directly to any given procedure, should a state decide to give itself one. Does it follow that the just-cause theory, and discussions of the morality of secession more generally, are irrelevant to the argument for domesticating secession? I think not. In some sense the just-cause theory is what you end up with once you have eliminated nationalist and choice theories from the field. I will not rehearse the critique of these theories here, but the value of that critique for this project is clear. For one thing, these two theories provide the self-justification for almost every democratic secessionist movement in the world. And as I noted earlier, the truth of either of these theories would virtually require a right of secession in the constitution of a just, democratic state. As Buchanan argues at the outset of his book, "A political philosophy [such as liberalism] that places a pre-eminent value on liberty and autonomy, that highly values diversity, or that holds that legitimate political authority in some sense rests on consent must either acknowledge a right to secede or supply weighty arguments to show why a presumption in favour of such a right is rebutted."[26] In effect, what we are calling just-cause theories are the outcome of these "weighty arguments" against permitting or requiring secession for any territorial group that fancies a state of its own.

III. DEMOCRATIC RULE-OF-LAW REASONS

The next set of reasons for domesticating secession in multinational states is based on (1) the possibility or probability that secessionist movements will arise within territories or subunits controlled by national minorities, whether there is an explicit recognition of a right to secede or not; and (2) the perceived advantages of handling secessionist politics and secessionist contests within the rule of law rather than as "political" issues that lie outside, or are presumed (by the secessionists) to supersede, the law.

In the preceding section we noted that even where a moral right exists (e.g., the right to secede if you have "just cause") it does not follow that there must be a constitutional expression of this right. In this section, in effect, we are considering the converse possibility: that there should be a legal provision for an activity (such as seceding or attempting to secede) even when there is no right to do it—in fact, even when the activity is morally objectionable. I will not make the case here that "vanity" secessions are morally objectionable,[27] but it will be a strong argument for legalizing secession that holds even if this is the case.

The groundwork for this argument comes from Daniel Weinstock's suggestion that we compare the legalization of secession to cases of legalizing other morally dubious activities. It is a pattern of argument that could be addressed to people who think that, for example, prostitution or selling of narcotics for recreational use is immoral. One might argue that these kinds of activities are going to happen whether they are legal or illegal and that there may be reasons to make them legal and bring them out of the black market and within the ambit of government regulation.[28] Weinstock argues that "there is a case to be made for making legal provision for people to engage in behaviour they have no moral right to engage in" when three conditions are met: (1) it is most likely that they will engage in this behavior even without the legal right to do so, or even if it is illegal; (2) "the behaviour in question does not involve the violation of an absolute moral prohibition"; and (3) "the consequences of legally unregulated behaviour of the kind in question are likely to be worse than the same behaviour engaged in within legal-procedural parameters designed to offset the foreseeable perverse consequences of granting the right."[29] This seems right as a claim about legitimate public policy formation in modern democratic states. The question is whether Weinstock is justified in claiming that secession satisfies these conditions. The first issue we have to clarify is what the relevant "behavior" is. Is it (1) advocating secession, (2) mobilizing for and demanding the right to secede, (3) attempting to secede, or (4) seceding? These are very different kinds of activities. Surely most people would see the mere advocating of secession, definition 1, to be something that falls within rights to free speech, just as advocating drug use, prostitution, theft, or even revolution does. Similarly, definition 2, mobilizing a peaceful secessionist movement that demands the right to secede, would seem to be an activity that would fall under rights to free speech, freedom of the press, and freedom of association, though obviously such activity would have to be carried out in ways that respected the law and public safety (as John Stuart Mill pointed out in *On Liberty*, freedom of speech does not protect every form of speech that might be bellowed out to an angry mob). At the other end of the spectrum, it cannot be definition 4, seceding itself, that is the "behavior" to be protected. For one thing, this certainly does not meet Weinstock's first, "inevitability" condition. For another, as a matter of fact and law, a group cannot secede of its own volition, any more than you can get divorced on your own (even if, in both cases, a territorial group or a spouse can separate de facto). Secession involves becoming a new state, and this requires recognition by other states. What, then, is the behavior that a constitutional secession procedure would be legalizing?

For the sake of brevity I have referred to this "behavior" or political phenomenon as "secessionist politics." It is a continuous spectrum of activities ranging from the legally innocuous activity of advocating secession to the legally and morally dubious activities of unilateral declarations of independence (UDIs) and armed insurrection, encompassing in between the creation of political parties with secessionist platforms, the contesting of elections by such parties, their organizing referendums on independence when they form regional governments, and so on. Within this spectrum the crucial point of constitutional interest is the question of whether there is a legal means for a regional government (or perhaps a federal party) representing a minority group to prove the democratic will of the group to secede and to trigger fair negotiations with the central government (and/or other partners in the state) to bring about a secession. This stage of "attempting secession," definition 4 above, is crucial because understandings about it will affect the dynamics of the activity at either end of the spectrum of secessionist politics: if popular demands for secession fall upon deaf ears in the central government, then, at one end of the spectrum, this could heat up the secessionists' rhetoric and increase the movement's sense of grievance along with its popularity; and at the other end of the spectrum, it could end up promoting the strategies of extremists in the movement who prefer extralegal options, such as violence or a UDI.

So does "attempting secession," or secessionist politics more generally, meet Weinstock's three criteria, above, for "legalization"? I will assume that it satisfies condition 2: that is, that it is not in violation of an absolute moral prohibition. Secessions from reasonably just democratic states are morally regrettable for many reasons, but surely they are not evil. When more than 99 percent of Norwegians voted to secede from Sweden in 1905, and the Swedes did not contest their wish to secede, it is hard to believe that something absolutely awful happened nonetheless. Of course, few cases would be this unproblematic, but in this case surely we would have been more concerned if Sweden had refused the request to secede, especially if it had reacted with force.

How about Weinstock's condition 1: Is secessionist politics in a multinational state *inevitable* whether or not there is a legal mechanism for secession? To some extent, this question is moot for my argument, since I am concerned only with those cases where there is already significant support for secession. Be that as it may, what is close to inevitable in multinational democratic states is that there will be movements calling for "self-determination," including the right to secede if that's what the group wants. (This is true almost by definition: we would not call these groups "national" minorities if their ethnocultural difference were not accompanied by a political will to some form of self-government.)[30] It is not inevitable that these movements will ever be strong (i.e., popular) enough to actually attempt, or even credibly threaten, to secede. In cases where they cannot rally strong support for secession, a constitutional procedure that allows secession will never be used. But in cases where strong popular support for secession is within the realm of possibility, it is unlikely that the lack of a constitutional procedure will dampen the support for the secessionist option.

And this leads us to consideration of Weinstock's third condition, that the consequences of not having a legal secession procedure may well be worse than the consequences of having one. There are two reasons for this: first, a popular secessionist movement without a legal means to pursue its political agenda will give rise to political uncertainty and possibly worse (in some cases, the certainty of violence); and second, a legal procedure of the right kind might actually diminish the chance that there will be an attempted secession or even a serious secessionist movement. I will say more about this second point in the next subsection. In the meantime, it is instructive to look at the case of Quebec and Canada as an example of the dynamics of a democratic secessionist movement within a constitutional order that was until recently silent on the legality of secession.

There is much to be learned from more than three decades of serious democratic secessionist politics in Quebec and Canada. Quebec's independence movement is an explicit model for other national minorities in western Europe and elsewhere. It is also, no doubt, seen by centralists in other multinational states as the example of what happens when "too much" autonomy is granted to a national minority. In the late 1960s the first major separatist political party in the province, the Parti Québécois (PQ), was founded with a former Quebec cabinet minister, René Levesque, as its leader. This party won the provincial election in 1976, promising not to attempt to secede without first winning a referendum. It held this referendum—which asked for a mandate to negotiate "sovereignty-association," a kind of state-to-state confederal arrangement—in 1980 and lost by a 60–40 margin. The party would nevertheless win three of the next six provincial elections in Quebec, although never with a majority of the votes, and one time with fewer total votes than the federalist Liberal Party of Quebec. In 1995 a PQ government held another quasi-independence referendum, and this time they came within a percentage point of winning. It is

worth reflecting on the wording of the question used in this referendum. The question on the ballot read: *"Do you agree that Quebec
should become sovereign, after having made a formal offer to Canada for a
new economic and political partnership, within the scope of the bill respecting the future of Quebec and of the agreement signed on June 12, 1995?"*
(Yes or No). Intense debate in the Quebec National Assembly could
not add the word *country* after the word *sovereign*, presumably because the majority PQ government knew full well that polls consistently show that support for Quebec's being "sovereign" is higher
than support for its becoming a "sovereign country." The bill referred to in the question was a long piece of proposed legislation
that called for a declaration of independence if the offer of confederal partnership was refused. The "agreement signed on June
12" was an informal one between the leaders of the three nationalist parties in Quebec. Given how fuzzy this question was—especially
as a basis for a UDI—it is perhaps not surprising that some leading
intellectual supporters of the "Yes" side expressed relief afterward
that they had *lost* by one percentage point rather than winning by
such a margin.

What was the federal government's response to this steady esca-
lation of democratic secessionist politics? Throughout this period
there were significant attempts to make French-speaking Quebecers feel more allegiance to Canada, including making French an
official language in Canada and expanding its use within the federal civil service; there was also a steady flow of "transfer payments"
into Quebec as part of a "regional equalization" scheme where the
wealthier provinces subsidized the poorer provinces, including
Quebec. There were also two major attempts by the federal government, with the agreement of most of the provincial governments, to explicitly recognize Quebec as a "distinct society within
Canada" in the constitution.[31] But on the question of secession itself, successive federal governments, like the constitution itself,
largely remained silent. Senior federal politicians played active
roles in both "sovereigntist" referendum campaigns (on the "No"
side), thus legitimizing them to a significant extent. But they never
laid out an official policy about how they would respond if more
than 50 percent of the voters voted Yes. They (literally) prayed that
that would not happen and were shocked when it almost did. Afterward, several academic conferences and think tanks debated

what might have happened if the separatists had narrowly won the referendum of 1995; and virtually no one imagined that things would have proceeded smoothly or "rationally." There would have been an unprecedented political stand-off between Ottawa (the federal government) and Quebec, with major economic consequences for both sides as international markets reacted. Several volatile issues—especially concerning the borders of a seceding Quebec state, which contained territories inhabited mainly by Aboriginal peoples or anglophones who had voted overwhelmingly against separation—had scarcely been aired in public debates.[32] On the border issue, for example, the federal government had neither challenged nor endorsed the separatists' assertion that a new Quebec state would retain the borders it had had as a province within Canada. There had been virtually no public debate on the issue of who would actually sit down to negotiate on behalf of Canada or the rump of Canada if secession negotiations took place (the government of Canada typically contains a significant number of members from Quebec, so it is not clear that it would be the appropriate body to represent the interests of Canadians outside Quebec). With issues like this unresolved in advance, many commentators refused to rule out the possibility of chaos and even violence during a period of attempted secession.

In a moment I will discuss some of the Canadian federal government's more recent attempts to clear up this uncertainty by laying ground rules and conditions for future secessionist attempts. At this point, however, it is worth drawing attention to three lessons from this case that could potentially apply in other open, democratic societies with serious secessionist movements.

First, this history illustrates the difficulty of fixing an arbitrary stopping point for the legality of secessionist politics. By this I mean that if it is permissible to advocate secession, to form parties with secessionist platforms, to have those parties form provincial governments, and to have those governments organize referendums that respect democratic norms, then it is very difficult for a central government to simply refuse to negotiate secession after a "victory" for the secessionists. To do so would be to declare that this whole decades-long democratic process was a charade. And that kind of response could only feed the indignation or *ressentiment* that lay behind secessionists' desire to be masters of their own house.[33] Yet there does not seem to be any obviously best place for central authorities to take a stand against secessionist politics in a free society—at least in a liberal democracy whose constitution is silent on secession. You cannot forbid people to advocate secession, and you cannot stop parties from putting secession in their platforms; and in most federations, you cannot prevent regional or provincial governments from holding consultative referendums. Antisecessionists can, of course, debate secessionists in all of the usual ways, but this hardly amounts to a strategy for containing secessionist politics.

From the perspective of ordinary citizens, who will have heard their politicians and opinion makers debate the secessionist option for years, a secessionist referendum campaign will look and feel very much like a normal election campaign, albeit one with much higher stakes. In all likelihood the "Yes" and "No" sides will be led by familiar political parties and politicians; they will have a concentrated campaign period, with the usual marketing mix of posters, TV ads, rallies, and televised debates; a vote in polling stations supervised by party workers and government election officials; and an outcome at the end of the evening with one side receiving more votes than the other, followed by victory and concession speeches from the two headquarters. If the "No" side wins, political life will return to normal. (Sort of. Referendums like this leave the body politic badly bruised.[34]) But if the "Yes" side gets more than 50 percent of the valid votes, citizens will find themselves in an entirely novel situation: a political contest has not just been *decided* according to the rule of law. Instead, a new contest for which there are no pre–agreed-upon contest rules has just been *initiated*. The seemingly familiar exercise of the referendum had the trappings of democracy, but it could also be described as a grand exercise in power politics masquerading as democracy. The secessionists will be asking for the referendum victory to be treated just like an election victory, entitling them to the "spoils." But in fact, when a constitution is silent on this issue of secession, all they will have received from their victory in a referendum is something equivalent to a show of hands at a trade union meeting in advance of contract negotiations. For example, "50 percent plus one" on referendum night might count for very little if it was known that there was a boycott by a substantial number on the other side, a fuzzy question, or if subsequent opinion polls showed the support for the "Yes" side to be slipping.

A second lesson from this Canadian case is that if there are no explicit constitutional rules in place to govern, for example, the process of holding a secessionist referendum—selecting the wording of the question, deciding the level of support needed for victory, and assigning rights and obligations of negotiating parties in the event of a victory by the secessionists—then secessionists will be able to set and in some sense legitimize many of the "rules" themselves. If the central government later declares the process flawed, or the majority insufficient, it will not be able to help looking as if it is trying illegitimately to move the goalposts while the ball is in the air, so to speak. As I will suggest later, the kinds of fair rules about secession that might be agreed to at the point of a federal state's founding or refounding would certainly be much more demanding than those that the separatists would set for themselves (e.g., procedures to prevent fuzzy or trick questions from being asked; qualified majorities for success; and possibly procedures for the democratic partition of the seceding territory if people living in border regions prefer to stay with the larger state). This suggests some clear advantages to setting those rules in advance in as legitimate a fashion as possible.

Finally—and this goes to Weinstock's third condition concerning the legalization of morally dubious behavior—there are several potential costs to having a secessionist political contest go entirely unregulated in this way, costs that are quite possibly worse than the costs of having a legalized secession procedure. We will discuss more of the costs to deliberative democracy of having ongoing secessionist politics a little later. At the very least, as Weinstock has emphasized, such long-running secessionist contests have a tendency to muscle many other issues off the political agenda; they also tend to polarize elections, so that voters will find themselves forced to vote for parties on the basis of whether they are separatist or not, rather than according to their policies on the usual range of socioeconomic issues.[35] Then there are the economic costs of political uncertainty, as well as the increased risk of violence. One of the lessons of the Canadian experience is that *ongoing, seemingly never-ending secessionist politics can be as unfortunate for the larger state as secession itself.* It is the kind of thing that constitutional engineers should be very eager to discourage at the point of founding or re-founding a multinational state.

In sum, a strong case can be made for making secession legal, under carefully constructed conditions, even for those who think (as I do) that secession from a reasonably just democratic federation is rarely justified. If secessionist politics is going to happen anyway, it is better that it take place within the rule of law—especially if a well-formulated secession clause actually takes away incentives to engage in secessionist politics. This latter point leads us to considerations of deliberative democracy and constitutionalism that we will explore in the next section.

Before moving on from this discussion of "rule-of-law reasons" for domesticating secession, it is worth exploring a "rule-of-law" objection and responding to it, in part, by commenting on the way Canadian courts and lawmakers have tried to domesticate secession in the years since the 1995 Quebec referendum.

Critics of constitutionalizing secession have cited a number of obstacles to formulating a secession clause. Some of these are objections *in principle* to constitutionalizing secession: for example, arguing that it violates the spirit and ideals of constitutionalism.[36] We will deal with some of these objections in the next section. At this point we will consider the objection that the real devil is in the details of a secession clause—where the particular details that will be relevant in some future secessionist contest are just too difficult to predict and too uncertain to fix in the text of the constitution. Part of this objection is well taken. Even the most enthusiastic supporters of constitutionalizing secession must recognize that, as Aronovitch puts it, "beyond whatever can be stipulated by rules and beyond whatever guidance can legitimately come from valid norms of law . . . there remains the core need, in the best of circumstances, for the parties to a potential secession to work out, on a partly *ad hoc*, contextualist basis, whether and how it is to happen."[37] But Aronovitch wants to go further and suggest that stipulating anything about secession in legal texts is ill advised. He raises three challenges in particular:

1. It would be impossible to spell out in a secession clause fair rules for dividing assets, debts, and properties. "This seems to require impossible prescience and/or to pre-

empt on all kinds of developments and innovations, economic, international, organizational, even moral; such
rules which—if formulable at all—might have seemed fair
at the outset may not be at all so after the fact."
2. "Similarly, how can there be, and why suppose there
should be, a clause deciding once and for all which units
or groups qualify for the right to secede?"
3. It is very likely there will be disputes between the secessionists and the central government about how to interpret a secession clause; but the Supreme or Constitutional
Court "seems an unlikely candidate for acceptance as an
impartial and effective arbiter for disputes about the right
to secession."[38]

I have so far avoided discussing how a secession clause should be
formulated, apart from suggesting that there are many different
options available. In the next section I will also suggest that a secession clause is best arrived at in constitutional negotiations that
include a wide range of constitutional provisions of interest to both
the minority (e.g., those promoting autonomy and recognition)
and the majority (e.g., those promoting unity and stability). The
most I will ever argue for in this chapter is that a well-formulated
secession clause could "fit" very comfortably within a package of
such provisions, perhaps even facilitating the final agreement. In
short, it could quite appropriately take many different forms. It is
nevertheless worth addressing some of Aronovitch's concerns here
because they go directly to the issue of whether a constitutional
clause can realistically and fairly enhance the protections of the
rule of law.
    All three of Aronovitch's concerns are legitimate worries, but all
three will be at least as worrisome in the absence of a secession
clause. For example, while it is possible to imagine a Supreme
Court failing to interpret contentious aspects of a secession clause
in ways that the secessionists will perceive as fair, it is surely much
more likely that the Court will side with an obstructionist central
government if there is no guidance whatsoever in the constitutional text. The same goes for Aronovitch's first concern, about the
difficulty in specifying precise constitutional formulas for dividing
assets, debts, and the like. In all likelihood, a secession clause would

not attempt to specify that level of detail—in which case, the negotiations over these issues would be no more difficult with than without a secession clause. But a secession clause might spell out some processes and principles for such negotiations, and these could be justiciable in the courts. Again, this could not be worse than having no secession clause at all. Finally, as for the concern about a secession clause having to specify which particular units, groups, or types of groups would be permitted to secede—this is indeed a difficult problem, with or without a constitutional clause. It is worth noting, however, that it is no more difficult in principle than many decisions that have to be made in federal constitutions concerning the types of units that qualify for special status, such as being a province, getting to send representatives to the second chamber of Parliament, getting to ratify or veto constitutional changes, and so on. In practice, it would be federal subunits that would be given access to a secession clause; but provisions could also be made for creating new subunits or for partitioning seceding subunits so that "federalist" counties could stay in the rump state.[39] Aronovitch is correct in highlighting just how much of the details in a secession would be up for negotiation. But negotiation is a fact of life in intergovernmental arrangements like federations or the European Union. Constitutions do not try to decide all these contests in advance, and constitutional courts gain legitimacy as arbiters precisely because they do *not* systematically favor the central government over the subunits.

Although it was published more than a year afterward, it appears that Aronovitch's article was written before the Canadian Supreme Court's 1998 Opinion on secession.[40] This thoughtful and lengthy document does much to highlight the close relationship between legal principles appropriate for secession and those already in place within multinational federal constitutions. After the sorry history of the Canadian federal government's neglect of the constitutional challenge of secession, discussed above—and, in particular, after the uncomfortably narrow federalist victory in the secessionist referendum of 1995—the Canadian minister of justice formally asked the Supreme Court to consider a number of questions about the legality of secession. The Court's subsequent Opinion, in effect, *read into* the constitution a modest secession clause, even though the constitution itself does not explicitly contemplate secession. I have discussed this Opinion at length elsewhere and will not rehearse all of that analysis here.[41] The Court's bottom line, so to speak, was that "[a] clear majority vote in Quebec on a clear question in favour of secession would confer democratic legitimacy on the secession initiative which all of the other participants in Confederation would have to recognize." They refused to spell out exactly what would constitute a "clear question" and what level of support would qualify as a "clear majority," but they left no doubt that the democratic legitimacy of such a result would require the federal government to negotiate in good faith.[42] Perhaps even more interesting than the bottom line is the reasoning leading up to it. The Court cited "four fundamental and organizing principles of the Constitution," namely "federalism, democracy, constitutionalism and the rule of law, and minority rights" (para. 32). The argument of the Opinion is then structured to show that *each one of* these fundamental principles entails the conclusion concerning the rights and obligations of secession negotiations.

Of course, there is no reason to think that most other constitutional courts would be as receptive to the legality of secession as Canada's. Still, Canada is the third oldest democratic federation, and with a tradition in constitutional law that, on the one hand, follows the American model and, on the other, recognizes the existence of multiple peoples within the state, it is hard to dismiss its relevance of the Court's Opinion on secession.[43] In the context of critiques of Aronovitch, Sunstein, Bauböck, and others, it is worth highlighting four aspects of the Opinion in particular. First, although the Court firmly rejected the legality of a *unilateral* secession attempt, it did not find the very idea of secession to be contrary to fundamental ideals or principles of constitutionalism (on the contrary). Second, while the Court would agree with Aronovitch that a complicated range of issues would have to be negotiated to effect secession, it also believed that there were fairly clear rights and obligations for the parties to these negotiations. Third, the Opinion gives some grounds for optimism that a constitutional court in a democratic multinational federation need not be hopelessly biased in favor of the federal government, especially when the court is able to consider these issues in "the cool hour" rather than in the throws of a constitutional crisis. As it turns out, the main political actors in both the federalist and secessionist camps found favor in the Opinion.[44]

A fourth and final lesson worth emphasizing here is based on the necessary shortcomings of the Opinion. The judges did not want to write new law and explicitly pointed out a number of issues that would have to be defined by political actors, especially concerning the clarity of the question asked in a secessionist referendum and the size of clear majority (although they hinted strongly that a supermajority would not be inappropriate).[45] In the next section I will discuss a number of distinct advantages to spelling out explicit conditions that would have to be met before a subunit could trigger secessionist negotiations.[46]

IV. DEMOCRATIC FEDERAL-UNION REASONS

It is now time to begin cashing some promissory notes that have piled up during the exposition and argument thus far. In particular, I have made two claims at a few points in the argument: first, that the strongest arguments for domesticating secession come, not from applying a moral theory of secession, but rather from thinking about appropriate conditions for a just federal union or partnership between ethnocultural or political communities sharing a democratic state. Second, I have claimed repeatedly that having such conditions entrenched and legitimized in the constitution would very likely reduce the incentives to engage in secessionist politics and would thereby decrease the social and political costs of secessionist politics and secession itself. It is time now to begin to cash out these notes.

Because entrenched secession clauses are so rare in the constitutions of modern states,[47] it is tempting to believe that they could be justified only by some special kind of argument—for example, an argument based on a moral theory of secession. Another approach is to ask what kinds of arguments or reasons are legitimate for justifying *any* features of constitutional design and then to ask whether, upon reflection, these reasons would, for certain kinds of states, justify some form of secession clause. Of course, the question of what constitutions are for, and how their provisions are justified, is a matter of great controversy in political philosophy and constitutional law. Fortunately, we do not have to settle most of those controversies for the issues at hand. Few would disagree with Cass Sunstein's general claim that "the central goal of a constitution is to create the preconditions for a well-functioning democratic order, one in which citizens are genuinely able to govern themselves."[48] While this may be the—or at least *a*—central goal of constitutions, there are other purposes for constitutions that are derived from or concomitant to this goal. Sunstein himself emphasizes that "a constitution should promote deliberative democracy, an idea that is meant to combine political accountability with a high degree of reflectiveness and a general commitment to reason-giving,"[49] and that it should create "structures that will promote freedom in the formation of preferences and not simply implement whatever preferences people have."[50]

More specifically, Sunstein urges that constitutional clauses should aim for

- The protection of rights central to self-government
- The creation of fixed and stable arrangements by which people order their affairs
- The removal of especially charged or intractable questions from the public agenda
- The creation of incentives for compromise, deliberation, and agreement
- The solution of problems posed by collective problems, myopia, and impulsiveness

Let us call Sunstein's view "deliberative constitutionalism." I have dwelt on Sunstein's account of constitutional justification in part because it is generally clear and sensible and in part because Sunstein is the most prominent opponent of constitutionalizing a secession clause. As it turns out, Sunstein believes that these goals collectively suggest "that a right to secede does not belong in a founding document."[51]

I would like to criticize this argument of Sunstein's in two rather different ways—first, in effect, by accepting his premises but denying that they lead to his conclusions. That is, we can accept his goal of deliberative constitutionalism but deny that a properly designed secession clause would undermine it. And second, I will consider the inadequacy of deliberative constitutionalism, on its own, for thinking through the constitutional challenges of the multinational state.

A. *Deliberative Democracy and Secessionist Politics*

The basic argument against Sunstein's case is this: he is absolutely right about the pernicious effects of secessionist *politics* on democratic deliberation and political stability—indeed, he may even underestimate the variety and potency of these effects—but he is too quick to assume that secessionist politics is necessarily encouraged by a secession clause and discouraged by its absence.[52] Secessionist politics can do all of the things Sunstein fears from an entrenched right to secede: namely

> increase the risks of ethnic and factional struggle; reduce the prospects for compromise and deliberation in government; raise dramatically the stakes of day-to-day political decisions; introduce irrelevant and illegitimate considerations into those decisions; create dangers of blackmail, strategic behavior, and exploitation; and, most generally, endanger the prospects for long-term self-governance.[53]

If anything, Sunstein and others underplay the corrosive effects of secessionist politics on deliberative democracy. One cannot fully understand the psychological and sociological dimensions of secessionist politics merely by imagining rational bargaining situations where one party threatens exit.[54] This is because of the ethnonationalist context of virtually every modern secessionist movement. For even cynical threats to secede to be credible, subunit leaders must first mobilize "their people" on inherently divisive nationalist lines. This kind of mobilization can take years and involves continuous agitation by secessionist entrepreneurs and other minority nationalists. They have an incentive to portray almost any decision or action by the central government as an example of insult, ignorance, humiliation, aggression, exploitation, or oppression. But unlike some other forms of "posturing" to back up threats in political bargaining, this kind of nationalist sentiment is not easily turned off; it can become a background feature of the political culture, guaranteeing that the pernicious effects described in the above quote from Sunstein become more or less permanent features of the political landscape. Even nonsecessionists in the political culture will find themselves appealing to these sentiments in the course of political argument.

But again, the issue here is not whether secessionist politics is bad for democracy and justice but rather what can be done through the constitutional engineering of a multinational state to take away the incentives for minority leaders to engage in secessionist politics. And again, part of this latter issue—perhaps only a small part—is the question of whether a legitimate secession clause would increase or decrease incentives for secessionist politics. This last question is, of course, largely an empirical matter, and the results would vary with the nature of the secession clause and the historical setting for which it is proposed. Much of Sunstein's argument is directed against entrenching what might be called a "simple right to secession," one that presumably could be exercised with something like bare majority support in the seceding subunit. But none of the supporters of constitutionalizing a secession clause are arguing for a simple right to secede. As I noted at the outset, the principal advocates for a secession clause have been political theorists who are philosophically opposed to secession in reasonably just democratic states. They propose what Sunstein calls a "qualified right to secede," one that might require, as I have noted, a substantial majority (two-thirds or three-quarters support) in the seceding region to be exercised, among other hurdles and qualifications. The hope would be that the qualifications on secession would be such that political leaders could not expect to mobilize enough support to make secessionist threats credible in the absence of genuine oppression by the central government. And with the prospects of a credible secessionist threat not in the cards, there would be less incentive to engage in the kind of nationalist mobilization that drives secessionist politics.

Sunstein does consider the usefulness of a qualified right to secede that would require a supermajority or an extended deliberation period. But he dismisses both qualifications with a sentence or two. He notes that "[a] requirement of a supermajority would certainly limit the occasions for, and seriousness of, secession threats. But in cases in which the subunit can be energized—for reasons of economic self-interest or ethnic or territorial self-identification— the protection would be inadequate."[55] But this is too breezy a reply. Surely we cannot dismiss a piece of constitutional engineering simply by imagining low-probability situations in which it might be used to overturn something we like about the status quo. We do not dismiss the legitimacy of a rigorous amending formula (such as that in the U.S. Constitution) simply by imagining that it could potentially be used to repeal some fundamental right. There are empirical conjectures relevant here. It is significant that there has never been a substantial majority within a subunit voting to secede from an advanced democratic state of the sort I described at the outset of this chapter. None of the most popular Western secessionist movements today—among the Québécois, Flemish, Scots, Catalans, Spanish Basques, and so on—has ever shown sustained levels of support for secession above 50 percent. It is also significant that there are no serious examples of secessionist movements within flourishing constitutional democracies that are based purely on economic self-interest—the other example cited by Sunstein, and also by economists who assume that this would be the natural and compelling reason for a territorial group to want to secede.[56] All of this suggests that a secession clause that demanded a supermajority significantly higher than 50 percent might be just the sort of mechanism that could help do something that Sunstein elsewhere cites as a legitimate aim of constitutional engineering: it would amount to "a decision to take certain issues [in this case secession] off the ordinary political agenda."[57] In Sunstein's own words, taking issues off the agenda in this way can "protect" and "facilitate" democracy. As the Canadian case illustrates, it is patently obvious that having a constitution remain silent on the issue of secession simply fails to do that.

In short, there is good reason to think—at least in the sorts of countries I am addressing here, in the first instance—that a "qualified right to secede" can serve as part of a constitutional precommitment strategy of the sort that Sunstein himself generally recommends. A crucial question, then, is, *Who* should be doing this precommitting? Constitution making is (thankfully) not left to philosopher-kings. In particular, an important consideration is whether the potentially secessionist minority itself would ever voluntarily precommit to an arrangement that made exit significantly more difficult. This question leads to a range of issues that are largely absent from most discussions of constitutionalism in the

American tradition, where multinational constitutional accommodation has never really been on the table.

B. *Beyond (or beside) "Deliberative Constitutionalism"*

All democratic states have an interest in constitutional structures encompassing precommitment strategies to facilitate stable, deliberative democracy. But in multilingual, multinational democracies, there is a range of constitutional issues that cannot be fully articulated in the language of deliberative democracy—even if addressing these issues successfully will also help facilitate stability and deliberative democracy. Most of these issues arise from the fact that such states have more than one "self" with a stake in self-government and self-determination. While it may have been a plausible dream that a common political and national identity would emerge in multiethnic countries of immigration (like the United States and Australia, where this has largely come to pass), this is a pipe dream (or a pipe nightmare) in multiethnic societies with historically rooted ethnocultural groups. As Walker Connor has argued, there are "no examples of significant assimilation . . . which have taken place since the advent of the age of nationalism and the propagation of the principle of self-determination of nations."[58] This suggests that if constitutions are seen as "pragmatic instruments,"[59] constitutional engineering in a multinational state cannot realistically have as one of its goals the creation of one (and only one) national community in a state in which there is already more than one. Among other things, no national minority would voluntarily assent to such a constitution. The constitution must find ways of reflecting and recognizing national pluralism and of providing concrete means for overlapping domains of self-government. (In what follows, I shall write as if such means necessarily include some form of federalism. I am using a fairly loose conception of federalism here, one that encompasses various forms of territorial autonomy for minorities—such as that enjoyed by the Scots or the Spanish Basques—even though some of these arrangements may not make the whole system federal according to some strict definitions of federalism.)

Obviously, this is not the place to develop a complete theory of multinational federal constitutionalism. I will suggest a few features of such constitutions that go beyond those necessary in the "uninational" state that seems to be the subject of most American writing on constitutionalism, including Sunstein's. The following list begins with some background principles or desiderata that may not find any explicit articulation in a constitutional text and moves on to items likely to involve some specific institutional mechanisms. (This list is not meant to be exhaustive. In fact, it is part of my argument in this chapter that a secession clause is something that belongs on such a list.)

1. *Collective Assent.* At one or more crucial stages in the founding or refounding of such states, it is important that constituent national or quasi-national groups assent to the constitutional terms of their association with the state. Otherwise, the arrangement will always be viewed as something akin to colonialism.

2. *Anti-assimilationism.* This principle lies behind most of the others, especially the ideals of assent, recognition, and autonomy. It is the principle that the majority should not be engaged in deliberate attempts to assimilate specific national minorities. It does not imply that other assimilationist policies (e.g., directed toward immigrants) are illegitimate or that the national minority's leaders can do whatever is necessary to prevent voluntary assimilation by individual members of their group into the majority culture. It is a requirement that the majority accept as legitimate and *normal* that their state contains more than one national group and that members of the national minority divide their loyalty and identity between their group and their larger state.

3. *Stability and Unity.* As in decentralized or federal "uninational" states—though with greater urgency—multinational federal constitutions must pay careful attention to balance autonomy and recognition of minorities and regions with the needs of a common cooperative political life and political identity in the state. A federation that is unstable or inefficient because it is overly decentralized is usually not in any partner's long-term interest.[60]

4. *Partnership.* It is likely that a multinational state that secures the assent of its minorities will see itself as a kind
of partnership of groups or communities or peoples,
and not just of equal citizens (although equal citizenship
in some form or other is also important). The ideal and
language of partnership may appear within the preamble of the constitution.[61]

5. *Territorial Autonomy.* Minority national groups (especially
territorially concentrated ones) will almost always demand, as a condition of their voluntary assent, a significant degree of autonomy over legislative and administrative jurisdictions of cultural and linguistic importance.
(Indeed, we probably would not call them *national* minorities or minority *nations* if they did not make such
demands.)[62]

6. *Recognition.* Minority national groups will also almost always demand recognition of their existence, and of their
status as partners, in the constitution and the major symbols of the state (including, possibly, the country's name,
flag, coat of arms, national anthem, official languages,
and so on).[63] Formal recognition can be a significant
sign of commitment to an anti-assimilationist principle.

7. *Special Representation.* Multinational federations may also
include permanent constitutional guarantees for special
representation of certain constituent groups in the central institutions of the state (e.g., in one or more of
the houses of Parliament, in the executive, the
supreme or constitutional court, the civil service, and
the military). Such representation may include limited
veto rights.

8. *Regional/Minority Role in Amending Formula.* Similarly,
consistent with the terms of partnership, autonomy, and
recognition, constituent groups are likely to demand a
special role, and perhaps a veto, over significant elements of constitutional change, especially those that
change the terms of the minority group's partnership.
Part of such a role may be the right to initiate formal negotiations over constitutional change.[64]

While I have worded some of these conditions as "demands," in general they will assume the status of principles and cherished ideals in the well-ordered multinational federation. Failure to meet any of them is likely to provide a serious and persistent source of friction and grievance. This is a fact of life in most multinational societies. And as such, these demands and objectives should figure in the deliberations not only of actual politicians conducting fair negotiations for constitutional reform but also of idealized parties negotiating a constitutional agreement behind a Rawlsian "veil of ignorance."[65]

As it turns out, most writers making a case for domesticating secession find it useful to think about why a secession clause might be selected by rational and reasonable parties drawing up a constitution behind a "veil of ignorance."[66] Even Sunstein, who does not take a Rawlsian approach to constitutionalism in general, is inclined to use thought experiments based on conjectures of how "people forming a new government" or "people in a newly formed nation" would select constitutional structures and precommitment strategies.[67] This is one way, according to Buchanan, to think of any of the terms appropriate for an ideal constitution.[68] We can, for example, "imagine a group of hypothetical agents who are asked to negotiate the terms of their political association, knowing that they will be members of a multination state, but not knowing which particular group they will belong to."[69] The "veil" here can be relatively thin: it is meant merely to model a degree of impartiality by ruling out agreements based on considerations of power and coercion, but it should allow the negotiating parties to take into consideration whatever there is to know about what makes democratic political systems effective and stable in a state shared by more than one ethnocultural or ethnolinguistic group.[70] In fact, much of the work of such a veil of ignorance could be done simply by imagining that the parties negotiating an original or a renewed constitutional agreement for the multinational state are enlightened and have the long-term interests of their citizens, their groups, and their progeny in mind. This is because, as I have noted, structural problems that lead to persistent perceptions of unfairness or injustice by some group or groups in the state are likely to create chronic sources of grievance and instability; and this kind of instability is in no group's long-term interest.[71]

Again, it is worth drawing attention to the fact that this kind of reasoning is recommended for *all* aspects of federal constitutionalism—from deciding on basic individual rights and the separation of branches of government to the federal division of powers and the selection procedures for Supreme Court judges. It is not some special kind of reasoning for thinking about whether to have a secession clause. Nevertheless, when we do think about a secession clause in this way, we can see at least five ways that a properly formulated secession clause could fit comfortably with the eight special features of multinational federal constitutionalism listed above and make the union stronger rather than weaker:

1. *Removing Secession as a Realistic Objective of Ordinary Politics.* Thus far, I have repeatedly drawn attention to one striking way that a rigorous secession clause might reduce the incentives for secessionist politics—namely by making the conditions for secession significantly more difficult than those that would be insisted upon by secessionist entrepreneurs in the absence of explicit rules. This could be thought of as a justification based on principle 3 from the above list, since it is attempting to use a secession clause as a way of facilitating unity and cooperation in the state. We have already discussed this argument in some detail. It is time to explore some less obvious ways a secession clause could facilitate a just federal union.

2. *A Mechanism for Voluntary Assent.* Even in the democratic world, almost none of the existing national minorities ever gave their initial, democratic assent to their membership in the larger state; and few have had a formal opportunity to assent since. In the less-than-fully-democratic world, of course, the situation for minorities is much worse. Most multinational states are the result of conquests, royal marriages, arbitrary colonial boundaries, and the like, from the distant past. When such conquests are of relatively recent vintage, as they were in the Baltics, minority nations will usually take their first democratic opportunity to exit—and rightfully so. In general, though, when peoples have been sharing the state for many generations, especially under conditions of equal citizenship

and democratic elections, exit is not the preferred option. The larger state provides more opportunities, and the intertwining of political and economic systems, not to mention populations and families, makes dismemberment messy and risky. But this acquiescence does not necessarily imply voluntary or enthusiastic assent on the part of minorities. When states are undergoing fundamental constitutional reforms, occasions for genuine assent present themselves. And an agreement between national minorities and the central government on a qualified right to secede is a powerful symbol of assent. Why is this? Because, for one thing, it mirrors a condition that would now be insisted upon by a sovereign state agreeing to enter a union. Some kind of qualified escape clause would almost certainly be necessary today to get any independent state to agree to surrender a significant degree of its sovereignty to join a new state or superstate organization, even a free-trade agreement. Second, an unused escape clause can become a symbol of continuous voluntary cooperation—roughly in the way that an amendable constitution is usually seen as tacitly accepted over generations even if it is only rarely amended. It must also be said that placing the possibility of a secession clause on the table during major constitutional reforms can provide a powerful means for making progress on other constitutional issues, as I shall describe below.

3. *Assent, Partnership and Recognition.* There are, of course, many symbolic and concrete ways that a constitution can enshrine ideals of partnership and recognition—including declarations in the preamble declaring the country to be a partnership, a "community of communities," or a federation of peoples, or the naming of specific roles for groups or subunits in, for example, constitutional amendment. Declaring that certain federal partners—whether by name or by subunit status—have a qualified right to secede is another meaningful way of recognizing such territorial groups as full and willing partners in the state. This is especially true in so-called asymmetrical federations (those in which one or more federal subunits are recog-

nized as homelands for particular national minorities and receive powers not shared by subunits occupied by members of the state's majority group). If only the national minorities' subunits are granted rights to secede, this will help satisfy their desire to be recognized as "not just another province." (Demands for such asymmetrical status have been historically important in Scotland, Quebec, and the autonomous territories of Spain that are the homelands for the Catalans, the Basques, and the Galicians.)[72]

4. *Trust Building, Antiassimilationism, and Stability.*[73] At the point when states are refounded—especially when this is an opportunity for the democratization of a previously undemocratic state—national minorities are often looking to emerge from a long history of oppression by the majority. In communist eastern and central Europe (ECE), as well as in Franco's Spain, for example, national minorities were subjected to extremely coercive assimilationist projects, typically including the denial of the right to use their minority language in schools and in public life (alas, much of this has continued in the postcommunist era in ECE). For true, voluntary democratic cooperation to work after such a history, an extended period of goodwill and trust building is needed. The minority is rightly suspicious of the majority; but the majority is also typically suspicious of the "loyalty" of the minority. In such a situation, an appropriately tailored secession clause could build trust in both directions. (In addition to a supermajority requirement, such a clause might also preclude any secession process for the first ten years.) It would assure the minority that the majority would change its assimilationist habits, and it could assure the majority that the minority would not use any breathing space it got to plot its escape.

5. *Fixing the Terms of Partnership.* I have already suggested ways in which a secession clause is not merely a constitutional *artifact* but can serve in a negotiating *process* to encourage constitutional reform. For example, some kind of secession procedure would almost certainly be demanded by independent states agreeing to join a new partnership, as there is implicitly in the European Union.[74] But for the

foreseeable future, federations are more likely to arise (or
be reformed) by decentralization than by the voluntary
union of previously independent states or colonies. And
putting a secession clause on the table in such processes of
reform creates some intriguing and largely unexplored
possibilities. In effect, a minority could agree to accept a
rigorous secession clause as a kind of quid pro quo in exchange for greater autonomy and recognition. Or to look
at it from the other side, majorities are often reluctant to
offer minorities a significant degree of autonomy or
recognition (e.g., constitutional recognition of the minority as a "people" or a "nation") because they fear that
this autonomy and status will be used by minority nationalists in nation-building projects leading to secession. Of
course, individual minority leaders demanding autonomy
and recognition will often verbally renounce secessionist
ambitions, but by agreeing to accept a secession clause
that would make secession an unrealistic goal in the absence of central government oppression, minority groups
would be making a concrete, long-term commitment to
the larger state; and in so doing they would be acknowl-
edging the fairness of *a particular level* of autonomy and
recognition.

This last idea suggests that thinking about the terms of secession
may be a very helpful way to think about the terms of union. It is a
truism in the literature on secession that one of the reasons secession is not usually justified is that it is possible for national minorities to enjoy a sufficient degree of self-determination and self-government within some kind of federal system. Some go even further
by suggesting that a national minority is done an injustice if it is not
granted a sufficient degree of autonomy and recognition within the
larger state.[75] But thus far political philosophers have given very little indication of how to evaluate whether the degree of autonomy
and the terms of federation more generally are just or appropriate.
"Veil of ignorance"–style contractual reasoning might give us some
very general guidelines, but there will always be too much particular sociohistorical information, and too much room for empirical
speculation, for us ever to hope to determine precisely from be-

hind a veil of ignorance the best terms of federation for any particular multinational state (e.g., its division of powers, constitutional amending formula, or subunit representation in the second chamber of Parliament). But in the rough-and-tumble world of actual constitutional negotiations between national minorities, federal subunits, and central governments, the creative use of a secession clause can help nudge a federation in the direction of arrangements that enhance both the autonomy of minorities and the stability of the state.

Now, it could be objected that if a central government is looking for some kind of guarantee that a minority will not use its newly granted autonomy and recognition in a nation-building project leading to secession, it will be better to have the minority agree, not to a rigorous secession clause, but rather to a clause that explicitly rules out secession altogether.

The first response to this objection is simply to accept that in certain situations there might be nothing wrong, from the perspective of multinational federalism, for a group to renounce all rights to secede in exchange for other forms of autonomy, status, or recognition. I am not arguing that a just multinational federal constitution *must* contain a secession clause but only that such a clause is potentially beneficial in a number of ways that matter in multinational democracies. That said, many minority groups can foresee no likely circumstances in which they will favor seceding from their larger state (perhaps this is the way most Welsh, Bretons, and Spanish Galicians feel), so in their constitutional negotiations they may very well be happy to renounce permanently a right to secede in order to receive other things they do desire. Other national minorities (and the politicians negotiating on their behalf), however, will find it much more difficult to renounce permanently the independence option, even if they are willing to agree to a clause that would make secession next to impossible.[76] So a second response to the objection is that it may be easier for a central government to secure a minority's agreement to a package of reforms if they demand that the minority accept a rigorous secession clause rather than renounce secession entirely. In circumstances where both sides are looking for an agreement—to end years or decades of constitutional disputes, from the point of the federal government, and to secure a more favorable status, from the point of view of the minority—the quid pro quo with a rigorous secession clause should look mutually advantageous.

It may also be a better hedge against secessionist politics in the future. In stable democracies, constitutional procedures have a way of gaining significant legitimacy over time, no matter how arcane. A secession clause that required, say, a three-quarters majority in the seceding province might sit unused for generations. But should a fairly popular secessionist movement ever arise, it is very likely that in a society that respected the rule of law, most would see the movement as bound to meet those conditions in order to trigger secessionist negotiations. (Consider how nobody seriously suggests ignoring the Electoral College rules in U.S. presidential elections, even when these rules dictate a result that goes against the more intuitively legitimate popular vote. People may advocate reforming the rules for future elections but not ignoring them while they are in place.) On the other hand, it is conceivable that a secessionist movement could arise long after the inclusion of a constitutional ban on secession, claiming some kind of extraconstitutional legitimacy. Simply put: we know that long-standing constitutional procedures—even arcane and inconvenient ones—are almost always adhered to in constitutional democracies but also that explicit bans on secession in otherwise open societies do not prevent the emergence of secessionist movements willing to move beyond the rule of law. We have already discussed, in Section III above, why it is generally preferable to deal with secessionist politics within the rule of law.

Perhaps the principal advantage to using a rigorous secession clause, rather than an outright ban in exchange for more autonomy or recognition for national minorities, is that this allows for some of the other important symbolic benefits described earlier. Entrenching even a heavily qualified right to secede in the constitution—particular if such a right is only granted to particular, named groups or subunits—can serve as a powerful and permanent symbol of that group's national status and willing partnership in the state. For a group to accept such a clause, restricting but not extinguishing its right to independence, is also a significant gesture of commitment to the state and to a political culture that precludes secessionist threats in negotiations between the subunit and the federal government.

Conclusion

I have tried to make a case for two points: first, that it would often make sense to include a secession clause in the constitution of a multinational democracy; and second, that the reasons for this are best understood not so much by thinking about the morality of secession as by thinking through the moral logic of multinational constitutionalism. If the case for the second point is plausible, then the case for the first point will necessarily be rather sketchy at this stage—because we are still a long way from having a very sophisticated theory of multinational constitutionalism.[77] Indeed, when it comes to issues about "entrenching institutional arrangements and substantive rights . . . constitutional theory remains in a surprisingly primitive state,"[78] even in the "cleaner" case of constitutional theorizing for the "uninational" state. I have argued that an appropriately qualified right to secession would often make sense within the framework of the deliberative constitutionalism that Sunstein advocates: it could provide a better disincentive for secessionist politics than would constitutional silence on the issue. It makes even more sense once we consider the additional roles a constitution plays in states containing more than one significant ethnocultural homeland. In these multinational states, we should think through the issue of whether to entrench a secession clause in much the same way that we think through issues such as whether to have a centralized state or a federation, how to divide the powers between federal and subunit governments, how to represent subunits in federal institutions, what role to grant subunits in the process of constitutional amendment, whether to give special powers or forms of recognition to particular groups or subunits, and so on. In a multinational state where these issues are open to free and fair negotiation, the demands of minority national communities will reflect their identities as peoples with their own needs for self-government and recognition—needs that must be balanced against their interest in participating within a stable, self-governing sovereign state. My argument does not conclude that multinational states *must* include a secession clause, nor does it have anything to say about whether "uninational" states would benefit from such a clause (presumably most would not).

NOTES

1. There was truth in advertising in the original working title of Daniel Weinstock's important recent article "Constitutionalizing the Right to Secede," *Journal of Political Philosophy* 9 (2001): 182–203. In draft form it was called "On Some Advantages of Constitutionalizing the Right to Secede." There is self-critique in this characterization of the "bullet-point" case. I am willing to include in this assessment a number of arguments I have advanced in two articles on the topic: Wayne Norman, "The Ethics of Secession as the Regulation of Secessionist Politics," in Margaret Moore, *National Self-Determination and Secession* (New York: Oxford University Press, 1998), and Wayne Norman, "Secession and (Constitutional) Democracy," in Ferran Requejo, ed., *Democracy and National Pluralism* (New York: Routledge Press, 2001).

2. A rationale for building a theory of secession out of a theory of federation that differs significantly from the one I present here can be found in Rainer Bauböck, "Why Stay Together? A Pluralist Approach to Secession and Federation," in Will Kymlicka and Wayne Norman, eds., *Citizenship in Diverse Societies* (New York: Oxford University Press, 2000), 366–71.

3. For more on the analogy between secession and divorce, see Jason Blahuta, "How Useful Is the Analogy of Divorce in Theorizing about Secession?" Dialogue 40, no. 2 (2001): 241–54, and Hilliard Aronovitch, "Why Secession Is Unlike Divorce," *Public Affairs Quarterly* 14, no. 1 (2000): 27–37.

4. Allen E. Buchanan, *Secession: The Morality of Political Divorce from Fort Sumter to Lithuania and Quebec* (Boulder, Colo.: Westview Press, 1991).

5. Walker Connor, *Ethnonationalism: The Quest for Understanding* (Princeton, N.J.: Princeton University Press, 1994), 29.

6. For a quick survey of autonomy arrangements across western and eastern Europe, see Will Kymlicka, "Nation-Building and Minority Rights: Comparing East and West," *Journal of Ethnic and Migration Studies* 26 (2000): 183–212, and "Western Political Theory and Ethnic Relations in Eastern Europe," in *Can Liberalism Be Exported?* ed. Will Kymlicka and Magda Opalski (New York: Oxford University Press, 2001), 13–105.

7. Of course, the truth of this claim depends on what one means by a serious secessionist movement. Possible examples of serious nonethnic secessionist movements in the last century include the comic-opera would-be secessionists in western Australia in the 1930s, as well as the secessionists wanting to break up the two-island confederation of St. Kitts-Nevis in the 1990s. Perhaps the most noteworthy nonethnic secessionist movement is that which has occasionally grabbed a substantial share of votes in north-

ern Italy. Most observers, however, attribute the secessionist rhetoric of the Northern League as a ploy to gain advantages for Italians in the north: in particular, to reduce their obligations to help those in the poorer south of the country. It may be (or have been) a serious movement, but it is not a serious secessionist movement.

8. For example, most of the former Warsaw Pact states as well as those that sprang out of the Soviet Union certainly have the ethnocultural potential for democratic secessionist politics, but they lack a history of democracy. The same could be said of most of the emerging democracies and nondemocratic states in Africa. India and the Philippines have somewhat patchy democratic track records and are also dealing with violent secessionists (and have a history of suppressing them with force). Even the United States might be concerned about secession procedures should the majority of citizens in Puerto Rico or in certain Canadian provinces (say, following a secession of Quebec) wish to enter the Union. For example, worrying about the future loyalty of such new states, it might at the very least want to avoid absorbing them without a qualified majority (say, 75 percent) of the new region's citizens agreeing in advance; and it might secure that agreement by allowing them to secede in the future with a similar qualified majority vote to secede. I shall not, however, be saying anything here about the desirability or feasibility of any of my suggestions for states in these other situations.

9. Note: this shorthand term is not meant to imply that the reasons and arguments in the following two categories are not also grounded in moral theories.

10. Buchanan, *Secession,* 127.

11. Although this is probably the most common justification used by secessionists themselves, it has relatively few philosophical apologists. See Kai Nielsen, "Secession: The Case of Quebec," *Journal of Applied Philosophy* 10 (1993): 29–43, and D. Copp, "International Law and Morality in the Theory of Secession," *Journal of Ethics* 2 (1998): 219–45.

12. See, for example, D. Gauthier, "Breaking Up: An Essay on Secession," *Canadian Journal of Philosophy,* 24 (1994): 357–72; Daniel Philpott, "In Defense of Self-Determination," *Ethics* 105 (1995): 352–85; C. Wellman, "A Defense of Secession and Political Self-Determination," *Philosophy and Public Affairs,* 24, no. 2 (1995): 142–71; and H. Beran, "A Democratic Theory of Political Self-Determination for a New World Order," in Percy B. Lehning, ed., *Theories of Secession* (New York: Routledge, 1998).

13. See, for example, Buchanan, *Secession;* Allen E. Buchanan, "Theories of Secession," *Philosophy and Public Affairs* 26, no. 1 (1997): 30–61; Norman, "The Ethics of Secession"; and Norman, "Secession and (Constitutional) Democracy."

14. See J. Costa, "On Theories of Secession: Minorities, Majorities, and the Multinational State," paper presented at the annual meeting of the American Political Science Association, San Francisco, 2001.

15. I explore each at some length in Norman, "The Ethics of Secession." See also Buchanan, "Theories of Secession," and Allen E. Buchanan, "Democracy and Secession," in Moore, *National Self-Determination and Secession*; Costa, "On Theories of Secession"; and Margaret Moore, *The Ethics of Nationalism* (New York: Oxford University Press, 2001).

16. See, for example, Cass R. Sunstein, *Designing Democracy: What Constitutions Do* (New York: Oxford University Press, 2001), 106. Sunstein readily acknowledges that "[w]hen oppression is pervasive, and not otherwise remediable, secession is a justified response; of course a subunit is entitled to leave a nation that is oppressing it." Another critic of constitutionalizing secession, Hilliard Aronovitch, also does not rule out the possibility that it may be appropriate for parties to negotiate a particular secession agreement. Aronovitch, "Why Secession Is Unlike Divorce," 33–34.

17. Buchanan, *Secession*, 138.

18. See Norman, "The Ethics of Secession," 50–51.

19. Ibid., 52.

20. See Weinstock, "Constitutionalizing the Right to Secede," 197.

21. The Flemish, of course, are not a minority in Belgium, but in all relevant respects their nationalist/secessionist movement can be compared to those of national minorities.

22. Moore, *Ethics of Nationalism*, 148.

23. Ibid.

24. Ibid.

25. A certain excessive enthusiasm about the constitutional implications of the just-cause theory is evident in some of my own previous arguments, especially as laid out in a portentously worded section "From the Just-Cause Theory to a Democratic Secession Clause." Wayne Norman, "The Ethics of Secession," 50–56.

26. Buchanan, *Secession*, 4.

27. Weinstock, "Constitutionalizing the Right to Secede," 187, summarizes some of this case in a paragraph.

28. For example, one might argue that brothels and prostitutes should be registered and required to meet various public health and safety standards and that heroin should be dispensed by licensed health clinics to addicts.

29. Weinstock, "Constitutionalizing the Right to Secede," 188.

30. Consider the case of the Friesian minority in the north of Holland—a territorially concentrated group with its own language and identity. They do not manifest such a political will for extensive self-govern-

ment, and this is why we do not tend to think of the Netherlands as a multinational state, even though it is plainly a multiethnic state.

31. Both of these attempts—known as the Meech Lake Accord (1987) and the Charlottetown Accord (1992)—failed because of extremely rigorous procedures for amending the Canadian Constitution combined with a lack of popular support outside Quebec. Both of these failed amendments were attempts to win Quebec's acceptance of a major overhaul of the Canadian Constitution that took place without its assent in 1982.

32. Other issues the federal government had never addressed included the question of whether Quebecers could retain their Canadian citizenship after secession, how the massive national debt would be divided between the two successor states, and whether Quebec would continue to use the Canadian dollar. Of course, the separatist Quebec government had a clear position on all of these issues: a 50 percent-plus-one vote would be sufficient to trigger the secession process, an independent Quebec would retain the borders it had as a province, Quebecers could retain their Canadian citizenship if they wanted to, and the new state would use the Canadian dollar and become an automatic member of NAFTA.

33. On the concept of *ressentiment* in nationalist politics, see C. Taylor, "The Politics of Recognition," in Amy Gutmann, ed., *Multiculturalism and the "Politics of Recognition"* (Princeton, N.J.: Princeton University Press, 1992); Philip Resnick, "Recognition and Ressentiment: On Accommodating National Differences within Multinational States," paper presented at the Europa Mundi Conference on Democracy, Nationalism and Europeanism, June 21–23, 2000, Santiago de Compostela; Philip Resnick, *The Politics of Resentment: British Columbia Regionalism and Canadian Unity* (Vancouver: UBC Press, 2000); Liah Greenfeld, *Nationalism* (Cambridge, Mass.: Harvard University Press, 1993).

34. It is interesting that opinion polls in Quebec consistently show a much lower level of support for holding another secessionist referendum than they show for preferring separation. In other words, a significant percentage of people who would prefer to live in an independent Quebec would rather not have the province go through another bruising referendum.

35. Weinstock, "Constitutionalizing the Right to Secede," 196.

36. See, for example, Aronovitch, "Why Secession Is Unlike Divorce," 33; Rainer Bauböck, "Self-Determination and Self-Government," manuscript, 32, quoted in Weinstock, "Constitutionalizing the Right to Secede," 191); or Sunstein, *Designing Democracy*, 95.

37. Aronovitch, "Why Secession Is Unlike Divorce," 34.

38. Ibid., 34–35.

39. Switzerland is one of the only federations to have democratic criteria for creating a new federal subunit (a canton), which it does through a cascading series of referendums. For an interesting proposal for how this could be used to democratically partition a seceding subunit, see Patrick Monahan and Michael J. Bryant, *Coming to Terms with Plan B: Ten Principles Governing Secession* (Toronto: C. D. Howe Institute, 1996), 15–17. See also J. Laponce, "Sovereignty and Referendum: In Defense of Territorial Revisionism," paper presented at the annual meeting of the Canadian Political Science Association, August 2000, Quebec City, Quebec; and Moore, *Ethics of Nationalism,* 206–7.

40. *Reference re Secession of Quebec,* S.C.C. no. 25506, Aug. 20, 1998, 2 S.C.R. 217.

41. See Norman, "Secession and (Constitutional) Democracy." See also Moore, *Ethics of Nationalism,* 208ff; James Tully, "Introduction," in Alain-G. Gagnon and James Tully, eds., *Multinational Democracies* (New York: Cambridge University Press, 2001), 1–33; C. Brown-John, "Self-Determination, Autonomy and State Secession in Federal Constitutional and International Law," *South Texas Law Review* 40 (1999): 567–601; and M. Walters, "Nationalism and the Pathology of Legal Systems: Considering the Quebec Secession Reference and Its Lessons for the United Kingdom," *Modern Law Review* 62 (1999): 371–96.

42. "[T]he conduct of the parties [in negotiations following a clear referendum victory for the secessionist side in Quebec] assumes primary constitutional significance. The negotiations process must be conducted with an eye to the constitutional principles we have outlined, which must inform the actions of all the participants in the negotiation process. Refusal of a party to conduct negotiations in a manner consistent with constitutional principles and values would seriously put at risk the legitimacy of that party's assertion of its rights, and perhaps the negotiation process as a whole." Secs. 94–95 of the Opinion.

43. See para. 59 of the Opinion for an example of the Court's explicit recognition that the majority of people in Quebec possess "a distinct culture" and constitute a "social and demographic reality . . . [that] explains the existence of the province of Quebec as a political unit and indeed, was one of the essential reasons for establishing a federal structure for the Canadian union in 1867." In para. 125 the Court recognizes that "much of the Quebec population certainly shares many of the characteristics (such as common language and culture) that would be considered in determining whether a specific group is a 'people,' as do other groups within Quebec and/or Canada." Aboriginal peoples are also given distinct constitutional rights in Canada.

44. For reactions by politicians, opinion makers, and academics to the Opinion, see David Schneiderman, ed., *The Quebec Decision: Perspectives on the Supreme Court Ruling on Secession* (Toronto: James Lorimer, 1999).

45. The judges consistently "hint" that a "clear majority" requires more than 50 percent plus one of the votes. The opinion contains expressions like "clear majority," "clear expression," "strong majority," "demonstrated majority," "enhanced majority," "substantial consensus," and "clear repudiation of the existing constitutional order" in at least twenty-two places.

46. After the opinion, the Canadian federal government took a small step toward clarifying how it would determine whether it believed that a secessionist referendum involved a "clear majority on a clear question." It did this in a piece of federal legislation, rather than through a constitutional amendment, which in Canada would have required the consent of most of the provinces. For some analysis of this "Clarity Act," see Norman, "Secession and (Constitutional) Democracy."

47. For good international surveys of this aspect of constitutional law, see Markku Suksi, *Bringing in the People: A Comparison of Constitutional Forms and Practices of the Referendum* (London: Martinus Nijhoff, 1993), and Monahan and Bryant, *Coming to Terms.*

48. Sunstein, *Designing Democracy,* 6.

49. Ibid., 6–7.

50. Ibid., 8.

51. Ibid., 114.

52. I have explored this argument in greater detail in Norman, "Secession and (Constitutional) Democracy."

53. Sunstein, *Designing Democracy,* 96.

54. Ibid., 102, and Russell Hardin, *One for All: The Logic of Group Conflict* (Princeton, N.J.: Princeton University Press, 1995).

55. Sunstein, *Designing Democracy,* 112.

56. For reasons explained earlier, I am ignoring here the debatable exceptions of the Northern League in Italy in the 1990s and the movement to break up the two-island federation of St. Kitts-Nevis. Of course, at least part of the explanation for the attempted secession of the Southern states during the U.S. Civil War is economic. This is one of many ways the case of the U.S. Civil War is sui generis in the history of secessionist movements.

57. In a recent reply to Weinstock, Sunstein concedes that he "cannot prove the (thoroughly empirical) conjecture that" that a secession clause would be more likely to fuel than dampen secessionist politics. And indeed he cites no empirical evidence. He concludes his reply to Weinstock's case for constitutionalizing secession by merely reasserting that "the more sensible prediction is that [a constitutional right to secede] would undermine,

rather than promote, the enterprise of democratic rule" (C. Sunstein, "Should Constitutions Protect the Right to Secede?" *Journal of Political Philosophy* 9 (2001): 355.

58. Connor, *Ethnonationalism*, 54.

59. Sunstein, *Designing Democracy*, 10, and "Should Constitutions Protect?" 350.

60. See Wayne Norman, "Toward a Philosophy of Federalism," in Judith Baker, ed., *Group Rights* (Toronto: University of Toronto Press, 1994); J. Linz, "Democracy, Multinationalism, and Federalism," paper presented at the annual meeting of the International Political Science Association, Seoul, South Korea, August 1997, 41–42; P. Van Parijs, "Must Europe Be Belgian? On Democratic Citizenship in Multilingual Polities," in Catriona McKinnon and Iain Hampsher-Monk, eds., *The Demands of Citizenship* (New York: Continuum, 2000), 235–53; and Bauböck, "Why Stay Together?" 381.

61. See Roger Gibbins and Guy Laforest, eds., *Beyond the Impasse: Toward Reconciliation* (Ottawa: Institute for Research in Public Policy, 1998), for an excellent collection of articles on philosophical, political, and economics perspectives on federal partnership.

62. For a survey of the recent literature on national autonomy, see Wayne Norman, "National Autonomy," in H. Lafollette, ed., *Handbook in Practical Ethics* (New York: Oxford University Press, 2003), 591–618.

63. See Taylor, "The Politics of Recognition"; J. Levy, *The Multiculturalism of Fear* (New York: Oxford University Press, 2000), chap. 5; Will Kymlicka and Wayne Norman, "Citizenship in Culturally Diverse Societies: Issues, Contexts, Concepts," in Kymlicka and Norman, *Citizenship in Diverse Societies*, 29–30; and A. Patten, "Liberal Citizenship in Multinational Societies," in Gagnon and Tully, *Multinational Democracies*, 293.

64. According to James Tully, "The effective right to initiate constitutional change is . . . an essential feature of the meaningful exercise of the right of internal self-determination." He argues that this is the central thesis of the Supreme Court of Canada's Opinion on secession. (Tully, "Introduction," 32).

65. See John Rawls, *A Theory of Justice* (Cambridge, Mass.: Harvard University Press, 1971), especially the use of this mode of reasoning at the stage of a constitutional convention (196–201).

66. See Buchanan, *Secession*, 130–31; Norman, "The Ethics of Secession," 47–50; Weinstock, "Constitutionalizing the Right to Secede," 198–200.

67. Sunstein, *Designing Democracy*, 97. Note that by *nation*, Sunstein clearly means "country" or "state." It is a consistent feature of his writing on constitutionalism that the nation and the state always coincide. Despite writing explicitly on the constitutional issues, and the question of secession, for multinational states like those forming or reforming after the col-

lapse of communism in Eastern Europe and the former Soviet Union, he never feels the need for a vocabulary that allows for the possibility of more than one group with a national identity sharing a state. See, for example, the original version of chap. 4 in Sunstein, *Designing Democracy,* which was published in 1991.

68. Buchanan, *Secession,* 130.

69. Weinstock, "Constitutionalizing the Right to Secede," 198.

70. The parties in Rawls's Original Position, for example, "know the general facts about human society. They understand political affairs and the principles of economic theory; they know the basis of social organization and the laws of human psychology. Indeed, the parties are presumed to know whatever general facts affect the choice of the principles of justice." Rawls, *A Theory of Justice,* 137. Hence, if they knew they were negotiating for principles and institutions for a multiethnic society, they would not ignore the probable dynamics of ethnocultural politics.

71. I have explored and defended this hypothesis in Norman, "Toward a Philosophy of Federalism," and in Wayne Norman, "Federalism and Confederalism," in Edward Craig, ed., *Routledge Encyclopedia of Philosophy* (New York: Routledge, 1998).

72. On asymmetrical federalism, see Ferran Requejo, "Cultural Pluralism, Nationalism and Federalism: A Revision of Democratic Citizenship in Plurinational States," *European Journal of Political Research* 39 (1999): 255–86, and Ferran Requejo, "Democratic Legitimacy and National Pluralism," in Requejo, *Democracy and National Pluralism.*

73. On the role of intercommunity trust in securing unity in multinational states, see Daniel Weinstock, "Building Trust in Divided Societies," *Journal of Political Philosophy* 7, no. 3 (1999): 287–307.

74. "For the European Community [sic], for example, a right to secede may therefore be more sensible, and indeed it will provide a greater incentive to join in the first instance." Sunstein, *Designing Democracy,* 105.

75. Bauböck, "Why Stay Together?"; Weinstock, "Constitutionalizing the Right to Secede," 189; Costa, "On Theories of Secession"; Moore, *Ethics of Nationalism,* 151.

76. See Weinstock, "Constitutionalizing the Right to Secede," 201, for an explanation of the moral psychology involved in this position.

77. There is a rich tradition of federalist philosophy stretching back to the Renaissance, the highlights of which are collected in D. Karmis and W. Norman, eds., *Theories of Federalism* (New York: Palgrave, forthcoming). But very few of these works combine sophisticated normative thinking about both federalism and constitutionalism. *The Federalist,* of course, is a notable exception.

78. Sunstein, *Designing Democracy,* 97.

9

THE QUEBEC SECESSION ISSUE: DEMOCRACY, MINORITY RIGHTS, AND THE RULE OF LAW

ALLEN BUCHANAN

I. The Canadian Supreme Court Reference Ruling

A. *The Reference Questions and the Court's Response*

In February 1998 the Governor in Council requested the Canadian Supreme Court to answer three questions:

(1) Under the Constitution of Canada, can the National Assembly, legislature or government of Quebec effect the secession of Quebec from Canada unilaterally?

(2) Does international law give the National Assembly, legislature or government of Quebec the right to effect the secession of Quebec from Canada unilaterally? In this regard, is there a right to self-determination under international law that would give the National Assembly, legislature or government of Quebec the right to effect the secession of Quebec from Canada unilaterally?

(3) In the event of a conflict between domestic and international law on the right of the National Assembly, legislature or government of Quebec to effect the secession of Quebec from Canada unilaterally, which would take precedence in Canada? (2)[1]

On August 20, 1998, the Supreme Court issued a closely reasoned opinion answering the first two questions in the negative and declining to answer the third on the grounds that no conflict exists in view of the negative answers to Questions 1 and 2 (147).

The Supreme Court's ruling is remarkable, not only because it is exceptionally well reasoned and lucid, but also because it attempts to do something of great importance that has not been done before: to subject the potentially destructive issue of secession to the rule of law by constitutionalizing the secession process, but in the absence of an existing explicit constitutional provision for secession.[2]

While scrupulous in its attention to existing law, the Court avoids a shallow legalism, basing its negative answer to the first question on an understanding of four fundamental principles that are assumed by the written text of the Canadian Constitution: (1) constitutionalism and the rule of law, (2) democracy, (3) federalism, and (4) protection of minority rights (49). The heart of the ruling is the simple and compelling premise that secession is a profound constitutional change, not a matter to be decided by a simple majority vote in the seceding region, and that as such it must be achieved by constitutional amendment through a process of negotiation.

The Court made no effort to specify the mode of constitutional amendment or the details of the process of negotiation. Instead, it concluded that if and when there is a "clear majority" in Quebec in favor of secession in answer to a "clear question" concerning secession, the Canadian government and other "participants in Confederation" will have a duty to negotiate the possible secession of Quebec in accordance with the four fundamental principles (87–90).

B. *The Case for Constitutionalizing the Secession Issue*

The Court emphasizes the deep commitment to constitutionalism in Canada that is present from the creation of the Confederation in 1867. Constitutionalism and the rule of law are intimately connected. The defining tenet of constitutionalism is that the constitution is the supreme law, while the core idea of the rule of law is to provide stability and continuity through the predictability of legal consequences, under conditions of impartiality. Given that secession would inevitably bring major social, political, and economic changes, there is a strong case for attempting to subject it to the rule of law. Given the commitment to constitutionalism, requiring that secession be achieved by constitutional amendment is equally plausible.

The Court strengthens the case for subjecting secession to the rule of law by invoking a nuanced understanding of the relationship between *legality* and *legitimacy*, a theme that has been articulated in more detail in a series of letters by Stephane Dion, minister for intergovernmental affairs.[3] For the difficult process of political divorce to be successful, goodwill and a spirit of cooperation will be necessary, and these in turn will depend in part upon whether citizens regard the secession as legitimate. The process of constitutional amendment, together with a commitment to negotiation guided by the four fundamental principles, is likely to enhance the perceived legitimacy of secession, thereby increasing the probability that the needed cooperation for successful secession will be forthcoming (89–92).

C. Consensual versus Unilateral Secession

The Court rejects the assertion that the Quebec authorities have a unilateral right to secede and contends that secession must be negotiated within the structure of an appropriate constitutional amendment process. In the words of the Court,

> [T]he secession of Quebec cannot be accomplished by the National Assembly, the legislature or government of Quebec unilaterally, that is to say, without principled negotiations, and be considered a lawful act. Any attempt to effect the secession of a province must be undertaken pursuant to the Constitution of Canada, or else violate the Canadian legal order. (104)

In stating that secession must be negotiated, the Court makes it clear that if secession is to occur it must be *consensual.*[4] Thus, while "the continued existence and operation of the Canadian constitutional order cannot remain unaffected by the unambiguous expression of a clear majority of Quebecois that they no longer wish to remain in Canada," the Court concluded that "the

primary means by which that expression is given effect is the constitutional duty to negotiate in accordance with the constitutional principles that we have described herein" (104). The
Court's conclusion that secession must be consensual rather than
unilateral—and that an offer to negotiate on the Quebec authorities' part would not be sufficient—follows simply from the premise that secession is a constitutional amendment and that constitutional amendment procedures require consent. Because the
Court does not specify the mode of constitutional amendment, it
is not clear whether only the consent of the Canadian federal
government and the Quebec authorities would be required or
whether seven of the ten provinces would have to consent.[5]

D. *"Remedial" Secession as Nonconsensual*

There is, however, a deeper consideration that adds further
weight to the Court's position that Quebec secession must be
consensual rather than unilateral. Quebec secession cannot be
regarded as the exercise of a *remedial right* to secede.[6] As the
Court states in its discussion of international law, the standard for
recognizing a right to "external self-determination" has been limited to

> situations of former colonies; where a people is oppressed, as for
> example under foreign military occupation; or where a definable
> group is denied meaningful access to government to pursue their
> political, economic, social and cultural development. In all three
> situations, the people in question are entitled to a right to exter-
> nal self-determination because they have been denied the ability
> to exert internally their right to self-determination. Such excep-
> tional circumstances are manifestly inapplicable to Quebec under
> existing conditions. (138)

Thus the justification for secession in the case of Quebec is *not*
that the people of Quebec are currently subjected to injustice at
the hands of the Canadian government and that secession is the
best remedy for avoiding continuation of that injustice. The chief
justifications for Quebec secession must appeal instead to (1) the
claim that Quebec is a distinct society or a nation and that as such
it is entitled to its own state if its people democratically choose to

have their own state, (2) the assertion that Quebec is entitled to
secede under international law through exercise of the right of
self-determination, and (3) the view that respect for the principle
of democracy requires a unilateral right to secede.

In cases in which secession is sought as a remedy for injustices
perpetrated by the state, it is extremely implausible to require
that the state consent to the secession. Requiring consent by the
state in such a case would make the unjustly treated group's access to the remedy conditional upon the cooperation of the per-
petrator of the injustice.[7] However, to repeat, this is not the case
with Quebec because Quebec secession cannot be justified on remedial grounds.[8] So, absent a "remedial right" case for Quebec
secession, the chief argument for unilateral secession simply does
not apply, and the Court's argument that secession must be subject to the rule of law, within the constitutional structure, remains in full force.

The same point can be framed in terms of legitimacy. A state
that respects the rights of all its citizens, both as individuals and
as members of groups, is generally presumed to be legitimate. In
a legitimate democratic state, the entire territory of the state is
the territory of the people of the state as a whole. It is the people,
not the government, to whom the territory belongs; the government merely acts as trustee for the people. Hence there is a presumption that any alienation of part of the territory of the state
must be achieved through a process in which the people as a
whole, not simply the people of the seceding area, are represented. Were the Canadian government to accede to unilateral
secession of Quebec without a process that secured consent from
representatives of the people of Canada as a whole, it would be
guilty of violating its fiduciary obligation to the people of Canada
by wrongfully alienating part of *their* territory.[9]

To put the same point somewhat differently, in cases of nonre-
medial secession, acknowledgment of a unilateral right to secede
is incompatible with popular sovereignty. No one, presumably,
would say that a majority vote in Quebec in favor of ceding Quebec to the United States would be valid. The explanation of *why* it
would be invalid relies on the notion that the people of Canada
are sovereign over the territory of Canada, including Quebec.
But if that is so, then the decision to remove part of the territory

of Canada should not be left solely to the people of one part of Canada.

I will argue later that the fact that Quebec secession cannot reasonably be viewed as the exercise of a remedial right also has important implications regarding the status of minorities in the negotiation process and in particular forms a premise in a compelling argument that the native peoples of Quebec ought to be principal participants in negotiations if they occur.

Thus far I have reviewed and supplemented the Court's main arguments in favor of constitutionalizing the secession issue and hence for rejecting unilateral secession. In the next section I examine more closely the chief arguments for unilateral secession by Quebec and conclude that the Court's rejection of a unilateral right to secede is justified. In Section III I argue that there are two important issues that the Court's ruling raises but does not adequately address: the risk that negotiations will break down, with the result that the goal of subjecting secession to the rule of law will not be achieved; and the standing of native peoples in Quebec in the negotiation process.

II. The Case for a Unilateral Right to Secede Examined

A. *The Simple Democratic Argument*

According to this putative justification for unilateral secession, the people of Quebec have a democratic right to secede, without consent and without negotiations, if a majority of them vote for independence. The implicit premise of this argument is that a decision to secede from Canada is within the domain of democratic decision making in Quebec. But this premise cannot stand scrutiny for a number of reasons. First, the legal rights that Quebec citizens have to participate in democratic decision making within the province are just that: rights to participate in the making of those decisions that, according to the constitution, are within the authority of the provincial government. This domain of authority does not include unilateral constitutional amendment, which, as the Court rightly points out, is what secession would be. The constitution specifies domains of decision making for the federal and provincial governments, and within each, democratic decision making has its proper place. Since a unilateral right to amend the constitution is not among the rights specified for provincial governments, a fortiori there is no right, under the constitution, for the people of Quebec to make this decision by majority vote or in any other way.

Proponents of the simple democratic argument might attempt to deflect this objection by claiming that the putative democratic right is not a legal right under the constitution but rather a moral right that follows from the principle of democracy, understood as a fundamental value that underlies majoritarian procedures at both the federal and provincial levels.

The Court's reasoning supplies a convincing refutation of this moral version of the simple democracy argument. The Court argues that "closer analysis reveals that this argument is unsound, because it misunderstands the meaning of popular sovereignty and the essence of a constitutional democracy" (75). In particular, the simple democracy argument ignores the importance of the principle of constitutionalism. In the words of the Court,

> Constitutionalism facilitates—indeed makes possible—a democratic political system by creating an orderly framework within which people may make political decisions. Viewed correctly, constitutionalism and the rule of law are not in conflict with democracy; rather they are essential to it. Without that relationship, the political will upon which democratic decisions are taken would itself be undermined. (78)

The principle of democracy is not the only fundamental principle; it must be balanced against the other fundamental principles. A decision by the majority may infringe the rights of minorities, so the democratic principle must be balanced by the protection of minorities. Similarly, a decision by the majority in Quebec would not in itself be sufficient to ensure that the principle of constitutionalism and the rule of law was adequately served, first, because, as we have just seen, using a majority decision within Quebec to make a fundamental constitutional change would violate the constitution by according Quebec powers that the constitution does not allocate to it, but second, and more importantly, because secession by majority vote, without negotiations guided by the four principles, would not achieve the goals of legal predictability, stability, and continuity in change that the rule of law aims to secure. Finally, allowing unilateral secession on the basis of a majority vote in Quebec alone would ignore the principle of federalism. That principle undergirds the constitutional requirement that constitutional amendments must involve all "participants in Confederation" unless the change affects only one province; yet clearly the secession of Quebec would affect all the other provinces.[10]

The main thrust of the Court's rejection of the simple democratic argument is that the decision to secede is unlike the ordinary decisions that are properly made within the democratic government of a federal unit. A simple majority referendum may be an appropriate device for making many types of decisions, but the decision to secede is no ordinary decision. There is a great difference between decisions that are made under the assumption that the territorial boundaries and membership of the polity are settled and decisions that determine what the territorial boundaries and membership of the polity are to be. A unilateral right to secede by majority decision would in effect use a decision procedure designed for quite different matters to empower a majority to determine not only the boundaries of the polity but also the fundamental citizenship of individuals, including those who fervently do not wish their citizenship to be changed. It is one thing to say that where individuals' rights as citizens are secured, majority rule has a proper place; it is quite another to say that the majority should be able unilaterally to deprive individuals of their most fundamental political status, in this case, their citizenship in their own country.

The Court's appeal to the principle of constitutionalism can also be deepened. The simple democratic argument also ignores the relationship between democratic procedures and the very idea of constitutionalism. In making a constitution, a people binds itself. Specific constitutional provisions erect barriers to prevent citizens from engaging in behavior that would undermine the most fundamental values they seek to achieve in a political society. One risk against which a well-crafted constitution should protect us is the temptation to use democratic procedures to engage in strategic behavior that would itself undermine the investment in democratic deliberation that is required if democracy is to function properly.[11] If "exit" from the state can be achieved unilaterally, by a simple democratic vote, then dissatisfied minorities who happen to be concentrated in a portion of the state's territory will be tempted to evade the demanding task of "voicing" their concerns within the process of public deliberation. Or they may be tempted to use the *threat* of "exit" to achieve a de facto minority veto over decisions that ought properly to be decided by the majority. Those who recognize the importance of sustaining a commitment to the project of creating and preserving a democratic polity will be careful to craft a constitution that achieves incentives for engaging in "voice"—that is, constructive engagement in public deliberation—while at the same time allowing the option of "exit." An "exit" procedure that required only a majority vote in a region of the state makes "exit" too easy, thereby undermining the commitment to deliberative democracy and encouraging strategic behavior that thwarts the purpose of democracy.[12]

Finally, there is an even more basic reason why it is a mistake to move from a general commitment to democracy to the very specific and problematic claim that there is a democratic right to secede for the majority in Quebec. The most cogent *justifications* for having democratic decision procedures within polities do not apply with the same force, if indeed they apply at all, to the decision to alter fundamentally the boundaries of the polity and the character of persons' citizenship. There are two chief justifications for democratic decision procedures. The first is that they are intrinsically valuable from the standpoint of equal respect for persons or equal consideration of persons' interests. The idea here is that the basic moral equality of persons requires that they have an equal say over at least the most important decisions that determine the character of their society or that they be able to participate as equals in making those decisions.[13] Yet clearly this justification for democracy does not imply that the decision whether to secede should be determined unilaterally by a majority decision in favor of secession in a part of the territory of an existing state. Indeed, if the intrinsic equality justification for democracy implies anything in this regard, it is that all citizens, not just those in Quebec, should have a say in the decision, on the premise that proper respect for the equality of persons requires that each should have a say on important political decisions. To put the same point somewhat differently: the first justification for democracy tells us why all those who are members of the polity should have an equal say in deciding the basic rules; democratic values cannot tell us what the boundaries of the polity should be because to implement them we must have already fixed the boundaries of the polity.

The second chief justification for democratic decision procedures is instrumental: the claim is that in general and over the long run, procedures that give every citizen a vote at least on the most important political decisions tend to produce better outcomes. In determining what counts as better outcomes, different political theories give greater or lesser weight to various values, including individual well-being and freedom and the goods of community. There is no reason to believe, however, that allowing unilateral secession by a majority vote within Quebec would produce better outcomes than a process of constitutional amendment. In fact, the opposite is more likely to be the case, at least so far as two uncontroversially important factors for evaluating outcomes are concerned: first, as we have already seen, the constitutional process better secures the benefits of the rule of law; second, that same process also includes provisions for ensuring the protection of minority rights that are absent in the simple majoritarian procedure. In sum, neither of the chief justifications for using democratic decision procedures within a polity whose territorial boundaries and membership are given does much to support the idea that those same procedures should be used to effect unilateral secession.[14]

It is important to emphasize that in rejecting the simple democratic argument for unilateral secession the Court does not discount the value of democracy. Rather, it argues that the democratic principle must be balanced against other fundamental principles and endorses a circumscribed but nonetheless essential role for democracy in the process of a negotiated, constitutionalized secession. According to the Court, the democratic principle, taken in the context of the constitution's provisions for amendment, comes into play in the process by which a proposal for secession is initiated. A clear "yes" majority in a Quebec referendum in response to a clear question on secession would both authorize the Quebec authorities to begin negotiations on secession and obligate the federal government and other "participants in Confederation" to join the negotiations.

However, even here the Court emphasizes that the democratic principle must be balanced against two other fundamental principles: a "clear" majority is needed both to provide an incentive for secession supporters to accommodate concerns of minorities in Quebec and to help ensure that there is sufficient resolve to carry through the project of negotiated secession in a way that minimizes disruptions and costs to all concerned, thus expressing a commitment to the rule of law (90–94). Moreover, the requirement of a "clear question" can in fact be justified on *democratic* grounds: if the purpose of the referendum is to allow the majority to decide for itself, the majority must know what it is voting for.

B. *The Effectivity Argument*

Some advocates of unilateral secession have appealed to the international legal principle of effectivity, according to which a secessionist entity becomes entitled to recognition in the system of states if and only if it secures effective control over the territory it claims.[15] In responding to this justification, the Court rightly distinguishes between the appeal to effectivity after the fact of unilateral secession as a criterion for recognition and the appeal to it as a putative justification for secession. As the Court points out, "to suggest that a subsequent recognition of an initially illegal act retroactively creates a legal right to engage in the act in the first place . . . is not supported by the international principle of effectivity or otherwise and must be rejected" (108). The applicability of effectivity as a criterion for recognition of a secessionist entity after successful separation in no way justifies the act of secession. Whether a secessionist entity that manages to secure control over the territory it claims is entitled to recognition simply on the basis of effective control is an entirely different question from whether it had the right to secede. In the Court's words,

Such a proposition . . . may or may not be true; and in any event is irrelevant to the questions of law before us. If, on the other hand, it is put forward as an assertion of law, then it simply amounts to the contention that the law may be broken as long as it can be broken successfully. Such a notion is contrary to the rule of law, and must be rejected. (107–8)

What the Court does not perhaps sufficiently emphasize is the problematic character of the principle of effectivity even when applied to the issue of recognition after the fact of secession. Put most simply, the principle of effectivity is a close relative of the transparently repugnant notion that might makes right. As such it ignores entirely the question of whether secession is justified, and it is unable to distinguish between legitimate and illegitimate secessions. In fact, the principle of effectivity is a vestige of an international legal system that did not prohibit the aggressive use of force and whose conception of state legitimacy lacked any normative content at all. In other words, until recently, states as conceived in the international legal system were little more than "gunmen writ large"—effective enforcers of rules within territories. Legitimacy, not just for secessionist entities but for states generally, was reduced to effective control. Given this normatively impoverished conception of state legitimacy, the principle of effectivity makes sense: it simply applies the criterion for existing states to the recognition of new states.

However, in the last fifty years or so, international law has made significant though halting steps toward a more normatively demanding conception of state legitimacy. Under current international legal doctrine—though not yet always in practice—states are required to respect the human rights of their own citizens and are prohibited from engaging in aggressive war.[16] Some international legal theorists have gone so far as to argue that an even more normatively demanding conception of legitimacy is beginning to emerge, according to which legitimacy requires democratic governance.[17]

The practice of international recognition of states can serve as a valuable instrument for moral progress. By making recognition conditional upon the satisfaction of normative criteria, such as the protection of basic human rights and democratic governance, the international system can provide powerful incentives for improving the behavior of states and would-be states. This line of thinking presumably underlay the attempt by the Council of Europe's Badinter Commission to require respect for minority rights as a condition for the recognition of new states emerging from the ruins of Yugoslavia.[18]

There are, in addition, noninstrumental reasons for requiring respect for the rights of all citizens as a condition for international recognition of states. It can be argued that only entities that respect the rights of all their citizens are justified in doing what claimants to the status of statehood attempt to do, namely, exercise a monopoly on the enforcement of laws within a territory. By making recognition conditional only on effective control, the principle of effectivity completely ignores the point that for the exercise of power to be legitimate it must meet certain minimal normative criteria.

For these reasons, any attempt to justify unilateral secession by appeal to the principle of effectivity is guilty of more than a confusion between the justification for seceding and the entitlement of a successful secessionist entity to recognition after the fact. To appeal to the principle of effectivity is to endorse regression rather than moral progress in international law.

C. The Argument from Uti Possidetis

The principle that "boundaries are to be respected unless changed by consent" has also been cited in support of unilateral secession by Quebec. The Court rejects this, arguing that "[t]here would be no conclusions predetermined by law on any issue. Negotiations would need to address the interests of other provinces, the federal government, Quebec and indeed the rights of all Canadians both within and outside Quebec, and specifically the rights of minorities" (151). It is important to note that the original domain of application for *uti possidetis*, and indeed the only context in which there is anything like consensus on its status as an international legal norm, is decolonization. First in Latin America and then in Africa, the principle was appealed to in order to limit fragmentation of newly liberated European colonies, whose boundaries were usually arbitrarily drawn, and which included several, and in some cases many, distinct and conflicting ethnic groups.[19]

Because the case of Quebec is so obviously different from that of decolonization, those who have attempted to enlist *uti possidetis* in support of Quebec secession have appealed to what they claim to be a more recent and relevant application of the principle: the dissolution of Yugoslavia. Here the "boundaries" that are to be respected are the internal boundaries that demarcate federal units.

It is important to note that even in the case of decolonization, where *uti possidetis* has been most frequently invoked, there are serious questions about whether the rationale for the principle provides adequate support for it. The rationale is that by precluding secessions from liberated former colonial states, the principle is a force for stability and peace. However, in its application in Africa it is far from clear whether the benefits of adherence to the principle outweigh the costs, or whether, at the very least, exceptions to it ought to be admitted. By ruling out revisions of colonial borders, *uti possidetis* contributes to the persistence of what may in some cases be intractable intrastate conflicts (the case of the civil war in Sudan is often cited as an example).

Perhaps out of recognition of the problematic character of appeals to the application of *uti possidetis* in colonial contexts and the fact that the "boundaries" in those cases are not the boundaries of federal units, advocates of unilateral Quebec secession have concentrated on the alleged precedent of the dissolution of Yugoslavia. But here there are three reasons to reject the appeal to *uti possidetis* as a justification for unilateral secession. First and most importantly, as the Court points out, the case of Canada and that of Yugoslavia are quite different in a crucial respect: Yugoslavia had ceased to function as a federation at the time that Slovenia and Croatia declared their independence. In other words, Yugoslavia broke down before it broke up. If Quebec secedes from Canada, it will be from a functioning federation, one that does an exemplary job of protecting minority and individual rights within the context of strong democratic institutions. As the Yugoslav federation collapsed, a situation of great uncertainty ensued, in which the most fundamental goods of the rule of law were put at risk. Under these conditions, there was some initial plausibility in the idea that if federal structures could no longer be relied on, the political infrastructures of the constituent republics were the best bet for maintaining some semblance of order.[20] Any such rationale is inapplicable to the case of Canada, which is not experiencing the slide toward anarchy that occurred in Yugoslavia just prior to the secessions. As the Court notes, "Nobody seriously suggests that [Canada's] national existence, seamless in so many aspects, could be effortlessly separated along what are now the provincial borders of Quebec" (96).

There is another difficulty with citing the international response to the breakup of Yugoslavia as affirmation of the applicability of *uti possidetis* to Quebec secession. To the extent that *uti possidetis* may have guided the decision of some states to recognize the seceding Yugoslav republics, this was a novel application of the principle, which previously had not been applied to the internal boundaries of states. One instance of the novel interpretation of the principle cannot be taken as sufficient evidence that *uti possidetis*, as applied to the internal boundaries of federal states, is indeed a principle of international law.[21]

Some who cite the Yugoslav case as a precedent for the application of *uti possidetis* to Quebec secession may have a different argument in mind. On their interpretation, international acquiescence to the dissolution of Yugoslavia along republic boundaries implies acknowledgment of a presumptive right to independence to federal units as such. This argument, however, is not cogent. There is nothing in international legal doctrine or practice, and certainly nothing in the concept of a federation, that imputes a presumptive right to independence to federal units. Moreover, there is a compelling reason why it would be a grave mistake for the international legal order to acknowledge any such presumption: doing so would create strong incentives for centralized states to resist any efforts to transform them into federations. If federal units are regarded as quasi-sovereign entities, with a presumptive right to independence, states will be unreceptive to initiatives for federalization, fearing that federalization will be the first step toward legitimizing secession of federal units.[22]

D. *The Argument from the Right of Self-Determination in International Law*

The Court correctly notes that there are at most three situations in which the international legal right of self-determination of peoples confers a right to secede: (1) cases of colonial domination, (2) cases of unlawful military occupation, and (3) cases in which a racial, religious, or ethnic group is excluded from participation in the government of the state in which they reside.[23] None of these circumstances hold in the case of Quebec. Quebec is not subject to colonial domination but rather is a full partner in a liberal democratic federal system, with significant spheres of autonomous political action; nor is it subject to occupation by a foreign military power. Finally, the population of Quebec enjoys broad rights of political participation at the federal, provincial, and local levels. Therefore, there is no case to be made that unilateral Quebec secession is authorized under the international legal principle of self-determination of peoples.

E. *The National Self-Determination Argument*

There is a quite different principle that is sometimes confused with the international legal principle of self-determination that some advocates of Quebec secession appeal to. This is the *nationalist principle*, according to which every nation (or "distinct people") as such has the moral right to political self-determination, where this includes the right to choose independent statehood.

The Court does not address this argument explicitly, arguing that

> it is not necessary to decide the "people" issue because whatever may be the correct determination of this issue in the context of Quebec, a right of secession only arises under the principle of self-determination of peoples at international law where "a people" is governed as part of a colonial empire; where "a people" is subject to alien subjugation, domination or exploitation; and possibly where "a people" is denied any meaningful exercise of its right to self-determination within the state of which it forms a part. (154)

Since the chief aim of this essay is to assess the Court's responses to the Reference Questions, limitations of space preclude a comprehensive analysis of various nationalist arguments for Quebec secession. However, given the importance given to the idea that Quebec is a nation in the current political controversy over secession,[24] it is worth pointing out how weak the argument for a unilateral right of secession based on the nationalist principle is.

The nationalist principle is vulnerable to a number of powerful criticisms that are well known in the literature of political theory. Before a brief survey of some of these objections, it is worth emphasizing two points. First, from the standpoint of Quebec secession, the nationalist argument is a two-edged sword: if francophone Quebec counts as a nation, then so do the native peoples of Quebec, and if the mere fact of nationhood (or being a "distinct people") confers the right to independent statehood on the former, then it does so as well on the latter. In a word, Quebec secessionists can consistently appeal to the nationalist principle only if they are willing to concede that the native peoples of northern Quebec may choose to have their own state or to exercise their right of self-determination by remaining, with their territory, in Canada. Second, even if, despite the objections to it, the nationalist principle were acceptable as a normative principle in political theory, this would do nothing to establish the legality of unilateral Quebec secession under international law. It is a gross mistake to confuse the nationalist principle with the international legal right of self-determination. The latter does not confer a right of self-determination on nations or "distinct peoples" as such. Instead, it confers this right only on "peoples" who meet the conditions satisfied in the three circumstances described above: colonization, unlawful military annexation, and exclusion from participation in government.

The most familiar objection to the nationalist principle is that its general application would entail excessive moral costs. There are simply too many groups that can plausibly claim to be nations (or "distinct peoples"). In most existing states there are several such groups, they are often mixed together rather than being neatly concentrated in separate regions, more than one group typically claims the same territory as its proper "homeland," and neither domestic nor international legal institutions are equipped to allocate territory in such a way that each group has its own territorial base for an independent state. Although for these reasons implementation of the nationalist principle cannot be achieved, even fairly limited attempts to implement it are likely to increase the number of ethnic conflicts and exacerbate their deadliness.

Proponents of the nationalist principle typically respond to this objection by retreating to a weakened version of the principle, according to which "nations [as such] have a strong claim to [some form of] self-determination [not necessarily independent statehood]."[25] The retreat to the weaker version signals a recognition that national self-determination is not an absolute value—that whatever presumptive claim nations may have to their own states must be balanced against other considerations, including peace and stability as requisites for the protection of human rights, as well as the conflicting claims of other nations for self-determination. Those who advocate the weaker nationalist principle therefore conclude that in many cases nations will not have a right to their own state but rather at most a right to some form of self-government short of independent statehood.

The weaker, more plausible version of the nationalist principle cannot justify *unilateral* secession by Quebec. To try to justify unilateral secession by a majority vote in Quebec by appeal to the notion of national self-determination is to give absolute weight to national self-determination—or rather it is to arbitrarily privilege self-determination for one nation and deny it to others. A negotiated, constitutionalized process of secession better reflects the limited and qualified case for national self-determination that the weaker version of the nationalist principle expresses. It does so in part by ensuring that the interests of one nation are not privileged to the exclusion of a proper weighing of the interest of others, under the requirement that negotiations be guided by the principle that minorities are to be protected. In sum, the appeal to national self-determination, even when it avoids confusing the nationalist principle with the principle of self-determination in international law, does not provide a sound justification for unilateral secession.[26]

F. Arguments from Cultural Preservation
or Cultural Autonomy

Some who endorse the nationalist principle place great weight on the claim that a nation (or "distinct people") is a cultural group and that for members of such a group this culture is constitutive of their identity. Some parties to the debate over Quebec secession dispense with the nationalist principle and assert that unilateral secession is justified because independent statehood is necessary for Quebec to preserve its distinctive culture.

At most, the appeal to the need to preserve the distinctive Quebec culture can establish that Quebec has the right, within the provisions for constitutional amendment, to initiate negotiations on secession. There is no *right* to cultural preservation, properly speaking, anymore than there is a *right* of every nation to its own state. There are morally important *interests* in cultural preservation, just as there are morally important interests in self-government on the part of nations. But in neither case do these interests rise to the level of absolute values for the simple reason that in various circumstances other morally important interests must be balanced against them. In the case of Quebec, the most obvious of these is the interest that native peoples in the province have in preserving their own distinctive cultures. So even if it is true, as proponents of the argument from cultural preservation assume, that achieving independent statehood is necessary for securing the survival of the distinctive francophone culture of Quebec, this does not show that unilateral secession by Quebec would be justified, nor even that the proper conclusion of negotiations over secession should be independence for Quebec.

A subtle shift in prosecessionist arguments based on the idea of culture may be occurring. In some cases advocates of Quebec secession speak, not of the need to preserve the culture from destruction, but of the need for cultural autonomy, for the members of the culture to be able to determine the development of that culture. The claim, then, is that independent statehood is needed to achieve this cultural autonomy.

This version of the cultural argument has one distinct advantage over the preservation version: it avoids having to provide evidence that Quebec's francophone culture is in fact in danger of destruction. For it can be argued that, according to reasonable indices, there is no evidence that this culture is "endangered." (A further problem for the cultural preservation argument is that it seems to trade on a naive and inaccurate view of cultures as static or at least fails to distinguish between cultural change and the death of a culture.) The cultural autonomy argument avoids having to make the empirical case that the culture is in danger and focuses instead on the importance of endogenous control over the culture's development.

However, in spite of this advantage, the cultural autonomy version of the argument is no more plausible as a justification for unilateral secession than the preservation version. First of all, the claim that every cultural group has a right to its own state is even less plausible (given the plurality of cultural groups intermixed in the same territories all over the world and the membership of the same individuals in more than one group) than the claim that every nation has a right to its own state. Even if the members of cultural groups have a legitimate interest in having the political means to shape the development of their culture, it does not follow that they have a right to independent statehood, much less that they have the right to effect independent statehood unilaterally by a simple majority vote. Once again, it is essential to recognize that there is more than one legitimate interest or important value at stake. And once again, a constitutionalized process of negotiation is more apt to achieve a proper balancing of conflicting interests and values than a unilateral act of secession.

G. *The Argument That What Is Not Prohibited Is Permitted*

Another putative justification for unilateral secession by Quebec runs as follows: under international law there is no prohibition against unilateral secession, but in international law whatever is not prohibited is permitted; therefore, under international law, Quebec has a right to secede unilaterally.[27] The first thing to note about this argument is that even if it were sound it would yield a rather weak conclusion. The only sense of the term *right* according to which the conclusion of the argument follows is that of a liberty or permission, not a claim right. To say that Quebec has a "right" in the liberty or permission sense is only to say that it is not obligated, under international law, *not* to secede unilaterally. Having a "right" in this very weak sense is compatible with the government of Canada having the "right" (in the same sense) to resist the secession by deadly force, and it is likewise compatible with other members of the system of states being permitted to assist the government of Canada in resisting the secession. In addition, to say that Quebec has a "right" in the liberty or permission sense does not imply any obligation on the part of any other state to recognize its independence if it does secede. In contrast to the liberty or permission sense of "right," a claim right is one that carries with it not only a liberty or permission on the part of the party who has the right but also correlative obligations on the part of others. If a group has the "right" to secede in the claim right sense, then not only does it have the liberty or permission to secede; in addition, other states, including the state from which it secedes, have an obligation not to interfere with its seceding. So at most the argument from the premise that what is not prohibited is permitted shows that unilateral secession would not be a violation of international law.

It is far from clear, however, that even this weak conclusion is valid. For it can be argued that international conventional (i.e., treaty) law does prohibit the unilateral secession of Quebec, even if the practice of states indicates that there is no clear customary international legal norm prohibiting such secession. As the Court points out, there are a number of important international conventions and UN resolutions that emphasize the importance of the territorial integrity of existing states and that strongly convey the idea that violations of territorial integrity are contrary to the fundamental purposes of the international legal system (112, 127–29). The Court also rightly notes that recent conventional international law emphasizes that the right of territorial integrity on the part of states that it affirms applies to all states that enable participation in government by all groups, rather than excluding some on the basis of race, religion, or ethnicity (126, 130, 138).

A case can be made, then, that even though there is no international legal prohibition against secession as such, there is, in conventional international law, a norm that prohibits unilateral secession from a democratic state. If this is the case, then there is not even an unambiguous "right" in the weak, permission or liberty, sense, to unilateral secession by Quebec under international law. It should be noted, however, that the opinion of international legal scholars may be divided on this issue and that not all would be convinced that conventional law includes a prohibition against unilateral secession from a democratic state such as Canada. Nevertheless, those who argue from the lack of a prohibition to a "right" to secede under international law should not overestimate the strength of their meager conclusion. Mere permissibility falls short of the normative force conveyed by what the Court calls a "positive" right or, more accurately, a claim right.

III. THE NEGOTIATION PROCESS: THE RISK OF NEGOTIATION BREAKDOWN AND THE STATUS OF NATIVE PEOPLES

A. *Unfinished Business*

So far I have argued that the Court is correct in concluding that unilateral secession by Quebec would not be legal under Canadian constitutional law and that it would not be authorized by international law as an exercise of the right of self-determination. Now I wish to argue that in spite of the cogency of its rejection of unilateral secession, the Court's ruling leaves two crucial problems unsolved.

B. *The Risk That Negotiations Will Break Down*

The Court's discussion of the process of a constitutionalized, negotiated secession distinguishes between the legal and the political spheres. Though the Court held that a clear majority vote on a clear secession question is needed to trigger negotiations, it also held that what counts as clarity on both counts is not justiciable but must instead be decided by the political actors, presumably those who would be parties to the negotiations if they occur (100). Similarly, the Court provided a basic, though highly abstract, legal structure for the negotiations by requiring that they involve constitutional amendment and be guided by the four fundamental principles but held that it is up to the political actors to judge what the four principles require and ultimately whether to consent to whatever terms of separation emerge. The Court cites two factors to support its constrained view of the proper domain of the legal: the fact that the political actors have an inalienable fiduciary obligation to their constituencies and the fact that neither domestic nor international law provides the resources for determining either the two clarities that trigger negotiation or the correct outcome of the negotiations (101–3, 151–53).

This admirable constraint comes at a price. Disagreement as to what counts as a clear majority or a clear question has already reached an impasse. Both the House of Commons of Canada and the Quebec National Assembly have proposed bills regarding the clarity question. The Canadian bill (Bill C-20) provides that the House of Commons shall determine the clarity of any referendum question on the secession of a province and shall determine, after a referendum has taken place, whether a clear majority has voted in favor of secession. The Quebec bill (Bill 99) states that 50 percent plus one vote will constitute a clear majority.[28] The Supreme Court's hope that the clarity issues would be settled by negotiation of the political actors appears to have been overoptimistic.

Even if this first hurdle is cleared, negotiations on the terms of secession might break down at any number of points (e.g., the shape of the boundaries of an independent Quebec or the proper division of the national debt). Presumably the Canadian government would take the position that, in the absence of agreement, adherence to the principle of constitutionalism and the rule of law requires that the status quo be maintained. If the Canadian government's default position (if negotiations break down) is the continued inclusion of Quebec in Canada, Quebec secessionists might understandably conclude that though each party has the right to accept or refuse terms, the deck is stacked against secession. The Quebec authorities might then unilaterally declare independence, in which case the goal of subjecting the secession process to the rule of law would be thwarted. The Court does not discuss alternative mechanisms that might be employed to reduce the risk that negotiations might break down.

There is a third alternative that lies between the complete judicialization of the process that the Court rightly eschews and the dangers of a process left solely to the political actors that the

Court endorses: mediation by a suitably composed international body. In fact, it can be argued that a consistent application of the core idea of the ruling—the thesis that if secession is to occur it should be subjected to the rule of law so far as possible—requires international mediation. My suggestion is that international mediation would reduce the risk that the benefits of the rule of law would not be obtained. In addition, I wish to suggest that international mediation would facilitate, not impair, another of the basic constitutional principles the Court says should guide the secession process: the protection of minorities.

International mediation must be distinguished from compulsory arbitration, which would almost certainly be rejected as being incompatible with the sovereignty of Canada and with the fiduciary obligation of the Quebec authorities to the people of Quebec. And regardless of whether they would have the right to do so, it is very unlikely that either party would agree to alienate final decision-making capacity to an external agent, no matter how impressive its credentials for impartiality.

International mediators could, however, play several constructive roles without having the power of compulsion. First, they could facilitate negotiations on what counts as a clear majority on a clear question, to try to break the current impasse in which the Canadian government and the Quebec National Assembly have each taken it upon themselves unilaterally to determine the answer to the clarity issue but with incompatible solutions. The hope is that the presence of mediators would tend to raise the level of discourse, requiring each party to make its case in a principled way, under conditions of publicity. If this first hurdle were cleared, the mediators could then set an orderly agenda for forging the terms of secession.

With regard to certain terms, what counts as an equitable agreement will depend in part on what are assumed to be the relevant facts. This is especially true in the case of the division of the national debt. One beneficial function of the mediators in this regard would be to establish what the relevant facts are, relying on the testimony of disinterested experts which it identifies.

The chief advantage of mediation is that it could approximate some of the virtues of the rule of law without demanding too much of the law and in particular of the judiciary. Chief among the virtues of the rule of law are impartiality, consistency, and the requirement that decisions must be supported by general principles. A properly structured mediation process could increase the probability that these values would be respected. In particular, the effects of requiring the parties not only to make their positions public but also to support them publicly with principled reasons should not be underestimated.

Mediation might produce benefits for both parties and for other states and international organizations as well. The process of mediation might do something to allay Quebec secessionist concerns that the Court has stacked the deck in favor of the status quo by making it more difficult for the Canadian government to demand unreasonable terms in hopes of scuttling the negotiations. In particular, mediated negotiation to determine what counts as a clear majority would seem to be more attractive to the secessionists than the attempt at unilateral determination after the fact, as specified in Canada's Clarity Bill. Similarly, the Canadian government would gain some assurance that if it negotiates in good faith, the publicity of the international mediation process will help ensure that the blame for failure lies squarely on the Quebec authorities. Furthermore, other states and organizations could look to the mediation process for guidance as to how they should respond if negotiations break down. And if mediation succeeds in producing an agreement acceptable to the parties, then the international community can be more confident that recognition of Quebec as a sovereign state would be appropriate.

C. The Status of Native Peoples: The Argument for Nonpaternalistic Protection of Their Rights

The Court is to be commended for emphasizing that the protection of minority rights must play a central role in a negotiated secession. However, the Court's position does not explicitly identify the native peoples of Canada or Quebec as parties to the negotiations. The Court says that the parties to the negotiations are to be the "participants in Confederation," but this phrase arguably refers only to the Canadian federal government and the provinces. Nonetheless, it can be argued that a constitutional convention exists for including the native peoples of Canada in deliberations concerning any constitutional changes or at least any that would affect their status.[29]

This appeal to constitutional convention fails to provide sufficient support for the status of the native peoples of Quebec in negotiations for two reasons. First, adherence to the constitutional convention in question is compatible with merely allowing representatives of native peoples to voice their concerns over the negotiations, without giving them any decision-making authority in the negotiations. Second, this constitutional convention would seem to require only that the native peoples of Canada (all of Canada) be consulted; it does not single out any special role for the native peoples of Quebec, who would be most directly affected by secession. More specifically, the constitutional convention fails to capture the significance of the fact that some native peoples of Quebec, especially the James Bay Crees and Inuit of northern Quebec, have achieved special rights of control over development and the exploitation of natural resources in their traditional homelands, rights that are specified in trilateral treaties that assign a role to the Canadian government to protect those rights.

The Court might reply that the key protection for the native peoples of Quebec lies in the fiduciary obligation of the Canadian government. The difficulty with this response is that it can be read as allowing a *paternalistic* mode of fulfilling the obligation—having the Canadian government speak for the native peoples rather than allowing them to speak for themselves in the negotiations.

There are three weighty reasons why such paternalism should be avoided in this case. First, to allow others to decide the fundamental political status of the native peoples is to perpetuate one of the evils of colonialism: treating native populations as if they were the property of others to be moved about or exchanged among white governments without their consent. Second, the long and often shameful history of whites attempting to act as surrogate decision makers for native peoples creates a strong presumption in favor of letting the native peoples decide for themselves. (An additional and not inconsiderable advantage of according these native peoples the status of principals in the

negotiations is that doing so would address the common com-
plaint of Quebec secessionists that the Canadian government is
using its professed concern for the native peoples as a "club" to
beat down the secessionist movement.) Third, it would be implausible to say that the native peoples of Quebec are incapable
of speaking for themselves effectively. In the process of defending their rights and interests over the past three decades they
have proved both articulate and skillful.[30]

The alternative under consideration is *not* that the native peoples of Quebec should be accorded an ex ante veto—a right to
decide in advance of any negotiations that they wish to remain in
Canada, within the system of rights they currently enjoy. Instead,
the less radical proposal has two parts. First, all native peoples of
Canada should be allowed to voice their views publicly in the
process of negotiations, in accordance with the constitutional
convention noted above. Second, those native peoples of Quebec
whose distinctive land, resource, and self-government rights
would be most affected by secession, primarily the James Bay
Crees and Inuit, have a duty to negotiate in good faith with the
goal of securing adequate protections for their existing rights, as
well as for legal structures within which they can reasonably pursue remedies for existing deficiencies in those protections. In addition, within the process of international mediation, these native peoples should have the right to propose a full range of alternative arrangements, including a condominium between Canada
and an independent Quebec in which they enjoy significant powers of self-government and share decision-making authority concerning development and the exploitation of resources and a status of autonomy within an independent Quebec. Finally, the ultimate decision as to whether to accept these or other alternatives
or to opt for the status quo—continued inclusion in Canada—
should be left to the native peoples.

This proposal will no doubt strike some as radical. Some who
advocate Quebec secession have suggested that it would suffice
for the Quebec authorities to offer assurances that the existing
rights of the native peoples, under the Constitution of Canada
and the James Bay and Northern Quebec Agreement, will be
honored by a sovereign Quebec. This reply, however, is inadequate. Given the long struggle for native peoples' rights gener-

ally, it would be imprudent of them—and irresponsible of their representatives—to accept paper assurances as sufficient, just as it would be inappropriate for them to acquiesce in the Canadian government's proposal to speak for them. Instead, the native peoples might reasonably require acknowledgment of a right on their part to appeal to an appropriate international body to oversee effective implementation of such an autonomy agreement in the event that they believe its terms are not being fulfilled. Anything less than this would make it unreasonable for the native peoples to forsake the protections they now enjoy under Canadian law.

Including the native peoples as principals in secession negotiations and making their autonomous status a matter of international concern would be of great significance not only for the indigenous peoples of Canada but for indigenous peoples everywhere. Many international legal and political theorists who take a rather constrained view on the rights of minorities or indigenous peoples to full independence have advocated instead various autonomy regimes that allow these peoples considerable powers of self-government in addition to protections for minority cultural rights. However, it is reasonable to expect such groups to be content with alternatives short of secession only if there is international support for intrastate autonomy regimes. Too often states have made autonomy agreements with minorities or indigenous peoples and then flaunted them with impunity. Examples include the autonomy agreement for Kurds in Northern Iraq, the autonomy agreement with Southern Sudan, the Serbian autonomy agreement with Kosovo, and the Ethiopian government's agreement to federal status of Eritrea. In each case the state violated the agreement, and massive violations of human rights and eventually civil war followed.

From this vantage point, Canada's response to the possibility of Quebec secession offers a hopeful opportunity for setting a progressive precedent. Given the strong culture of human rights and respect for minority rights found in Canada, this case provides a favorable venue for taking a significant step toward making support for the implementation of autonomy regimes for indigenous peoples and minorities a matter of international responsibility.

Those who may be tempted to dismiss the foregoing proposal as too extreme should keep in mind the premise upon which it and the whole analysis of this essay is based: that Quebec secession cannot be viewed as the exercise of a remedial right to secede but instead must be regarded as a negotiated and hence consensual secession. Given the legitimacy of the Canadian state and the absence of persistent and serious violations of the rights of Quebecois that could justify secession on remedial grounds, secession must be consensual. The proposal offered here only concerns who should be required to consent to this momentous constitutional change. The point is that the special historical vulnerability of the native peoples and the need to avoid perpetuating the deficiencies of paternalistic modes of protecting them imply that they should be principal participants in any negotiations over secession. It is the special vulnerability of native peoples, the continuing economic and social legacy of historical injustices they have suffered, that singles them out from other minorities in Quebec who may oppose secession.

This last point warrants emphasis. The proposal for recognizing the native peoples of Quebec as principals in the negotiations does *not* rest on any general principle to the effect that every minority group has the right to veto secession. In any secession, there will be some who dissent from the decision to separate. The point, rather, is that the situation of this particular minority is special. So the proposal advanced here does not imply, for example, that the anglophone minority in Quebec has the right to veto secession.

One final consideration, though somewhat speculative in character, may help to allay the concerns of some who regard principal status for native peoples as inappropriate. Native peoples participating in public negotiations would presumably be subject to pressures for moderating their demands not only by members of the international public generally but by other indigenous groups in particular. It seems likely that there would be significant pressure for the native peoples involved in the negotiations to act fairly and reasonably. To fail to do so would be to lose the opportunity to forge a valuable precedent in the struggle for indigenous peoples' rights and to supply ammunition to those governments who wish to continue treating indigenous peoples paternalistically or ignoring their claims altogether.

IV. Conclusion

This essay has critically evaluated and supplemented the justifications for the Canadian Supreme Court's reference ruling on Quebec secession, while pointing out that the ruling raises but does not directly address two important issues—the need to minimize the risk that negotiations will break down, thereby defeating the goal of subjecting the secession conflict to the rule of law, and the status of native peoples in negotiations over secession. The analysis presented here agrees with the Court's main conclusions in response to the three reference questions but provides a more comprehensive examination of both some of the arguments for and against unilateral secession that the Court does consider and some additional arguments that it omits but that have figured prominently in the scholarly literature about secession and in some cases in the public discourse in Canada. With regard to the danger that negotiations will break down, I have suggested the possibility of international mediation of the negotiations over the terms of a secession referendum (the clarity issues) and the terms of secession itself. Finally, I have argued that a proper understanding of the relationship between the right to secede, democracy, and minority rights in the case of the possible secession of Quebec requires full partnership for those native peoples whose distinctive rights would be directly affected by separation.[31]

NOTES

I am grateful to Cindy Holder for her excellent assistance in the preparation of this essay.

1. *Reference re Secession of Quebec* ([1998] 2 S.C.R. 217). Numbers in parentheses in text refer to paragraph numbers from this source.

2. Explicit secession provisions exist, for example, in the Ethiopian Constitution and the Constitution of St. Kitts–Nevis. The Soviet Constitution also contained a special constitutional provision for secession from 1917 until the demise of the Soviet Union.

3. Letter from Stephane Dion to Lucien Bouchard, premier of Quebec (August 11, 1997); Letter to Bernard Landry, deputy premier of Quebec (August 26, 1997); Letter to Jacques Brassard, ministre delegué aux affaires intergouvernementales canadiennes (November 19, 1997).

4. The proposed Quebec legislation that prompted the Governor in Council to submit the reference questions to the Court proposed that the Quebec authorities could effect secession after offering to negotiate a treaty of economic cooperation to the Canadian government but reserved for the Quebec authorities the right to declare independence unilaterally if in their opinion the negotiations were not successful.

5. If secession is taken to fall under the General Procedure for Amending the Constitution outlined in sec. 38(1), it will require (in addition to resolutions from the House of Commons and the Senate of Canada) resolutions from the legislatures of at least two-thirds of the provinces comprising at least 50 percent of the population of Canada. If, on the other hand, secession is taken to fall under sec. 43 (Amendment of Provisions Relating to Some but Not All Provinces), it will require (in addition to resolutions from the House of Commons and Senate of Canada) only those provinces affected to pass resolutions on the matter. See Constitution Act, 1982, secs. 38(1), 43.

6. The growing literature on secession often relies on a distinction between the right to secede as a remedial right only and the right to secede as a primary right, one that a group can have in the absence of a valid grievance that it is subject to serious and persisting injustices at the hands of the state. Allen Buchanan, "Theories of Secession," *Philosophy and Public Affairs* 26, no. 1 (1997): 31–61.

7. In 1991 Gorbachev made the unpersuasive proposal that the Baltic Republics could secede from the USSR if a majority of the Politburo and of the other republics agreed.

8. Some might argue, however, that the case for Quebec secession can be made on grounds of injustice, in either or both of two ways: by arguing that the English conquest was unjust and that secession is an appropriate remedy for this injustice; or by arguing that the fact that the 1982 constitution went into effect without Quebec's consent constitutes an injustice. Both of these claims are problematic. With regard to the first, some would question whether an event as remote in time as the conquest could supply a justification for current secession. In any case it is hard to see how this remedial claim could justify secession of all of Quebec, since much of Quebec was not settled by the French at the time of the conquest. With regard to the second claim, it can be argued that the

majority of constitutional scholars hold that Quebec's lack of consent to the 1982 constitution does not affect its validity and that hence there is no injustice in current constitutional arrangements on that score.

9. In the case of a legitimate state, and absent a valid case for remedial secession in the face of injustices, the "internal" aspect of the international legal right of self-determination of the whole population precludes unilateral secession.

10. Constitution Act, 1982, Part V, Procedure for Amending the Constitution of Canada, especially secs. 38 (1), 42(1), and 43.

11. See Cass Sunstein, "Constitutionalism and Secession," *University of Chicago Law Review* 58, no. 2 (1991): 633–70; Allen Buchanan, "Democracy and Secession," in *National Self-Determination and Secession,* ed. Margaret Moore (New York: Oxford University Press, 1998).

12. See Allen Buchanan, *Secession: The Morality of Political Divorce from Fort Sumter to Lithuania and Quebec* (Boulder, Colo.: Westview Press, 1991), chap. 4; Daniel Philpott, "Applying Self-Determination," in *Rethinking Nationalism,* ed. Jocelyn Couture, Michel Seymour, and Kai Nielsen (Calgary: University of Calgary Press: 1997).

13. See Thomas Christiano, *The Rule of the Many* (Boulder, Colo.: Westview Press: 1996).

14. It can be argued that a permanent minority that was always outvoted on issues that were most important to it would have a case for secession. I consider the case for unilateral secession by a permanent minority in Allen Buchanan, *Justice, Legitimacy, and Self-Determination: Moral Foundations for International Law* (New York: Oxford University Press, forthcoming, 2003).

15. This is, for example, the position argued by the *amicus curiae*; see *Factum of the Amicus Curiae,* sec. 2.1 (b), paras. 82–91.

16. See, for example, Article 2(4) of the UN Charter (which requires states to refrain from the threat or use of force against other states), in Basic Documents in International Law and World Order, ed. Burns H. Weston, Richard A. Falk, and Anthony A. D'Amato (St. Paul, Minn.: West Publishing, 1980), 6–23; the Vienna Declaration and Program of Action, June 25, 1993, UN Document A/Conf. 157/23, July 12, retrieved from the Web site of the Office of the United Nations High Commissioner for Human Rights, www.unhchr.ch/huridocda/huridocda.nsf/(Symbol)/A.CONF.157.23.En?OpenDocument; the International Covenant on Civil and Political Rights, UN Document A/6316 (1966), in Weston et al., *Basic Documents,* 201–10; and the European Convention for the Protection of Human Rights and Fundamental Freedoms (1955), in Weston et al., *Basic Documents,* 164–72.

17. See Thomas Franck, "The Emerging Right to Democratic Governance," *American Journal of International Law* 86 (1992): 46–91.

18. See "Guidelines on the Recognition of New States in Eastern Europe and in the Soviet Union," December 16, 1991, *I.L.M.* 31 (1992): 1486.

19. See Antonio Cassese, *Self-Determination of Peoples* (New York: Cambridge University Press: 1995); Ian Brownlie, "The Rights of Peoples in Modern International Law," in *The Rights of Peoples,* ed. James Crawford (Oxford, England: Clarendon Press, 1988); and Hurst Hannum, "Rethinking Self-Determination," *Virginia Journal of International Law* 34 (1993): 1–70.

20. However, it can be argued that in the Yugoslav case rigid adherence to *uti possidetis* was a mistake because it precluded more constructive alternatives by ruling out a redrawing of boundaries that would have left fewer minorities in a vulnerable position.

21. It would be implausible to explain international acceptance of the secession of the Baltic Republics as affirmation of the principle of *uti possidetis* because these secessions were better regarded as restoration of previously sovereign states conquered by the Soviet Union.

22. See Donald Horowitz, "Secession: Law, Politics, and Philosophy," in *National Self-Determination and Secession,* ed. Margaret Moore (New York: Oxford University Press, 1998).

23. See Hannum, "Rethinking Self-Determination"; Cassese, *Self-Determination of Peoples*; Christian Tomuschat, ed., *Modern Law of Self-Determination* (Dordrecht, the Netherlands: M. Nijhoff, 1993).

24. The existence of a Quebec people is, for example, an important component of the argument presented by the *amicus curiae*; see *Factum of the Amicus Curiae,* Part I, Statement of Facts, and Part III (2.2), Second Question in Question 2, especially paras. 93, 95–99, and 105–9.

25. This formulation is found in what is perhaps the most systematic and influential contemporary case for national self-determination, David Miller's *On Nationality* (Oxford, England: Clarendon Press, 1995).

26. There are a number of other objections to the nationalist principle. One is that the principle leans heavily on the importance of nationality for persons' identity but overlooks the fact that in the modern world many individuals' identities are constituted by membership in several communities or cultural groups, that these group-based identities change, and that it is simply false that for all or even most persons their membership in a nation is the most important source of identity. The nationalist principle, then, appears arbitrarily to privilege one form of identity. If the proponent of the principle retreats to the weaker claim that nations, among other communities important for identity, have a

"claim" to some form of self-government, not necessarily independent statehood, then a large gap opens between the (weakened) nationalist principle and the desired conclusion that Quebec has a unilateral right to secede. Harry Brighouse, "Against Nationalism," and Allen Buchanan, "What's So Special about Nations?" both in Couture, Seymour, and Nielsen, *Rethinking Nationalism*.

27. *Factum of the Amicus Curiae*, Part III (2.1) a, paras. 75–81.

28. House of Commons of Canada, 2d Session, 36th Parliament, 48 Elizabeth II, 1999; National Assembly of Quebec, 1st Session, 36th Legislature, 1999.

29. See, for example, Peter Hogg and Mary-Ellen Turpel, "Implementing Aboriginal Self-Government: Constitutional and Jurisdictional Issues," in *Aboriginal Self-Government: Legal and Constitutional Issues*, ed. Patrick Macklem et al. (Ottawa, Canada: Royal Commission on Aboriginal Peoples, 1995), 378–430; Royal Commission on Aboriginal Peoples, *Report of the Royal Commission on Aboriginal Peoples: Renewal: A Twenty-Year Commitment* (Ottawa, Canada: Royal Commission on Aboriginal Peoples, 1996); Alan Cairns, "Dreams versus Reality in Our Constitutional Future," in *Reconfigurations: Canadian Citizenship and Constitutional Change: Selected Essays*, ed. Douglas E. Williams (Toronto: McClelland and Stewart, 1995), 339–41.

30. See, for example, Grand Council of the Crees EEyou Astchee, *Never without Consent: James Bay Crees' Stand against Forcible Inclusion in an Independent Quebec* (Toronto: ECW Press, 1996).

31. This chapter is based on an essay prepared by the author at the request of the Office of the Privy Council, Government of Canada in 1998.

10

SECESSION, CONSTITUTIONALISM, AND AMERICAN EXPERIENCE

MARK E. BRANDON

I.

Is secession ever justified in constitutional terms? To ask this question incites conceptual dissonance. For to say that secession might be constitutionally permissible seems inconsistent with conventional wisdom about what a constitution or constitutional order is supposed to do—to hold a political world together, not to permit it to fall apart. As Robert Post has put it, the point of a constitution is to establish a "unity of agency" in a constitutional state. Secession, he argues, "fracture[s] the pre-existing collective agency of a democratic state."[1]

We may add to that conceptual intuition an empirical observation: any society of almost any degree of complexity will display differences among the people who constitute it. Typically, for reasons of interest, morality, or a sense of common enterprise, people simply live with diversity. In fact, if sufficiently numerous and cross-cutting, differences can promote a kind of stability and balance that make secession unnecessary, perhaps undesirable.[2]

Sometimes, however, societies cannot rely on complexity and differentiation for stability. Sometimes people who are joined in political society find that they are divided by something they consider important, that the division is of long standing and appears to be enduring, that the division aggregates along geographic

272

lines, and that the people do not want to live together anymore. When those conditions hold, secession is a practical option, not least because, in extreme cases, it can avert the annihilation of large numbers of people. But practicality is not equivalent to constitutionality. Again, then: Is secession ever constitutionally justified? If so, how and why?

To address those questions, I pursue a case study of the breakdown of the American order in 1860–61. This is a hard case in several respects. First, the Constitution of the United States did not expressly permit or provide for secession. Second, the method for pursuing secession was unilateral. Third, some of the seceding states refused to offer reasons for their separation, relying instead on presumptively authoritative formal acts. Fourth, the order being dissolved was a kind of liberal democracy, though there were ticklish problems concerning the status of slaves, women, and the native tribes. Fifth, and most powerfully, the American secessions aimed to continue a regime whose dominant mode of production was immoral, by our lights.

For these and other reasons, American scholars have a genuine aversion to taking secession seriously as a constitutional matter. Cass Sunstein, for example, has proclaimed that "no serious scholar or politician now argues that a right to secede exists under American constitutional law."[3] At the very least, American scholars have had difficulty talking coherently about the matter in the face of secessionist movements in the Soviet Union, eastern Europe, the Middle East, South Asia, Africa, and even Canada.

Reinforcing the scholastic aversion to or confusion about secession is the figure of Abraham Lincoln. Even today he casts a long shadow across the American constitutional stage. In fact, with respect to secession, he casts shadows in two directions. With respect to the first, consider Sunstein's position, which is essentially a version of Lincoln's theory of perpetuity. Secession is unconstitutional, says Sunstein, for two reasons. First, we (in the United States) have judicial precedent on point, specifically the Supreme Court's pronouncement in *Texas v. White*,[4] which held that "[t]he Constitution, in all its provisions, looks to an indestructible Union, composed of indestructible States." Second, and more important for understanding Lincoln, Sunstein says that secession is barred by principles of constitutionalism. Thus, "whether or not secession might be justified as a matter of politics or morality, constitutions ought not to include a right to secede," and "courts should not find such a right to be implicit in constitutions." In the American case, Sunstein says, this position arises out of the "spirit of the original document, one that encourages the development of constitutional provisions that prevent the defeat of the basic enterprise."

But the argument from perpetuity was not Lincoln's only position. In our own time, Akhil Amar has staked out ground that falls within Lincoln's second shadow. Amar's constitutional strategy is strongly textual but ultimately rests upon a nationalist theory of the Constitution. Amar borrows a prop from John Marshall to support Lincoln's insistence that "the People" of the Constitution were the people of the nation as a whole. Consequently, he says, secession could not be accomplished simply on the motion of the seceding states but had to rest on a decision of the nation as a whole.[5]

I shall argue that both of these positions are wrong. Perpetuity is wrong in principle. And the weaker claim is wrong in the context of the Southern secessions from the United States in the mid-nineteenth century. Constitutionalism supplies the ground for my argument.

Constitutionalism is a political theory that is concerned with a kind of enterprise in which people (or a people) self-consciously attempt to conceive, articulate, and implement the design for a new political world.[6] In functional terms, then, constitutionalism is concerned—must be concerned—not only with creating and maintaining but also with dissolving political orders. In terms of both method and substance, it takes its baseline from Alexander Hamilton, who posited that the proposed Constitution of the United States was an experiment in whether it was possible to establish government through "reflection and choice" instead of through "accident and force."[7] This baseline suggests that political power should be authoritative, purposeful, and bounded; that the operation of power should be principled and traceable to a constitutional text; and that the regime should be capable of generating voluntary attachment among citizens, even if they have not formally consented to it. The institutions, norms, and procedures of the regime should reflect these considerations. There are many ways to arrange institutions, norms, and procedures that are compatible with constitutionalism; some may even be illiberal or disagreeable. To be clear, slavery is inconsistent with constitutionalism; secession, however, is not only consistent but logically required.

This logical requirement follows from accounts that constitutional regimes supply about their own origins. That is, the most powerful arguments for secession derive from the character of the founding of the regime from which secession is sought. This claim trades on the tendency of constitutional orders to rationalize themselves and to justify their existence by referring to the manner in which they were created. The ostensible manner of entering into constitutional union becomes the means also for leaving.

In the lore of the United States, not to mention the Preamble and Tenth Amendment to the Constitution, the authors of constitutional text were "the people." But much depends on how the people are configured for constitutional purposes. From the beginning, there were at least two accounts of who the people were (and on whose behalf they acted in creating the new constitutional order). Both accounts were visible in the dispute between federalists and antifederalists over the ratification of the Constitution. Of course, ratification did not end the dispute but merely transplanted it and revised the concrete issues over which it would be conducted. With respect to secession, the foundational myths presupposed by the federalist and antifederalist accounts of constitutional authority pointed in different directions. But under either account, I argue, secession is permissible. At stake in the difference between the two accounts is simply the institutional method by which secession may be authorized.

I should distinguish this conception of constitutionalist justification from three alternative modes that scholars have used to argue for (or against) secession. The first is geopolitical, or what Akhil Amar calls "geostrategic."[8] Geopolitical argument gives primacy to considerations of national defense (paying attention to both military and geographic concerns) and the strategic balance of power within the nation. No one can doubt that such considerations are of constitutional significance in the

Aristotelian sense of the word. Nor can one deny that the
founders of the American constitutional order were exquisitely
sensitive to their role in sustaining security from without and stability within. And considerations of geopolitics bear directly on
strategic calculations of both the conservators of a regime and
would-be secessionists.[9] But those considerations do not speak directly to the principles that must undergird the authority and
maintenance of a constitutionalist enterprise.

The second mode is moral. It justifies or criticizes acts of secession by resorting (1) to principles of moral philosophy or (2) to
moral standards that transcend the Constitution or the logic of a
particular constitutional order. Allen Buchanan supplies a per-
ceptive and wide-ranging example of a moralist mode of the first
type, justifying secession through liberal political theory.[10] Arguments for self-determination as a human right—grounded, for
example, in international law—are transcendental in the second
sense.[11] Clearly, any constitutional argument for secession is, in
some form or fashion, moral in character. Nevertheless, I resist
the inclination to rely on transcendental moral arguments. First,
the moral justifications cut more than one way in the American
case. Second, such arguments are usually insufficiently tied to
constitutional text, the logic of the order, or the basic principles
of constitutionalism to permit them to qualify as potent constitutional arguments. Third, thickly textured moral arguments tend
to be weak in times of social, economic, or political crisis, which
are precisely the times in which we typically find secessionist
movements.

The third mode is fundamentally economic. James Buchanan
argues that the right to secede was originally implied in the Constitution of the United States as a hedge against excessive taxation, incursions on free trade, and restrictions on the movement
of capital.[12] Apart from his general and largely unsupported invocation of original intent, however, his ultimate justification for secession is a form of theory whose rationality is exclusively economic, and a narrow version of economic rationality at that.[13]
Consequently, it leaves precious little room for politics or, as
Charles McIlwain called it, "gubernaculum."[14] Thus James
Buchanan's is not an autonomously constitutional theory.

II.

When a group of people finds that it no longer wants to belong to a particular polity, that its members insufficiently sense the "mystic chords of memory" that bind a nation both institutionally and culturally, there are several options open to it.[15] It may persevere within the system, hoping for (or despairing of) a change in the political character of the nation through a change either in constituency or of ethos. In the nineteenth-century United States, radical Southerners believed that the South had already suffered too long as an oppressed minority, and they were beginning to find converts among moderates as well.[16]

If the disaffected group is small in number or widely dispersed geographically, its members might consider simply leaving. In his critique of tacit consent as a justification for political regimes, David Hume recognized some of the profound practical impediments to expatriation—the cost of travel and resettlement and the difficulty of learning a new language and manners—which are especially burdensome for people who often have the most reason to leave.[17] Hume did not mention the deterrents to procuring employment that provides a decent wage (including the difficulty of securing permission even to enter another country and to work there) or the risks of statelessness in a world in which citizenship has been described as "the right to have rights."[18] And there are the psychic costs of uprooting self and family from one's home, which is especially traumatic for people possessing a strong sense of place, as did many in the South. For some Southerners expatriation would have been a rejection not only of their nation but also of their country, their home.

If the group is especially large, is convinced of its moral or technological superiority, or believes its mission divinely sanctioned, it might opt for revolution. Revolution might take on more than one meaning in this context. It might take the form of a *radical alteration* in the government's structure or purposes, most radically by dismantling entirely the nation's government and erecting a new one in place of the old. Alternatively or even additionally, it might imply the willingness of opponents of the existing regime to use *systematic violence* to achieve their aims.

John Brown's attempt to seize the U.S. military garrison at Harper's Ferry was revolutionary in both senses. Both geographically and politically, however, his aims were not necessarily to take on the nation but simply to bring down the slave government of the state of Virginia and to incite insurrections by slaves throughout the South.

Certainly, secession can be revolutionary in either sense. In the end, however, the South's attempt to secede was revolutionary only in the second sense, not in the first. For one thing, most Southern secessionists, despite fanciful pretensions to a national slave empire before 1860, were content to leave be the national government and the rest of the nation. They were content, that is, simply to leave. For another, the Southern aim, at least in several respects, was hardly a radical alteration of existing relations, even within the seceding states. The aim instead was to preserve what many saw as the extant order and hence was conservative in many respects.

Even so, by 1860 there was some authority for considering such a move revolutionary, even if it were conducted peacefully. Kenneth Stampp argues that the conceptual foundations for the constitutional illegitimacy of secession were laid between 1830 and 1833—not surprisingly, in response to the crisis over nullification. Daniel Webster, he notes, considered secession an act of treason. Edward Livingston, senator from Louisiana, said it was "extralegal," as the states had transferred their "attributes of sovereignty . . . to the General Government . . . ; the States have abandoned and can never reclaim them." Under the Constitution, he argued, the national government was "sovereign and supreme." Secession was revolution.[19]

John Quincy Adams derived from a theory of consent the notion that consent could not be withdrawn. He traced the origin of the Union to the Declaration of Independence. That "primitive social compact of union, freedom and independence" committed all the "States whose people were parties to it" to membership in the Union forever. Adams's doctrine would have covered the infidelity of South Carolina in the early 1830s; however, it would not have reached Alabama, Mississippi, Louisiana, Texas, Arkansas, Florida, or Tennessee, as none of them had been a "party" to the Declaration of Independence.[20]

In his *Commentaries,* published in 1833, Joseph Story joined Livingston in explicitly linking arguments against secession to a theory of the Constitution. He argued that the Constitution had been intended to serve "as a permanent form of government, as a fundamental law, as a supreme rule, which no State was at liberty to disregard, suspend, or annul." It was "designed for perpetuity." In his later years, James Madison seemed to agree. Secession, he said, was never permissible merely as an act of political will but was justified only for "intolerable oppression" under accepted theories of revolution.[21]

In the context of the crisis over nullification, the most important argument against secession was President Andrew Jackson's. He pressed a nationalist theory of the historical origin and theoretical foundation of the Union that even his sometimes enemy John Marshall would have embraced. Union, Jackson said, antedated the existence of the states. Departing from Adams's theory that the Declaration of Independence was binding on the states because they consented through their predecessors, the colonies, Jackson argued that the Declaration was binding on the states precisely because they were *not* present (in fact or by proxy) when the Declaration created the Union. Because the Union was *historically* prior to the states, he said, it was *theoretically* preeminent as well. Thus the Constitution did not alter the relative primacy of the Union and the states. It reinforced the primacy of the Union by establishing the nation as supreme. National supremacy was a function of the manner in which the Constitution was ratified: by the people. The Constitution was not simply a treaty or compact among the states. It was a national charter creating a national government that bound the people directly because it owed its existence to them. Secession, then, at least in the case of the United States, would "not break a league, but destroy[] the unity of a nation."[22]

Adams, Story, Madison, and Jackson were inclined to conflate secession with nullification. The conflation was partly a function of American experience: talk of secession had almost invariably accompanied talk of nullification. From a psychological standpoint, the two were undoubtedly motivated by the same interests or impulses. For example, in debates during the crisis over nullification, some Southern radicals, though not John C. Calhoun, had sometimes seemed to argue that nullification and secession were kindred theories. Indeed, some modern scholars have suggested that secession is a logical extension of the doctrine of nullification.[23]

In fact, however, the two are almost mutually exclusive in that each tends to ameliorate the impulse that generates the necessity of the other. Under almost all conceivable circumstances, nullification would have provided such security for local self-determination that it would have practically nullified the need for an exit. Especially in Calhoun's hands, nullification was an attempt to reconstruct the notion of a national majority so as to render secession unnecessary and to defuse it as an explosive constitutional issue.

III.

Just as a discontent or alienated minority has certain options, a nation trying to hold itself together has two general strategies short of permitting secession (or, of course, dissolution altogether): (1) It might permit some sort of nullification or local control on matters of constitutional import; or (2) it might employ the coercive power of the nation to preserve union. Both solutions seek long-term cohesion. The first achieves cohesion in exchange for a short-term sacrifice of national supremacy in the national application of constitutional standards. The second achieves cohesion by putting at risk one of the basic tenets of constitutionalism: choice. Both risk further disintegration over time, but the second may well remove evidence of that disintegration from sight. In the United States in 1861, the most extreme version of the first solution, nullification, had been rejected so often for so long that it was widely considered politically untenable.[24] The more moderate version, rooted in antifederalist localism, had been rendered inaccessible, at least with respect to the status of slavery in the nation and the territories, by the increasing tendency of both sides of the debate to seek out national solutions, especially after *Dred Scott*. Lincoln opted for a pragmatic combination of the two strategies, invoking localism on the question of slavery, while emphasizing the supremacy of national authority generally.

But nationalism is a double-edged sword, for secession is ironically most plausible as a strategy in the context of a strongly nationalist constitutionalism. This irony may begin to explain why some Southern radicals were inclined to resort to secession in 1860–61. *Dred Scott* stood partly for the proposition that the only logical or practical solution to the cleavages that slavery was exacerbating was a national one. Certainly Taney's opinion displayed a strongly nationalist rhetoric, and its rationale threatened to obliterate geographical limits to the institution of slavery within the nation. Such nationalism might have satisfied Southerners, even the most committed firebrands, as long as *Dred Scott* was law.[25]

But when Abraham Lincoln was elected president in 1860—having argued two years earlier both that "a house divided against itself cannot stand" and that he opposed the extension of the Supreme Court's decision in *Dred Scott* as precedent binding the Court or the polity—the substantive content (or consequence) of nationalist constitutionalism seemed ready to turn on its head. Some Southerners perceived Lincoln as committed to the adoption and enforcement of a national antislavery policy. His election, they erroneously believed, demonstrated that a majority in the nation was now committed to the same thing.[26]

Fear, necessity, and hope can motivate radically different interpretations of the same text or event. Many Southerners, and certainly most secessionists in the South, were disposed to read Lincoln's positions on nationalism and abolition through the lens of fear rather than hope. So they also chose to read him, but with more justification, when he spoke on secession. In his First Inaugural Address, the same speech in which he pledged to support a constitutional amendment explicitly protecting slavery, he said that "in contemplation of universal law, and of the Constitution, the Union of these States is perpetual."[27] He cited no specific tenet of universal law but did offer three other reasons, one concerning the logic underlying the creation of nations, one concerning the history of the Union and the definition of "perfection," and one grounded in specific presidential obligations under the Constitution. Four months later, in his "Message to Congress in Special Session," he would add two more arguments of substance, one from a theory of democracy and one implicating the right of self-preservation.[28]

First, said Lincoln, every nation ever created presupposed perpetuity. "It is safe to assert that no government proper, ever had a provision in its organic law for its own termination. Perpetuity is implied, if not expressed, in the fundamental law of all national governments." In other words, the proposition of perpetuity went without saying. Because the Constitution did not speak explicitly to the legality of secession, perhaps even if it had, the nationalist presumption prohibited secession, according to Lincoln. At one point in his First Inaugural, Lincoln subtly suggested that there might be a constitutional mode for accomplishing secession, but only by "all the parties who made it." He derived this mode from his assumption that the Constitution's ratification procedures required unanimity. But he did not say who the parties were or how their will might be represented. Nor did he indicate the slightest willingness to engage the mode as a practical possibility.[29]

Second, "[t]he Union is much older than the Constitution." Lincoln traced its origin unbroken to the Articles of Association of 1774, through the Declaration of Independence and Articles of Confederation, to the Constitution, whose Preamble stated its object to be "to form a more perfect Union." "But if destruction of the Union, by one, or by a part only, of the States, be lawfully possible, the Union is *less* perfect than before the Constitution, having lost the vital element of perpetuity."[30]

Third, he insisted that the Constitution did not confer on the president the authority "to fix terms for the separation of the States." Moreover, it imposed on him an oath, to "preserve, protect and defend," as he put it, "the government" of the nation. Consistent with his reading of the oath, he would defend the government against the dissolution that secession threatened.[31]

Fourth, the United States, he said, was engaged in "an experiment" in "popular government." Popular government is democratic government. Democratic government requires that a majority govern and that the minority acquiesce in majoritarian decisions. The only permissible response to policies with which a minority disagrees is to try to change policy at the next election. "[T]here can be no successful appeal, except for ballots themselves."[32]

Fifth, and following from the fourth, is this oft-quoted series of questions, which I can frame no better than Lincoln:

[T]his issue embraces more than the fate of these United States. It presents to the whole family of man, the question, whether a constitutional republic, or a democracy—a government of the people, by the same people—can, or cannot, maintain its territorial integrity, against its own domestic foes. It presents the question, whether discontented individuals, too few in numbers to control administration, . . . can . . . break up their Government, and thus practically put an end to free government upon the earth. It forces us to ask: "Is there, in all republics, this inherent and fatal weakness?" "Must a government, of necessity, be too *strong* for the liberties of its own people, or too *weak* to maintain its own existence?"[33]

Although at the time of his inauguration Lincoln foreswore "bloodshed or violence . . . unless it be forced upon the national authority," there was no question that he considered secession illegal, "that no State, upon its mere motion, can lawfully get out of the Union,—that *resolves* and *ordinances* to that effect are legally void." More than simply illegal, though, secession was on his terms a "dissolution," an act of revolution "against the authority of the United States." "I therefore consider that, in view of the Constitution and the laws, the Union is unbroken."[34] He would continue to hold that view throughout the Civil War.

His principal claim, moreover, was not simply that the Union was unbroken in this case. It was that Union could not be broken in *any* case, at least not constitutionally. The weaker version of Lincoln's position might have left room for a constitutionally justified theory of secession. But when he implied that there might be a constitutional way out of the Union, his vehicle—the consent of "all the parties"—was more stringent than a fair reading of Article VII might allow. And even if his reading of Article VII were supportable, Lincoln's public position consistently undermined and finally rejected the notion that secession might be constitutional. His ultimate position—the one he held to most firmly and the one he relied upon in prosecuting the War—was that union was perpetual.

IV.

For more than a century, Lincoln's doctrine, reinforced by Union military victory and the Supreme Court's confused blessing after the War, has made national perpetuity and the illegitimacy of secession appear to be brute constitutional facts. The emphatic character of the military solution, the ascent of the myth that the forces of Union had all along fought the Civil War to free the slaves, and the martyrdom of Father Abraham tended to obscure the constitutional weakness of Lincoln's claims. I shall address his claims seriatim in this section. Beginning in this section and continuing in the next, I shall explain why the logic of constitutionalism requires a theory of secession.

First, constitutionalism and (ironically) written constitutions themselves attest to the notion that some things go without saying. One function of constitutional theory is to articulate and justify those unsaid things. Lincoln was correct, then, that the creation of a nation, whether by written constitution or not, might presuppose one or more principles that are fundamental to the enterprise of state building or constitution making. But he was wrong in assuming that perpetuity is logically necessary or experientially universal in the creation of nations generally or in the formation of American Union.[35] Even his weaker claim, that the dissolution of the Union requires the consent of "all the parties," is a dubious account of what Article VII requires, and it begs for a description of who must consent to secession and how they may do so. Lincoln's assumption that secession was equivalent to dissolution was at best only partially accurate, for nonviolent or "constitutionalist" secession accomplishes merely the withdrawal of a geographic part of the nation and leaves the old national government intact over the rest.

Second, Lincoln's account of the unbroken pedigree of national union was historically and theoretically suspect. As Stampp points out, apart from the question whether the states or the Union was older, the Constitution itself undermined the notion that the Union's existence was unbroken from 1774 (or 1776 or 1781). The very process and product of the Philadelphia Convention were illegal from the standpoint of both the Articles of Confederation and the Convention's charter granted by Congress under the Articles. Moreover, the procedures for ratifying the proposed Constitution did not require that all the states consent to the new plan of government before it became effective. Under Article VII, the Constitution was "valid" after only nine states had ratified it, although only within those states that had ratified it. Nonunanimous ratification would have meant that there were at least two "national" governments (and hence two unions)—one under the aegis of the Constitution and the other under the Articles of Confederation—controlling two separate territories where once there had been one. If, on the other hand, the Constitution's nonunanimous ratification operated to dissolve the Confederation, as a secession or revolution would under Lincoln's theory, then there may have been as many as five governments (and arguably five unions) where once there was one. Each of the four nonratifying states, bound neither to the Constitution nor to the Articles, would have exercised its own sovereign authority.

And as Stampp and others have noted, the Constitution's self-described purpose of forming "a more perfect Union" does little to acknowledge continuity of the Union if one emphasizes the word *form*.[36] Besides, the idea that perpetuity is a necessary adjunct to perfection would seem silly but for the fact that so many intelligent people have recited it. Why might perfection not permit the *abandonment* of old, imperfect forms of association in favor of new and better ones? At the very least, the congruence of perfection and perpetuity needs more than simple assertion to support it.

Third, while Lincoln's contention that he was bound by his oath to protect the national government was probably deep-felt, it was nonetheless incompatible with the text and theory of the Constitution. The oath set out in Article II, Section 1, requires that the president "preserve, protect and defend the *Constitution*" (italics added), not the national government. Lincoln would shortly convert his conflation of national government and Constitution into a hierarchy in which the former was superior to the latter. For example, in justifying his suspending the writ of habeas corpus, he suggested that the preservation of government was the end of constitutionalism, the Constitution itself only a means; thus the Constitution could be suspended in the interest

of the latter. This hierarchy, of course, ran counter to the constitutionalist notion, framed poignantly by Frederick Douglass, that
the Constitution and its processes and values were distinct from
government, in part because they were designed to serve as standards against which to measure the actions of government.[37] The
Constitution may well be an instrument or means, but not in the
way that Lincoln suggested.

Fourth, Lincoln's argument from democracy assumed too
much in two ways. On the one hand, it assumed that the Constitution had institutionalized a radical form of democratic politics
in which majority ruled and minorities must submit. If Lincoln
were correct in this regard, then Calhoun's fears of a "national
consolidated democracy" were justified. In fact, however,
notwithstanding the polity's pretensions to democracy and the
South's constant carping about its status in the Union, the Constitution supplied a large number of institutional constraints on
majoritarianism. Whatever else it did, the Constitution did not
institute radical democracy. In fact, it could not have done so and
still been true to either of its prevailing foundational myths.

On the other hand, Lincoln's democratic theory, standing
alone, cannot account for a deeply alienated, potentially permanent minority. It is one thing for a democracy to say that the majority's will must govern in most circumstances. It is another for it
to insist that on a range of issues going to the heart of a people's
constitutive political identities, the people must nonetheless submit. At that point, democracy takes on an authoritarian, totaliz-
ing character that may be incompatible with constitutionalism's
principle of limits and that radically undermines the conditions
under which constitutional attachment can occur. Constitutional
politics rests upon authority but is not authoritarian in the sense
suggested by Lincoln's claim.

Fifth, then, Lincoln's argument from self-preservation touches
one of the deepest, most vexing problems of constitutionalism:
Must constitutional government be too weak to preserve itself? I
cannot provide a comprehensive answer to such a difficult question in this context, but I might venture two observations that cut
against the answer that Lincoln proposes. First, in every iteration
of the question, Lincoln presupposed that the issue was fundamentally one involving a challenge to national authority *by violent*

means. It may be that the firebrands of South Carolina dug their own graves on this issue by provoking Lincoln to resist force with force. But had the South Carolinians resisted resorting to violence, they would not have triggered Lincoln's argument from self-preservation, at least not in the form in which he offered it.

The other observation about self-preservation is this: violence to one side, the answer to Lincoln's question is Yes. Plainly, government may coerce obedience when it acts authoritatively and when those upon whom it acts are citizens, denizens, or wards of the polity. But when the people presume to act, not as mere citizens, but as constitutional sovereigns, then government must respect and submit to those people, even to the point of its own dissolution. Otherwise, at least according to the foundational myths that have underwritten the Constitution of the United States, constitution making itself is a theoretical and practical impossibility. There are times when government must permit its authority to be destroyed. Perpetuity is at odds with these notions.

But the profound success of perpetual union has effectively buried part of the American constitutional tradition. Throughout the nineteenth century, secession was a recurrent theme of constitutional arguments, especially in New England. Unhappy over Jefferson's election as president in 1800 and incensed over his purchase of Louisiana from the French three years later (arguing that the nation would soon be overrun with what they termed "negro boroughs"), Federalists in the Northeast began to talk of disunion as early as 1803. The talk intensified after the adoption of the Embargo of 1807, which Federalists considered a threat to Northern capital.[38]

The War of 1812 provoked an especially strong reaction in New England. Some states refused to the United States the use of their militias and discouraged capitalists from lending money to the nation to support the war effort. In December 1814, atop a wave of secessionist sentiment, delegates from Massachusetts, Connecticut, Rhode Island, two counties in New Hampshire, and one in Vermont met in what became known as the Hartford Convention. One month later, they produced a "Report" that detailed the conditions under which they would remain in the Union. These conditions included the adoption of seven constitutional amendments that, ironically for the Federalists, would have excluded slaves from computations for the apportionment of representation, required a supermajority for the admission of new states, and radically reduced national governmental authority. The Convention's report concluded with a thinly veiled threat to reconvene and proceed with secession if the proposed amendments were not adopted and the War not ended.[39]

Between 1819 and 1821, the admission of Missouri provoked another crisis of faith, both North and South.[40] So did the Mexican War, which invigorated debates over the disposition of the Western territories. These debates in turn provoked threats of secession by the South. And when it appeared in 1850 that California would be admitted as a free state, some Southern radicals, some bent on disunion, called a convention of Southern states for June 1850, though unionist sentiment held sway.

But the most persistent talk of secession, both before and after the Mexican War, came from the Garrisonian wing of the antislavery movement. As early as 1837 Wendell Phillips had anticipated Lincoln's "house divided" speech, warning that the North as well as the South was corrupted by slavery, that the two systems could not coexist, that unless slavery were eradicated "there must grow up a mighty slaveholding State to overshadow and mildew our free institutions." Disunion must follow from Southern supremacy.[41]

Secession was a natural corollary to Garrisonian nonresistance. But though Garrison had repudiated the Constitution in the earliest days of *The Liberator* as "the most bloody and heavendaring arrangement ever made for the continuance and protection of a system of the most atrocious villainy ever exhibited on earth," disunion did not become an official tenet of Garrisonianism until 1843. Then the Massachusetts Anti-Slavery Society adopted a resolution, championed by Garrison himself, "[t]hat the compact which exists between the North and the South is 'a covenant with death, and an agreement with hell'—involving both parties in atrocious criminality; and should be immediately annulled." At its annual meeting the following year, the American Anti-Slavery Society ratified resolutions encouraging abolitionists "to withdraw from this compact . . . and by a moral and peaceful revolution to effect its overthrow." The Society said the constitutional order was so corrupted by slavery that the only way for the North to avoid responsibility was to secede. "NO UNION WITH SLAVEHOLDERS!" became the Garrisonian battle cry. As the Mexican War wound down, Garrison intensified his disunionist position in the most impassioned terms.[42]

Garrisonian incitement to secession continued throughout the 1850s. Garrison himself publicly burned a copy of the Constitution in 1854 and proposed a National Disunion Convention in 1857.[43] In 1857 and 1858, there was even more talk of disunion among Garrisonians and among other Northerners outside the Garrisonian camp.[44]

Henry David Thoreau had his own peculiarly individualistic brand of secession. Drawing on transcendentalist moral philosophy rooted in Protestant Christianity, he raised the ultimate question of civic duty: What should be an individual citizen's obligation toward a government that participates in, perpetuates, and promotes the expansion of slavery? Thoreau supplied an answer in his essay on "Resistance to Government." The scope of a citizen's allegiance to government followed from his moral duty as a human being.

> It is not a man's duty, as a matter of course, to devote himself to the eradication of any, even the most enormous wrong; he may still properly have other concerns to engage him; but it is his duty, at least, to wash his hands of it, and, if he gives it no thought longer, not to give it practically his support. If I devote myself to other pursuits and contemplations, I must first see, at least, that I do not pursue them sitting upon another man's shoulders. I must get off him first, that he may pursue his contemplations too.[45]

Here he parted company with Garrison. For to argue, as the Garrisonians did, that Northern states should dissolve the Union was to ignore one's individual moral responsibility. "Why do they [the Garrisonians] not dissolve it themselves,—the union between themselves and the state . . . ? Do they not stand in the same relation to the state that the state does to the Union?" Abolitionists, he said, should not wait for a majority in Massachusetts to secede from the Union. "[A]ny man more right than his neighbors constitutes a majority of one already."[46]

Nor did antislavery secessionism stop at mere talk. The City of Lawrence, Kansas, declared itself independent from the state in

1857. And at least four localities attempted to secede from the South after the start of the Civil War, although they were motivated more by fidelity to the Union than by opposition to slavery. With the help of Union troops, the region we now call West Virginia seceded from Virginia in 1861.[47] In 1861, a unionist meeting in eastern Tennessee called for the secession of that region from the state of Tennessee. The call came to naught.[48] In 1862, citizens in Winston County, Alabama, met to consider declaring the county the "Free State of Winston" but never formally ratified the proposal.[49] And there is a legend that Jones County, Mississippi, seceded from the Confederacy in 1863, declaring itself the "Republic of Jones." In truth, from the beginning of Southern secessions, the people of Jones County displayed a mixture of unionist sentiment and populist opposition to virtually all forms of political authority. And after the War began, the county became a home to anti-Confederate guerrillas. But although it did not formally secede, had it done so, it would have concretely demonstrated a philosophical heritage of sustained lineage.[50]

V.

Political regimes form, they fall apart. Nations are born, they die or break apart. The sun also rises. The very fact of birth or of founding would seem to rebut any pretense of eternal existence. Why should we hold, then, that a union born as recently as 1774 or 1776 or 1781 or 1789 is perpetual? Never mind the arrogance or presumptuousness of the belief. What of its incompatibility with what we see in the world?[51] Impossibility is a substantial problem for any norm or theory that claims to be practical. Moreover, if an impossible norm is essentially a pretext for forcibly maintaining a regime, it threatens to violate Alexander Hamilton's constitutionalist principle of reflection and choice. It is also potentially incompatible with constitutionalism's concern with creating new political orders, for creating new orders requires dissolving old ones. But how?

Political regimes—even constitutional ones, including the United States—arise to some degree from illegality. (That is not to say that they must arise from coercion or violence, although almost all do to some extent.) Their illegality is one characteristic that distinguishes them, that makes them recognizable as distinct from their predecessors. Were they legal, they would continue to seem part of the existing regime. But as Robert Cover noticed, if the way of founding a new regime resides in illegality (from the standpoint of an existing regime), in acts incoherent or incompatible with the logic of the old regime, it supplies a potential way out of the new regime as well.[52] The illegality for getting in becomes the legality for getting out. That illegality has this capacity lies partly in its authority as precedent.

Precedent is not intrinsically binding. It has no intrinsic moral value, although it may make claims on morality because of its congruence with (or its eventual acceptance as part of) people's felt sense of what is right.[53] To the extent that people rely on that congruence or acceptance to justify a regime, the mode of founding becomes a measure of the regime's legitimacy. In a constitutionalist order, the founding is not simply a brute fact of the matter; it is an event that begs for explanation by any political order that tries to justify itself. This is one reason for the appearance and power of mythical stories of political foundings. The founding, or its story, becomes a means for self-justification. It becomes a part of the logic (or phenomenologic) of the new regime that estops it from denying the constitutional authority of the mode by which it was founded and by which it justifies itself.

In the American context, the need to justify the new constitutional regime fueled debates throughout the antebellum period over the authority of the Constitution, the status of states in relation to the nation, and the role of the people both as authorizers and as participants. The debates were important and persistent, not as academic exercises in the creation of myth and not merely because the character of the American myth was such that the content of the debates revealed (and disguised) what was at stake in justifying the creation and maintenance of the constituted order, but also because the chosen myth was perceived to bind the order itself even when the issue was the very survival of the order. More simply, myth helped describe a logic for exit.

To argue, though, that a myth of the order's creation supplied a logic for getting out only begins the inquiry, for from the beginning there were at least two such accounts competing for primacy.[54] They differed from each other over two fundamental elements of the story: Who was the creator, and how was the creation accomplished?

VI.

By our present lights, the story that might have seemed most mythically plausible was the familiar federalist account of the founding, which was perfected by John Marshall and extended by Lincoln. Marshall held that the Constitution was a document of special, national significance. Although he conceded that states possessed attributes of sovereignty, the Constitution authorized the nation to supersede the authority of states within certain domains of action. Consequently, the Constitution required a special mode of ratification. It required ratification by the people of the whole nation. Making a nation was an act of sovereignty superior (but not entirely oblivious) to the sovereignty of the people of a state.

Lincoln expanded and intensified the nationalist implication of Marshall's federalism in two ways. First, Lincoln pushed the creation of the nation backward, past the ratification of the Constitution to the adoption of the Declaration of Independence. This permitted him to make a second, crucial move concerning the sovereignty of states. This move resembled Andrew Jackson's claim in the crisis over nullification. Put briefly, in the beginning in North America, there were no states, only dependent colonies. At a critical moment in history, there arose from those colonies a unitary people—a Union—who threw off their bonds of dependence through a Declaration of Independence and forged new collective bonds of independence in the Revolution. The states did not exist until after the formation of the Union. The Constitution reinforced the antecedent bonds of the Union, and states continued to exercise authority under the Constitution, which was basically an instrument of national union.

As Lincoln put it: "The Union is older than any of the States; and in fact it created them as States." Thus "[o]ur States have neither more, nor less power, than that reserved to them, in the Union, by the Constitution—no one of them having been a State *out* of the Union." "Tested by this, no one of our States, except

Texas, ever was a sovereignty. And even Texas gave up the character on coming into the Union."[55]

The logical implication of either version of the federalist myth was that secession could not be accomplished by a mere state, for secession was not a matter of simple separation. It was instead a dissolution of the bonds of nationhood that could not be accomplished authoritatively except by the national people as a whole.[56] But how might the will of the national people be expressed? The institutional possibilities were numerous: the vote of at least a majority of the people in every state,[57] the approval of a majority of the people or of the delegates to conventions in nine-thirteenths of the states,[58] the vote of a majority in conventions or in legislatures of three-fourths of the states,[59] the vote of majorities in both houses of Congress,[60] or most simply the vote of a majority of people in the nation regardless of residence.[61]

As an added protection against precipitous action, one might convert majoritarian decisions in any of the preceding modes into supermajoritarian decisions. Some combination of modes might also have been conceivable. For example, if the *admission* of states to the Union required concurrent ratification of the national legislature and of some representative body of the states to be admitted, perhaps the *withdrawal* of states required some similar expression of concurrent majorities (or supermajorities). Under the most stringent version of concurrent majorities, a majority in Congress would have had to combine with a representative majority in *all* of the states, since all were conceivably affected by any state's withdrawal.

Some version of the federalist myth might well be intuitively appealing to many of us today. But we should remember this about the manner in which myth binds: myths rely for their authority (and therefore their power) on the extent to which they comport with perceived reality, which in turn relies partly on the reality that people *want* to see or believe in. For a variety of reasons, much of the country during the period preceding the Civil War was either unprepared to believe in the federalist myth of the popular founding or unwilling to commit to its nationalist implications.

Despite the nationalist dimensions of proslavery constitutional doctrine after *Dred Scott*, many Southerners and others sympathetic to slavery would have been suspicious of extending nationalist constitutionalism to other arenas. Some may have suspected that a national power strong enough to protect slavery would have also been strong enough to destroy it. For other proslavers, quite happy to indulge in nationalism where slavery was concerned, the impulse for a weak central government persisted for reasons including an inherited Jeffersonian constitutional tradition, a continuing antagonism to Northern capital and its own consistent demand for the assistance of a strong national government, and an intensifying regional identity. The growth of Southern identity cut two ways, depending on context. From within the constitutional union, it supported a distinctly localist constitutionalism, consistent with a tradition traceable to Calhoun and other Southerners; but from an external perspective—external to the Constitution, though internal to the Southern region—it became the foundation for an emergent "Southern nationalism."

Abolitionists and other opponents of slavery also were wary of the implications of nationalism, but for different reasons. First, Marshall's antiseptic myth of the popular founding was largely incompatible with the Garrisonians' pessimistic account of the Constitution as "a covenant with death." Second, and related to the first, lawyers, judges, and even members of Congress who helped enact fugitive slave laws had converted—antislavery constitutionalists would have said "perverted"—nationalism into a tool of "the slave interest." Third, and a consequence of the first two points, opponents of slavery had their own localist constitutional tradition. They wanted a vehicle for mitigating the harsh effects of Taney's nationalist constitutionalism on the issue of slavery, when they did not want a way out of the Union entirely.

Other people, neither proponents nor opponents of slavery, might also have understandably resisted the myth of the popular founding and its implications. As if to emphasize the point, people regularly treated the term used to denominate the nation— the United States—as if it were plural rather than singular.[62] Hence "We the People of the United States" were not necessarily the people of a single union or nascent nation. They were the people of *states*, then united, but perhaps not always so. And some, including Lincoln, referred to the United States as a "confederacy."[63] Secessionism to one side, the United States was not yet a nation, as late as 1861.[64]

These considerations lent force to the antifederalist story that the founding was an act of sovereign states, or, if popular, an act of the *people* of those states. If the Union had been continuous over time, so this account went, it was not the Union that Lincoln invoked as a device for preventing secession. It was something more closely akin to a Swiss-style confederation of states. And if states (or the people of states) could get into the Union, they could get out as well. But how?

VII.

There were two possible constitutional ways out, both riding atop the antifederalist account of the constitutional founding. The first and most directly constitutional mode of exit was for a convention in each state to adopt an ordinance of secession, just as state conventions over the years had ratified the Constitution as a condition of the admission of states to the Union. South Carolina had employed a convention for proposing its Ordinance of Nullification thirty years earlier, as it had in an abortive attempt to secede in 1852. The state activated the device once more to adopt, on December 20, 1860, its "Ordinance of Secession" "dissolv[ing] the Union between the State of South Carolina and other States united with her under the compact entitled 'The Constitution of the United States of America.'"[65]

As this self-description made clear, South Carolina's account of the origins of constitutional Union rejected any notion that the Constitution was a covenant of a national people. The Constitution was instead a compact, resembling a treaty, among the states and could be rescinded for cause on the motion of one of the states. This account assumed a great deal concerning conventional legal distinctions between a compact or contract (which could be dissolved on the motion of one party in the event of a breach by another) and a national constitution or covenant (which, presumably, could not so easily be dissolved).

In rapid succession during the first two months of 1861, Mississippi, Florida, Alabama, Georgia, Louisiana, and Texas followed

South Carolina's lead. Conventions in each state adopted ordinances of secession dissolving ties between the state and the Union. Eventually, after hostilities erupted, Arkansas, North Carolina, and Virginia followed suit, largely out of a sense of loyalty to the region. Most of the ordinances also included provisions specifically rescinding or repealing prior ratifications of the Constitution and its amendments as well as declarations that the state "resumed" the exercise of what Virginia called "all the rights of sovereignity which belong and appertain to a free and independent State." Some absolved their citizens and public officials of responsibility to abide by their oaths or allegiances to the Constitution of the United States. In an apparent but notoriously vague reference to constitutional rights to own slaves, Mississippi, Louisiana, and Arkansas cautiously ensured that rights acquired and vested under the U.S. Constitution would continue in force despite the repeal of the Constitution within the states' territories. The ordinances of Texas and Virginia were ratified by popular votes. In Texas's case, the referendum was an attempt to cure a defect in the selection of the convention. In Virginia's, it was an expression of the location of sovereign authority.

Within a few days after adopting its ordinance, South Carolina's convention approved a Declaration of Causes justifying the state's secession from the Union. The Declaration provided a list of abuses that were unified by twin themes. First, the states of the North had violated the "compact between the States," thus justifying its rescision. Almost every example of the breach of the compact pertained to slavery. Second, the national government, which was now in the hands of a political party beholden solely to the Northern states, had "become[] destructive of the ends for which it was instituted," thus justifying its "abolition" within the territory of South Carolina and its replacement with a government compatible with principles of self-government. So the two bases for of Southern insecurity, previously distinct, were now joined: self-government (the battle for which on the national level had been virtually lost in the 1830s with the demise of nullification as a plausible constitutional theory) and the protection of slavery (the battle for which seemed about to be lost on the heels of Lincoln's election). Had it been ratified, the proposed Corwin Amendment—which purported to provide perpetual constitutional protection for slavery—might have partially assuaged fears concerning the latter; but it would not have addressed worries about the loss of self-government, unless slavery had been the sole constitutive characteristic of Southern political identity.[66]

Four of the nine other states that resorted to conventions as vehicles for seceding also recited reasons for their separation. But unlike South Carolina's Declaration, the reasons these other states offered were brief, underdeveloped, and sometimes little more than afterthoughts. Two of the four states, Louisiana and Arkansas, did not directly mention threats to slavery as a justification for secession. Self-government and solidarity with the rest of the region were the most prominent themes, even of the two states, Texas and Alabama, that did recite threats to "property" or to "domestic institutions."

The five other states that seceded by convention did not give any reasons for their action. Perhaps some things, including slavery, had simply ceased to need saying. But why would that have been so? Part of the answer may lie in the character of the device by which secession was accomplished. South Carolina's ambivalent approach to secession—adopting first an ordinance that recited no reasons and then a declaration listing causes—indicated the confusion that some felt over the character of the act. The form of the Declaration of Causes, even some of its language, looked back to the Declaration of Independence, ostensibly an act of *revolution*. Without exception, however, the ordinances of secession appeared in the form of *legal* enactments. They were ratified by the same constitutional, now legal, process defined in the basic law.

Perhaps the "real" impulse for secession was the protection of slavery. Or perhaps it was nothing more than a selfish and petty preoccupation with national political processes: if we cannot nullify your laws, we shall nullify your Constitution. It was the strategy of one who was either dissatisfied with substantive outcomes, which in the Southern case would have been unwarranted, or unwilling to continue to play by basic rules that he perceived to systematically disadvantage him, which had been Calhoun's claim all along. Even so, it was part of a search for a "constitutional" way out of the Constitution. Some might argue that if that were the character of the act, constitutional *reasons* were required. But it may be the peculiar characteristic of secession as a constitutional device that it needs no substantive justification. It is justified constitutionally if it is compatible with the process by which the Constitution was ratified. If it is the constitutionally defined sovereign act of a sovereign, it is justified by that fact. It needs no further justification.[67]

VIII.

The second way out relied on a different account of the founding. It combined Lincoln's claim that the Union antedated the Constitution with an antifederalist account of the character of that Union. In February 1861, the legislature of Tennessee submitted a proposition to the citizens of the state that would have authorized calling a convention to decide whether Tennessee should secede from the Union. The proposition lost by a vote of 69,675 (55 percent) to 57,798 (45 percent), a fairly substantial margin. The unionists had held the day. But after South Carolinians fired on federal troops at Fort Sumter in April, Lincoln called up a militia of seventy-five thousand troops and declared his commitment to use force to suppress the "combinations" of the states of the Deep South. In Tennessee, unionist moderation succumbed to regional solidarity. In special session in May 1861, Tennessee's legislature ratified a "league" with the Confederacy—whose Congress had approved a new constitution on March 11 and submitted it to the seceded states for their ratification—and adopted a "Declaration of Independence" by which it "dissolv[ed] the Federal relations between the State of Tennessee and the United States of America."[68]

The legislature adopted its Declaration rather than an ordinance of secession out of a quixotic desire to avoid being drawn into debates over "the abstract doctrine of secession." Instead, it chose simply to assert its "right as a free and independent people to alter, reform, or abolish our form of Government in such manner as we think proper." The notion clearly drew part of its force from its association with Thomas Jefferson's Declaration of Independence eighty-five years before. If that association made it appear that Tennessee's Declaration, like South Carolina's Declaration of Causes, was revolutionary instead of constitutional, the appearance rested partly on assumptions about the character of the American Revolution itself. It is tempting to imbibe the myth that the Revolution was part of a new creation, that its aims and principles were universalist innovations made possible because the political world was being reinvented on the North American continent.

In important (perhaps crucial) ways, however, the American Revolution was not so radical at all. For Locke's principles for justifying revolution, which were an unmistakable part of Jefferson's Declaration of Independence, were actually quite conservative. They demanded that acts of resistance would occur not for "every little mismanagement of public affairs" but only after "a long train of abuses."[69] And if Locke's *Second Treatise* was an anticipatory justification for the Glorious Revolution, that event was hardly revolutionary and was "glorious" only in that it efficiently replaced one monarchical house with another without the spilling of blood.

Second, notwithstanding Jefferson's maxim prohibiting revolution for "light and transient causes," it is striking just how insubstantial some of the causes for the Revolution now seem and how conservatively most of the revolutionaries framed their demands. The claims of the colonists were primarily claims about self-government and the proper nature of representation under the British Constitution. They were demands that the colonists be accorded the rights of British subjects.[70] The Revolution was less a revolution than a constitutionally justified secession that could not be accomplished without the assistance of arms. Edmund Burke may have been right: the colonists in separating were being truer to principles of the British Constitution than were the British themselves.[71] In drawing on that aspect of the American Revolution, Tennessee's Declaration of Independence may have been similarly true to principles of the Constitution and of constitutionalism.

Nevertheless, there was one aspect of Tennessee's Declaration that distinguished it from Jefferson's and emphasized its constitutional character. Like most of the ordinances of secession, Tennessee's Declaration offered no reasons to the world, candid or otherwise. It was not a justification to (or from the perspective of) the outside. It was a simple statement, as if for consumption from the inside. It contained no argument. It opened with a terse statement of the source of its authority ("We, the people of the State of Tennessee"); it "abrogated and annulled" all prior "laws and ordinances by which the State of Tennessee became a member of the Federal Union of the United States of America"; and it "resume[d] all the rights, functions, and powers which . . . were conveyed to the Government of the United States." It did not say so, but it might have traced its constitutional pedigree to the principle textually embodied in the Constitution's Tenth Amendment.[72] It was, or purported to be, an authoritative statement of the political rights of the people and state of Tennessee. As confirmation of its self-stated authority, the citizens of Tennessee ratified it in a popular referendum by a margin of 104,913 (69 percent) to 47,238 (31 percent). Like the ordinances, it required no further justification.[73]

These secessions were constitutional not simply because of their method, by which an ostensible sovereign was acting in a manner consistent with constitutional precedent (consistent, that is, with the logic of the existing order). Nor were they constitutional simply because of their subject matter, which pertained to the deconstitution and reconstitution of a people. They were also constitutional in their aims. Many in the South argued that their purpose in seceding was either to recapture or to secure rights that they thought had been lost or were in jeopardy under the Constitution of the United States, just as one aim of the Revolution had been to secure for Americans the rights of British subjects. Secession was their way of recovering *their* constitution.

In their ordinances of secession, the conventions of Alabama and Mississippi authorized their states to become part of a new "Federal Union," formed "upon the principles of the Constitution of the United States."[74] Perhaps not surprisingly, the Constitution of the Confederacy was almost identical to the Constitution of the United States, except for a couple of items that the Confederate framers would not permit to go without saying. First, the sovereign authority for the Confederate Constitution was expressly acknowledged to derive from "the people of the Confederate States, *each State acting in its sovereign and independent character*"[75] (italics added). Second, "the institution of negro slavery" was guaranteed national constitutional protection without euphemistic evasion.[76] Third, and ironically, the Confederate Constitution took as its explicit purpose "to form a permanent government."[77]

IX.

There would seem no stronger example of the failure of a constitution than that one or more ostensibly constituent parts of the regime that it formed and regulated would separate from the whole by dissolving the political ties that once bound it. Even if carried out peacefully, such a separation clearly evinces a failure of the constitutional order. But the failure of the order is not necessarily a failure of the Constitution or of constitutionalism (the principles that undergird the constitutional enterprise). On the contrary, secession may well signal the *success* of constitutionalism and of the Constitution itself. It does so if, drawing on Alexander Hamilton's maxim in *Federalist*, No. 1, it permits the *de* constitution of politics through "reflection and choice" rather than through "accident and force."

To press the point to conclusion, let me return to the five characteristics that make the Southern secessions such hard cases, at least for one who would defend the constitutionality of secession. The first problem is that the text of the Constitution did not explicitly authorize separation. As I have indicated, however, the "right" to secede does not depend upon text for its authority. Text may supply evidence of such a right, but it is not a prerequisite.[78] In some respects this claim is parallel to the notion that certain rights and principles may be binding despite their absence from explicit constitutional text.[79] But secession can cut more deeply than some such rights or principles because its justification arises directly from the authority of a constitution itself. This authority is pretextual, not in the sense that it is insincere (though it might be), but because it is theoretically (perhaps temporally) prior to the constitution. I have tried to show in this essay how that logic works generally and how it worked specifically in the American case.

Second, if my account is apt, secession is permissible if the order is constitutionalist in the sense of its being an autochthonous principled order, if it is democratic with respect to political process, or if it is liberal in respecting particular rights of individuals.[80] Similarly, secession is permissible even if the regime sees itself as the last best hope on earth for limited self-government or imagines itself to be an expression of divine will or a manifestation of moral righteousness.

We might consider, for example, other self-governing (though not necessarily constitutionalist) institutions that have been able to persist and flourish despite the success of secessionist movements. The Christian schism from Judaism did not spell the end of the latter, though it is true that many Christians through the ages have sought to eradicate Jews. Nor did the Protestant Reformation destroy Roman Catholicism. Nor, to press the point homeward, did the eighteenth-century American secession incite the demise of Great Britain. The point, however, is not whether constitutionalism (whether democratic, liberal, or other) is desirable but whether any particular order is entitled to a presumption of permanence strictly because it happens to be constitutionalist (whether democratic, liberal, or other). It is not. Constitutionalist orders are entitled to defend themselves against certain sorts of challenges—violent, for example, or lacking authority—to their existence. But they are required to respect other challenges that are consistent with constitutionalist process and with the authority on which the orders themselves rest.

The third characteristic that makes the Southern secessions hard cases is that they were unilateral. As I have argued, however, unilateral secession is permissible on at least one understanding of the authority of the Constitution of the United States. That understanding was dominant in the country in the nineteenth century. This claim of dominance does not rest on a philosophical commitment to antifederalism; for purposes of this study, I am agnostic as between the federalist and antifederalist accounts of the Constitution's authority. The claim rests instead on a reading of nineteenth-century American political culture, a culture in which two myths, each of which was logically possible, vied with each other for primacy. On the antifederalist account, the Constitution's authority derived from a compact among antecedent sovereigns whose sovereignty was not dissolved (though it was limited in certain domains) by ratification of the Constitution; consequently, those sovereign entities could withdraw from the compact on their own motion. Again, this was not the only theory in play; but, on my reading, it was the dominant one; and it was the one that the regime itself relied upon generally (though, history being messy, there were exceptions to this reliance). This, to paraphrase Robert Post, does shatter a collective national agency, an agency established for important purposes. But the dominant understanding of the character and authority of the constitutional founding leads me to conclude that the collective national agency, whose authority derived from that founding, was constitutionally obliged to accede to these unilateral secessions, precisely because they were consistent with the agency's own authority.

The fourth difficulty the secessions present is that some of them were perpetrated without the decency of reasons. I confess admiration for the giving of reasons generally and worry about consequences of not doing so. I also confess, however, that as long as the authority of an order is framed in terms of sovereignty, as it usefully has been in the American case, I see no logical requirement for giving reasons *when the sovereign speaks as sovereign*. This is the authority of God with respect to the creation of the cosmos; it is also the authority of the "mortal God" with respect to the constitution of politics. There may be, lurking in shadows that point toward the future, a brave new world in which the people who are governed are not—theoretically or practically—the sovereign authors of their government, but I am not confident that it is a constitutionalist world.

The final difficulty is the most uncomfortable one. It is that the secessions of the Southern states aimed at protecting slavery, which is wrong by our lights. That fact makes the Southern secession appear not only perverse but morally bankrupt. There are several things to say about this. The first is that slavery is inconsistent with constitutionalism. It is so, not because slavery denies human dignity nor because it is incompatible with the metaphysic that posits a property in one's person and labor, but because it denies slaves the means to attach to the constitution that presumes to bind them. It denies them these means as a political matter, as a matter of material economy, and as a psychological matter.

Second, however, the Constitution and constitutional order of the United States violated this principle of constitutionalism. They did so through explicit but euphemistic support in the constitutional text, through policies of the nation and states, and through decisions of the Supreme Court of the United States. If the Southern secessions were impermissible because they aimed to perpetuate slavery, so too was the colonial secession from Britain, and so was the Constitution itself.

Third, until the end of the Civil War, Abraham Lincoln's constitutionalism reinforced this violation. He was, of course, no abolitionist, despite Southern paranoia on the point. The thrust of his position on the territories was that they might elect to protect slavery after they were admitted to the Union.[81] He plainly supported the Corwin Amendment—proposed by Congress and ratified by three states that would soon fight on the side of the Union—which would have perpetually prohibited Congress from interfering with slavery. In his First Inaugural Address, Lincoln said the proposed amendment was already "implied constitutional law" but that he had "no objection to its being made express, and irrevocable."[82] And his Emancipation Proclamation, if legal, freed slaves everywhere in North America except in the Union.[83] Lincoln, like most white Northerners of his time, loved the Union more than constitutionalism.

Thus, but for the Civil War, slavery likely would have persisted, protected in the South without or within the Union, although many Southerners feared things would be otherwise. Slavery might not have survived in perpetuity, as its proponents imagined in 1860–61. It might have lasted "only" one hundred years, which Lincoln said he was willing to tolerate.[84] But it would have persisted had secession never been dreamed or attempted.

That secession in the United States was ultimately used to attempt to support and perpetuate a system of slave labor, however, was not predestined. It was historically contingent on a number of factors, including patterns of immigration and settlement, the remarkable success of Northern capital, and political and cultural developments both planned and unexpected. There were times in the country's history that the movement for secession was every bit as strongly and conscientiously pursued in New England as it was in the South.[85] Had New England seceded to form a slaveless commercial republic, or had the Garrisonians persuaded the North and West to secede and establish a new republic of free citizens, we might well now view secession as an institution of liberty and righteousness. In American constitutional thought, it might have become a sword against tyranny and oppression, as John Brown certainly intended his foray at Harper's Ferry.

We should frankly acknowledge, however, that constitutions can help form us without making us good (or liberal). Some constitutions might well help make people better, even good, and perhaps not solely by accident or force. But they do not *have* to do so. Similarly, as a constitutional institution, secession might make a people better, but there is no guarantee. Given people's temptations to violence and destruction, not to mention their propensity for short-sightedness and miscalculation, the constitutional possibility of secession may be valuable if it makes the disintegration of politics somewhat safer for human beings. Some have argued that one aim of liberalism is to lower the stakes of politics in order to make it safer for human habitation. Secession may serve a similar function in reverse. Instead of lowering the stakes of politics and political and constitutional debate per se, the constitutional possibility of secession might ironically help to raise them. It might do so because it can lower the stakes of political disintegration, so that nations break apart without disaster. But if the possibility of secession does not raise the stakes of politics, even if it does debase them, that does not make it any less constitutional.[86]

NOTES

1. Quotations come from Professor Post's comments at the annual meeting of the American Society for Political and Legal Philosophy, January 3, 2001, San Francisco. In general terms, his position derives from the confluence of democracy and community as constitutional domains. See Robert C. Post, *Constitutional Domains: Democracy, Community, Management* (Cambridge, Mass.: Harvard University Press, 1995), 3–10. More

specifically, see Post, "Democratic Constitutionalism and Cultural Heterogeneity," *Australian Journal of Legal Philosophy* 25 (2000): 185.

2. In American constitutional thought, James Madison noted the virtues of social diversity. See, for example, Madison, *The Federalist*, No. 10 (1787). See also Walt Whitman's paean to disharmony: "Do I contradict myself? / Very well then I contradict myself." Whitman, *Song of Myself* (1858). On the value of cross-cutting cleavages, see E. E. Schattschneider, *The Semi-Sovereign People: A Realist's View of Democracy in America* (New York: Holt, Rinehart and Winston, 1960).

3. Cass Sunstein, "Constitutionalism and Secession," *University of Chicago Law Review* 58 (1991): 633.

4. *Texas v. White*, 74 U.S. 700 (1869). This decision was an attempt to harmonize Lincoln's theory of the Union with the radical Congress's policy of Reconstruction. Because the two were irreconcilable, however, the opinion is fundamentally incoherent and—putting aside questions about the bindingness of judicial pronouncements of constitutional principles—of little value.

5. Akhil Amar, "Of Sovereignty and Federalism," *Yale Law Journal* 96 (1987): 1455–62. For reasons set out more fully below, while Amar's claim is constitutionally defensible, it is in important respects a twentieth-century imposition on nineteenth-century constitutional thought.

6. See Mark E. Brandon, *Free in the World: American Slavery and Constitutional Failure* (Princeton, N.J.: Princeton University Press, 1998), 10–11.

7. Alexander Hamilton, *The Federalist*, No. 1 (1787).

8. Akhil Amar, "Some New World Lessons for the Old World," *University of Chicago Law Review* 58 (1991): 486.

9. Amar seems to treat Lincoln's observations in his First Inaugural Address as dispositive of the geopolitical feasibility of the secession of the Southern states. Ibid., 490–91. While such a conclusion is sustainable only by supplying substantially more evidence and argument than Amar or Lincoln supplies, it is beyond my purpose to address the issue in greater detail here.

10. Allen Buchanan, *Secession: The Morality of Political Divorce from Fort Sumter to Lithuania and Quebec* (Boulder, Colo.: Westview Press, 1991).

11. See S. James Anaya, "Self-Determination as a Collective Human Right under Contemporary International Law," and Diane F. Orentlicher, "International Responses to Separatist Claims," both presented at the annual meeting of the American Society for Political and Legal Philosophy, January 3, 2001, San Francisco. See also Jonathan I. Charney and J. R. V. Prescott, "Resolving Cross-Strait Relations between China and Taiwan," *American Journal of International Law* 94 (2000): 453. The challenge for international law, as I see it, is fourfold: (1) it lacks an

established mechanism for generating authoritative norms; (2) it is conflicted over where sovereignty resides (i.e., whether in people or in the state); (3) it is conflicted over the criteria for establishing sovereignty (i.e., whether sovereignty is a function of power or of authority); and (4) it lacks an adequate institutional means for enforcing norms. These deficiencies may be remediable at some future time; for now, however, they weaken international law's claims to effective authority.

12. James M. Buchanan, "Europe's Constitutional Opportunity," in *Europe's Constitutional Future,* ed. Graham Mather (London: Institute for Economic Affairs, 1990), 4–7.

13. Ibid., 7–9. To confirm the essentially economic foundation for Buchanan's position, see James M. Buchanan and Roger L. Faith, "Secession and the Limits of Taxation: Toward a Theory of Internal Exit," *American Economic Review* 77 (1987): 1023.

14. Charles Howard McIlwain, *Constitutionalism: Ancient and Modern* (Ithaca, N.Y.: Cornell University Press, 1947), 67–92.

15. A word of caution: in much of the theoretical and comparative literature on secession, *national* refers to separatist movements, which are sometimes impelled by ethnic, national identities against an established "state." To flirt with confusion, I shall follow here American constitutional usage, in which *national* connotes interests, values, or government of the United States; its antonym refers to local or sectional interests or values, which are often embodied, institutionally, in "states."

16. Jesse T. Carpenter, *The South as a Conscious Minority, 1789–1861* (1930; reprint, Columbia: University of South Carolina Press, 1990), esp. 181–84, 190–94.

17. David Hume, "Of the Original Contract" (1748), Essay 12, in *Social Contract: Essays by Locke, Hume, and Rousseau,* ed. Ernest Barker (Westport, Conn.: Greenwood Press, 1948), 155–56.

18. As to the latter, see Chief Justice Warren's plurality opinion in *Trop v. Dulles,* 356 U.S. 86 (1958), 101–3.

19. Kenneth Stampp, "The Concept of a Perpetual Union," *Journal of American History* 65 (1978): 28–29.

20. Ibid.

21. Cited in ibid., 30–31.

22. Andrew Jackson, "Proclamation by Andrew Jackson, President" (December 10, 1832), in *A Compilation of the Messages and Papers of the Presidents, 1789–1897,* vol. 2, ed. James D. Richardson (New York: Bureau of National Literature, 1896), 640–56.

23. Arthur Bestor, "State Sovereignty and Slavery: A Reinterpretation of Proslavery Constitutional Doctrine," *Journal of the Illinois State Historical Society* 54 (1961): 119; Stampp, "The Concept."

24. The rejections, for the most part, were justified. Although constitutionalism may permit nullification or concurrent majorities, it does not require them. Moreover, with limited exceptions, neither institution is supported by the text of the Constitution or the logic of the American order. (Among the exceptions are the amending process of Article V, the election of the president in Article II and the Twelfth Amendment, and the institution of judicial review.)

25. Madison and Livingston had argued almost thirty years earlier that states were obliged to respect decisions of the United States Supreme Court, while the Southern nullifiers were attacking the Court. By 1860, ironically, the South was fully committed to upholding *Dred Scott* while Northern abolitionists were talking of flouting the decision.

26. This belief was not necessarily inconsistent with the fear that appeasement by the nation on the question of slavery would derail secession. For example, secessionists might have worried that the motives for appeasement were weak, insincere, or short-lived, or that parchment guarantees would henceforth be so weak that as soon as the movement for secession was stopped, pressures on Southern institutions would revive.

27. Abraham Lincoln, "First Inaugural Address—Final Text," in Abraham Lincoln, *The Collected Works of Abraham Lincoln*, vol. 4, ed. Roy P. Basler (New Brunswick, N.J.: Rutgers University Press, 1953), 264.

28. Abraham Lincoln, "Message to Congress in Special Session" (July 4, 1861), in Lincoln, *Collected Works*, vol. 4, 421. Lincoln offered two additional claims in his "Message to Congress." The first was an invocation of the slippery slope: if one state can secede, then all might secede; where will it end and who will pay the bills? (436). The second raised the improbable specter of the destruction of republican government: the national government is obliged to guarantee to the states a republican form of government; however, if the states secede, they might adopt nonrepublican institutions at some time in the future; therefore, the nation is obliged to prevent the possibility (440). Because these claims are exceedingly weak, I shall not answer them in this essay.

29. Lincoln, "First Inaugural Address," 264–65.

30. Ibid., 264–65.

31. Ibid., 270, 271.

32. Lincoln, "Message to Congress," 439.

33. Ibid., 426.

34. Lincoln, "First Inaugural Address," 265–67. At one point in his final text, he inserted the word *revolutionary* in place of *treasonable,* which he had used in his first draft (cf. 253 and 265). It is not entirely clear whether he considered secession carried out without violence to be revo-

lutionary. There are intimations in his First Inaugural that he did and that the secession of the states of the Deep South was simply unjustified revolution (267). He reiterated these intimations in Lincoln, "Message to Congress," 432–34.

35. Compare the Federal Republic of Germany's Basic Law, which explicitly provided for its own death upon reunification but did not die, with the Articles of Confederation of the United States, which proclaimed a "perpetual" Union but did die.

36. See the helpful discussion on some of these questions in Stampp, "The Concept," 8–9. Stampp notes that some of the Constitution's framers, attempting to avoid responsibility for dissolving the Union, argued that the Union had already been "destroyed by the failure of certain states to respect their obligations under the Articles of Confederation."

37. Lincoln, "Message to Congress," 429–30; Frederick Douglass, "Comments on Gerrit Smith's Address" (March 30, 1849), in *The Life and Writings of Frederick Douglass*, ed. Philip S. Foner (New York: International Publishers, 1950), 374–79. Lincoln's nationalist hierarchy has been repeated by others over the years. See, for example, Herbert D. Croly, *The Promise of American Life* (New York: Macmillan, 1909), 75, 77. Croly's devotion to nation stemmed partly from what he considered the intrinsic value of the Union, partly from his contention that devotion to the Union was also devotion to another good—democracy. Both notions, for different reasons, are problematic. See also Nevins's claim that whatever else the Civil War might have accomplished, it was justified because it saved the Union. Willard L. King and Allan Nevins, "The Constitution and Declaration of Independence as Issues in the Lincoln-Douglas Debates," *Journal of the Illinois State Historical Society* 52 (1959): 7. But see David Donald, "Died of Democracy," in *Why the North Won the Civil War,* ed. David Donald (Baton Rouge: Louisiana State University Press, 1960), 79.

38. William M. Wiecek, *The Sources of Antislavery Constitutionalism in America, 1760–1848* (Ithaca, N.Y.: Cornell University Press, 1977), 107–8; Stampp, "The Concept," 23–25.

39. "Report of the Hartford Convention" (1815), in *American History Leaflets, Colonial and Constitutional,* ed. Albert Bushnell Hart and Edward Channing (1906), no. 35, 1–2, 25–27.

40. Stampp, "The Concept," 25–26.

41. Wendell Phillips, "The Right of Petition," speech at Quarterly Meeting of the Massachusetts Anti-Slavery Society (March 28, 1837), in Wendell Phillips, *Speeches, Lectures and Letters* (Boston: Lothrop, Lee and Shepard, 1891), 4–5.

42. Walter M. Merrill, *Against Wind and Tide: A Biography of William Lloyd Garrison* (Cambridge, Mass.: Harvard University Press, 1963), 204–14. See also Truman Nelson, ed., *Documents of Upheaval: Selections from William Lloyd Garrison's "The Liberator," 1831–1865* (New York: Hill and Wong, 1966), 202–7; Robert M. Cover, *Justice Accused: Antislavery and the Judicial Process* (New Haven, Conn.: Yale University Press, 1975), 170; Louis Filler, *The Crusade against Slavery, 1830–1860* (New York: Harper and Brothers, 1960), 178; David M. Potter, *The Impending Crisis, 1848–1861* (New York: Harper and Row, 1976), 48.

43. See Filler, *Crusade against Slavery,* 205–6, 216.

44. Ibid., 258–59, 303. Filler's assertion that by 1857 disunion was a "popular northern view" is overstated but rightly emphasizes that secessionism was not simply a Southern phenomenon.

45. Henry David Thoreau, "Civil Disobedience" (1849), in *Walden and Other Writings by Henry David Thoreau,* ed. Brooks Atkinson (New York: Random House, 1950), 642.

46. Ibid., 643, 645, 651.

47. James M. McPherson, *Battle Cry of Freedom: The Civil War Era* (New York: Oxford University Press, 1988), 297–99.

48. Eric Foner, *Reconstruction: America's Unfinished Revolution, 1863–1877* (New York: Harper and Row, 1988), 13.

49. Samuel A. Rumore, "Building Alabama's Courthouses: Winston County," *Alabama Lawyer,* November 1989, 320.

50. Richard Aubrey McLemore, ed., *A History of Mississippi,* vol. 1 (Hattiesburg: University and College Press of Mississippi, 1973), 518–25; Rudy H. Leverett, *Legend of the Free State of Jones* (Jackson: University Press of Mississippi, 1984).

51. Rousseau put it this way: "If we would set up a long-lived form of government, let us not even dream of making it eternal. If we are to succeed, we must not attempt the impossible, or flatter ourselves that we are endowing the work of man with a stability of which human conditions do not permit." Jean-Jacques Rousseau, *Social Contract,* book 3, chap. 11.

52. Robert M. Cover, "Foreword: NOMOS and Narrative," *Harvard Law Review* 97 (1983): 15–16. Although Cover refers to secession as "revolutionary" (23–24), secession sometimes also derives from the same "jurisgenerative" properties that he associates with acts of interpretation (albeit extrainstitutional acts). At the very least, the impulse to secession derives from the same impulse that produces jurisgenerative interpretations.

53. In this context, *precedent* might refer either to the process of relying on previously established outcomes or to the substantive outcomes themselves. Or it might refer to some combination of the two.

54. A myth is in one sense partly a fiction or an illusion. Nevertheless, it is a story that people take to be true about themselves or their origins. In this latter sense, myth becomes, in Mircea Eliade's words, an "exemplary model." See Wendell C. Beane and William G. Doty, eds., *Myths, Rites, Symbols: A Mircea Eliade Reader,* vol. 1 (New York: Harper and Row, 1975), 2–3. It becomes a story that, while perhaps not literally true, is to be made true in people's actions, including people's attempts to (re-)create themselves.

55. Lincoln, "Message to Congress," 433–35.

56. *Cohens v. Virginia,* 19 U.S. (6 Wheat.) 264 (1821), 413–14.

57. This was consistent with Lincoln's conclusion that Article VII required unanimity.

58. This mode would have been consistent with Article VII.

59. This mode would have been consistent with the procedures set out in Article V.

60. Hortensius (1814), in Stampp, "The Concept," 24.

61. No one suggested this as a mode for authorizing secession, and it would have had little foundation in the constitutional text.

62. Concededly, such usage could simply be a holdover from British usage or could be explained in other ways. It is possible, after all, for language to explain too much. But the usage is suggestive. See James M. McPherson, *Abraham Lincoln and the Second American Revolution* (New York: Oxford University Press, 1990), viii.

63. Abraham Lincoln, "Reply to the Illinois Delegation" (March 5, 1861), in Lincoln, *Collected Works,* vol. 4, 275.

64. McPherson, *Abraham Lincoln,* viii.

65. "An Ordinance to dissolve the Union between the State of South Carolina and other States united with her under the compact entitled 'The Constitution of the United States of America,'" in Albert Bushnell Hart and Edward Channing, eds., *Ordinances of Secession and Other Documents, 1860–1861,* American History Leaflets, no. 12 (New York: A. Lovell, 1897), 3.

66. On the Corwin Amendment, see Mark E. Brandon, "The 'Original' Thirteenth Amendment and the Limits to Formal Constitutional Change," in *Responding to Imperfection: The Theory and Practice of Constitutional Amendment,* ed. Sanford Levinson (Princeton, N.J.: Princeton University Press, 1995).

67. See Exodus 3:13–14: Then Moses said to God, "If I come to the people of Israel and say to them, 'The God of your fathers has sent me to you,' and they ask me, 'What is his name?' What shall I say to them?" God said to Moses, "I AM WHO I AM." And he said, "Say this to the people of Israel, 'I AM has sent me to you.'"

312 MARK E. BRANDON

68. Hart and Channing, *Ordinances of Secession*, 1–2, 16, 19; Ralph A. Wooster, *The Secession Conventions of the South* (Princeton, N.J.: Princeton University Press, 1962), 179–80.

69. John Locke, *Second Treatise of Government*, ed. C. B. Macpherson (1690; reprint, Indianapolis: Hackett, 1980), sec. 225.

70. Gordon S. Wood, *The Creation of the American Republic, 1776–1787* (Chapel Hill: University of North Carolina Press, 1969), 3–17.

71. Edmund Burke, "Speech for Conciliation with the Colonies" (March 22, 1775), in *Burke's Speech on Conciliation with America*, ed. Hammond Lamont (1897), 19–20. David A. J. Richards argues that the Revolution was basically a dispute over interpretation of the English "constitution." See his *Foundations of American Constitutionalism* (New York: Oxford University Press, 1989).

72. Louisiana's declaration was explicit on this point.

73. Hart and Channing, *Ordinances of Secession*; Wooster, *Secession Conventions*, 188.

74. Compare Marshall L. DeRosa's account of the "American" origins of the Confederate Constitution. He argues that the political theory of the secessionists was essentially antifederalist and that "the fundamental constitutional principle that distinguishes the C.S.A. Constitution from the U.S. Constitution is the locus of sovereignty." DeRosa, *The Confederate Constitution of 1861: An Inquiry into American Constitutionalism* (Columbia: University of Missouri Press, 1991), 5, 120, et seq. My differences with DeRosa are subtle but significant. First, the Southern romance with the antifederalists was deeply ambivalent, especially after *Dred Scott*, as Southerners came increasingly to a nationalist stance on questions pertaining to slavery. Second, although a conception of sovereignty was important to Southern constitutional identity, it was not the sole principle distinguishing it from Northern identity. The division between the constitutions of the United States and the Confederacy occurred along two axes. One was sovereignty. The other was slavery. (And within the orbit of these two issues were constitutional questions concerning congressional authority and the character of citizenship.) While the Constitution of the United States was not opposed to slavery, even by prevailing Northern interpretations, its proslavery elements tended to be interpreted as localist, not nationalist. It was precisely on this point that Taney's opinion in Dred Scott drove a wedge between Northern and Southern constitutional cultures. The eventual nationalist stance of some Southerners on slavery was ratified in the Confederate Constitution. Third, therefore, the secession of the Southern states and the formation of a new Confederate nation can be understood not merely as antifederalist but also as compatible on some fronts with federalist philosophy.

75. Constitution of the Confederate States of America, Preamble.

76. Ibid., Article IV.

77. Ibid., Preamble.

78. I am tempted to the position that an explicit textual provision denying a right to secede would be of no effect. This is only a temptation, however, and in any event the justification for the position would take me beyond the confines of this essay, so I shall not pursue it here.

79. A complete account of this position would require a theory of constitutional interpretation, which I shall refrain from offering here. Suffice it to say that some rights or principles may be binding, despite their absence from constitutional text, because they are necessary to, presupposed by, or logically entailed in other (explicit) rights or principles.

80. With respect to liberalism, one contrary position I have heard is that the appearance of the Bill of Rights renders illegitimate any antifederalist account of the origins of the American order. The point of this position, if I understand it correctly, is that the antifederalist myth makes it too easy to leave a liberal order and therefore to forsake rights. I believe this position is misguided in several respects. First, as an historical matter, it overlooks the fact that antifederalists were instigators and authors of the proposals that became the Bill of Rights. That fact, of course, does not make the Bill of Rights the property of antifederalists; but it does suggest that the Bill of Rights was not the exclusive property of the federalists. Second, in the years before the Civil War, the first eight (or ten) amendments to the Constitution were consistently interpreted to be limits on the national government, not the states. This reading, by federalists and antifederalists alike, not only did not bar but positively reinforced an antifederalist gloss on a significant part of the Constitution. Third, the Bill of Rights was a quirky quilt of provisions, some significant and others less so. Thus, even if one is committed to the ontological primacy of liberal rights, the Bill of Rights is not the only or even the most sensible or powerful expression of those rights. It is possible to imagine, then, a secession that could produce a new order improving on the Bill of Rights from a liberal perspective. It is possible to imagine, moreover, that an antifederalist approach to secession could protect (or disregard) rights of individuals just as well as a federalist approach. Fourth, if the response to the preceding point is that liberalism entails (or follows from) the primacy of nation-statism, then liberalism, to that extent, is anticonstitutionalist. Fifth, the liberal position I have described seems to presuppose either a metaphysic in which the point of any political order must be to protect individual rights or a "ratchet" theory in which political change that might abjure extant rights is prohibited. There are several

things to say about this position. First, as I have already suggested, there might be many ways to protect liberal rights, including ways that abandon parts of the Bill of Rights. Second, and regardless, we cannot assume anything about the character or status of rights in a new regime from the mere fact that its existence is traceable to a secession or from the fact that the secession is achieved by a particular mode. Finally, and more fundamentally, once a secession occurs, there follows an opportunity for reconstitution. Constitutionalism imposes some limits on what the new order may embrace if it is to be a constitutionalist order, but the limits are not those of liberalism; the opportunity for reconstitution is autochthonous and radical. These facts suggest that the constitution of a new order is a fearsome undertaking, fraught with danger and possibility.

81. For a general discussion of Lincoln's position, see Brandon, *Free in the World,* 116–34.

82. Lincoln, "First Inaugural Address," 270.

83. Lincoln, "Preliminary Emancipation Proclamation" (September 22, 1862), in Lincoln, *Collected Works,* vol. 5, 433–36; "Emancipation Proclamation" (January 1, 1863), *U.S. Statutes at Large,* vol. 12, 1268–69.

84. Lincoln, "First Joint Debate (Ottawa) and Fourth Joint Debate (Charleston)," in *Political Debates between Abraham Lincoln and Stephen A. Douglas* (Cleveland, Ohio: Burrows Brothers, 1894), 94, 188–89. One hundred years roughly corresponds to the period after which most forms of legal racial segregation were abolished and sharecropping declined as a form of economic organization.

85. Filler, *Crusade against Slavery,* 303.

86. This chapter draws substantially from Mark E. Brandon, *Free in the World: American Slavery and Constitutional Failure,* (Princeton: Princeton University Press, 1998). Thanks to Princeton University Press for permission to use portions of that argument.

INDEX

Aaland Islands, 21–22, 40–41n, 48n, 59–60, 78
Abkhazia, 54
Aboriginal peoples, 92, 104–5, 120, 131, 133, 207, 234n. *See also* Indigenous (autochthonous) peoples; Native Americans (U.S. and Canada)
Adams, John Quincy, 278–79
Afghanistan, 196
African Union, 80, 85n
Agency for International Development, 81
Alabama, 278, 290, 295, 297, 300
Amar, Akhil, 274–75, 306n
American Anti-Slavery Society, 288
American Revolution, 292, 299–300
Amnesty International, 81
Apartheid, 23
Arkansas, 278, 296–97
Arnold, Thurman, 73n
Aronovitch, Hilliard, 210–13, 230n, 232–33n
Articles of Association, 282
Articles of Confederation, 282, 284–85, 309n
Assembly of First Nations (Canada), 110, 125, 134n
Assimilation, 102, 129, 137, 149, 219, 225
Atlantic Charter, 51
Australia, 90–91, 94, 101–3, 109, 118n, 120, 122, 124, 131, 133, 219, 230n
Authoritarianism, 29, 52

Autonomy: group, 1–2, 6, 8, 51, 56, 65, 71, 89, 93, 100, 108, 114n, 195, 205, 219–21, 225, 227, 256–57, 265; individual, 6, 8, 91–92, 137, 156, 161, 183. *See also* Cultures and cultural preservation; Federalism and antifederalism; Minority groups; Rights; Secession; Self-determination; Self-government
Azerbaijan, 52

Badinter Commission, 34–38, 46–47n, 49n, 52–53, 250
Baltic states, 69, 115n, 223, 268n, 270n
Bangladesh, 39n, 52, 54, 57, 62, 69
Banton, Michael, 73n
Bauböck, Rainer, 213, 230n, 233n, 236n
Belgian Congo, 62
Belgium, 11, 109, 174, 196, 199, 232n
Bentham, Jeremy, 27
Beran, H., 231n
Berman, Nathaniel, 83n
Biafra, 53, 61–62
Big Bear, 113n
Bill of Rights, 313–14n
Blahuta, Jason, 230
Boldt, Menno, 117n
Bosnia and Hercegovina, 31, 35–37, 45–47n, 54, 56, 82n, 196
Brandon, Mark, 2–3, 11, 14–15, **272–314**
Brazil, 106

315

Briffault, Richard, 43n
Britain, 58, 62, 75n, 95, 102, 299–300,
    302, 304
British Colombia, 90, 117n
British North America Act (1867), 99
Brittany, 170n
Brown, John, 278, 305
Brown-John, C., 234n
Brownlie, Ian, 67, 75n
Bryant, Michael J., 234n
Buchanan, Allen, 1–15, 43n, 73n, 98,
    114n, 194, 197, 199, 201, 222, 231n,
    238–71, 276
Buchanan, James, 276
Bureau of Indian Affairs (U.S.), 112n,
    126, 128
Burke, Edmund, 299
Burma, 120
Byrd, Joe, 126

Cairns, Alan, 115n
Calhoun, John C., 279, 286, 294, 297
California, 288
Canada, 9, 11, 25–26, 31–32, 34, 62–63,
    91, 99, 102–4, 108–10, 116–18n,
    119–20, 132, 134n, 145–46, 149,
    153, 155, 157, 174, 176, 181, 196,
    199, 205–7, 209–10, 212–13, 218,
    231n, 233–35, 238–67, 268n, 273;
    Canadian Charter, 155, 170n;
    Supreme Court of, 13–14, 23,
    31–32, 84n, 117n, 212–14, 236n,
    238–41, 243–45, 247–54, 259–62,
    267. *See also* Constitution, Canadian;
    Language rights and policy; Que-
    bec; Secession; Self-determination
Cantonese immigrants, 9
Carens, Joseph, 171n, 188–89n
Cassese, Antonio, 42n, 60, 64–67, 73n,
    79, 83–84n
Catholicism, 302
Charlottetown Accord (1992), 233n
Cherokee, 91, 126
Cherokee v. Georgia, 128
Choudhry, Sujit, 188n
Christianity, 302

Citizenship, 20, 28, 245, 277, 312n
Civic virtue, 28, 161
Civil War, U.S., 235n, 283–84, 290, 293,
    304, 309n, 313n
Clarity Bill (Canada), 262
Clinton, Bill, 81
Cobban, Alfred, 43n
Colonies and colonization, 6, 24, 26,
    55, 61, 65–69, 89–91, 94–95, 101,
    143, 223, 253–54
Columbus, Christopher, 90
Commission of Rapporteurs, 21, 40n,
    60, 78–79
Common good, 28
Confederacy, 300–301, 312n
Conference for Peace in Yugoslavia, 34
Conference on Security and Co-opera-
    tion in Europe, 20
Congo, 107
Connecticut, 287
Connor, Walker, 219
Constitutionalism. *See* Secession; *and
    constitutions*
Constitution, British, 299
Constitution, Canadian, 238–40, 264
Constitution, U.S., 135n, 158, 218,
    273–76, 278–79, 281–89, 291–92,
    294–98, 300–304, 308n, 312–13n
Contact Group, 20
Copp, D., 231n
Corruption, 7, 143
Corwin Amendment, 296, 304, 311n
Cosmopolitanism, 186
Costa, J., 232n
Council of Europe, 37, 167n, 250
Cover, Robert, 291, 310n
Crawford, James, 69, 75n, 83n
Cree Indians, 9, 90, 181, 263–64
Croatia, 30–31, 34–36, 45–49n, 56–57,
    172n, 251
Croly, Herbert D., 309n
Cultures and cultural preservation, 6,
    8–10, 90–93, 99, 103, 106, 110,
    112n, 117n, 120–21, 125–27, 132,
    137–47, 149–54, 156–64, 171n, 180,
    183–85, 187, 189n, 256–57. *See also*

Autonomy; Rights, group and cultural; Secession; Self-determination
Cutler, Lloyd, 46n
Czechoslovakia, 19, 33–34, 45n, 51–52, 58
Czech Repbulic, 19, 33, 45n

Dahl, Robert, 43–44n
Darwinism, 102
Dawes Act, 112n
Declaration of Causes, 296–97
Declaration of Independence, 278–79, 282, 292, 298
Declaration of Independence (Tennessee), 298–99
Declaration on Friendly Relations (1970), 22–23, 60–68, 79, 83–84n
Declaration on Minorities (1992), 68
Declaration on the Granting of Independence to Colonial Countries and Peoples (1960), 111n
Declaration on the Rights of Indigenous Peoples (draft), 94
Declaration on Yugoslavia (1992), 35
Decolonization, 19, 22–23, 51–52, 60, 63–64, 68, 103–4, 250–51
Democracy, 10, 24, 70, 79–82, 106, 123, 161, 163–64, 185, 187, 194, 213, 217, 231n, 239, 243–45, 247, 249, 267, 272, 281–83, 286, 309n; consociational, 71–72; democratic accountability, 105; democratic deliberation, 12, 28, 32–33, 44n, 209–10, 215–16, 219, 244, 246; democratic principles, 3, 5, 25–29, 34–38, 59, 77–82, 101, 106–7, 115n, 118n, 148, 242, 248. *See also* Rights, to democratic governance; Secession, and democratic principles
Democratic National Committee, 126
Denmark, 119
Department of Indian Affairs (Canada), 108
Department of the Interior (U.S.), 128
DeRosa, Marshall L., 312n
De Varennes, F., 147, 170n

Dewey, John, 193
Dignity, 141, 303
Dion, Stephane, 240
Discrimination, 4, 8, 125, 152
Diversity, 28, 136, 148, 162, 167n, 174–75, 201, 272
Douglass, Frederick, 286
Dred Scott, 280–81, 294, 308n, 312n

East Timor, 19, 45n, 82n, 120
Education, 92, 99, 105, 109–10, 129, 144–45, 148–50, 152, 154, 156, 160, 164, 170–72n, 175, 180, 187, 225. *See also* Language rights and policy
Eliade, Mircea, 311n
Emancipation Proclamation, 304
Empathy, 28
Environmentalism, 148
Epstein, Richard, 135n
Equality, 24, 28, 64, 66, 92, 96, 112n, 155, 186, 246
Equal opportunity, 148
Equal protection, 20
Eritrea, 19, 52, 56, 69, 265
Esperanto, 173n
Estonia, 159, 172n
Ethiopia, 19, 52, 56, 196, 265, 267n
Ethnic cleansing, 56, 58
European Charter for Regional or Minority Languages (1992), 167n, 169n, 170n
European Community, 19–20, 34–37, 46–49n
European Union, 37–38, 48n, 79–80, 106, 140, 148, 176, 196, 212, 225

Federalism and antifederalism, 32, 51, 56, 89, 104, 106, 108, 119, 127, 196, 213, 219, 222, 227, 239, 245, 252, 275, 287, 290, 293, 295, 298, 302, 312–13n
Federalist, The, 237n, 301, 306n
Filler, Louis, 310n
Finland, 22, 40–41n, 48n, 59
First Inaugural Address (Lincoln), 281–82, 304, 306n, 308–9n

Flanagan, Tom, 117n
Flanders, 200
Fleras, Augie, 112n
Florida, 151, 172n, 278, 295
Founding, 14–15, 220, 225, 275, 287,
    290, 292, 294–95, 298, 302
Fox, Gregory H., 42n, 85–86n
Framework Convention for the Protec-
    tion of National Minorities (1995),
    167n
France, 39n, 62, 102, 170n, 196
Franck, Thomas, 24–25, 42n, 47n,
    68–70, 73n, 79, 81, 84n
Franks, C. E. S., 112n
Fugitive slave laws, 294

Garrison, William Lloyd, 288–89, 294,
    305
Gauthier, D., 231n
Genocide, 62
Georgia (post-Soviet state), 39n, 52
Georgia (U.S. state), 295
Germany, 47n, 52, 102, 309n
Gibbins, Roger, 236n
Glenny, Misha, 45n
Glorious Revolution, 299
God, 311n
Golove, David, 73n
Gorbachev, Mikhail, 268n
Greece, 48n
Greenland, 90, 119–20
Green, Leslie, 171n
Guidelines on the Recognition of the
    New States in Eastern Europe and
    in the Soviet Union, 35
Gutmann, Amy, 44n

Habeas corpus, 285
Haiti, 24, 69, 81
Halperin, Morton H., 73n
Hamilton, Alexander, 274, 290, 301
Hannum, Hurst, 42n, 74n
Harper's Ferry, 278, 305
Hartford Convention, 287–88
Hart, H. L. A., 122, 134n
Hawaii, 39n

Holmes, Stephen, 133
Homelessness, 185–86
Horowitz, Donald, 1–5, 11, 39n, **50–76**,
    77–79, 81–82, 82–84n, 111n, 134n
Human rights, 20, 35, 37–38, 249, 255,
    265, 276. *See also* Language rights
    and policy; Rights
Hume, David, 277

Ibo, 58, 61–62
Identity, ethnic and national, 20, 28,
    95, 103, 109, 137, 142, 145, 149,
    157–58, 162–63, 169n, 170–71n,
    175, 177, 184, 196, 219–20, 229,
    237n, 256, 270n, 294, 307n, 312n.
    See also Cultures and cultural preser-
    vation; Immigration and immi-
    grants; Language rights and policy;
    Minority groups; Nationalism;
    Rights, of minorities
Immigration and immigrants, 2, 8–10,
    138–44, 147–54, 157–59, 161–63,
    165, 170n, 172n, 176, 178–85,
    187–88, 195, 304. *See also* Cultures
    and cultural preservation; Identity,
    ethnic and national; Language
    rights and policy; Minority groups;
    Rights
Incentive theory, 72
India, 39n, 54–56, 58, 62–63, 90, 118n,
    119–20, 122, 127, 130–32, 173n,
    174, 231n
Indian Reorganization Act (1934), 122
Indian Self-Determination Act (1975),
    122
Indigenous (autochthonous) peoples,
    1–2, 6–7, 14, 89–110, 112–18n,
    119–24, 126, 128–29, 132–33,
    138–39, 144, 146–47, 153–54, 156,
    158–60, 164, 168n, 170n, 265–67.
    See also Aboriginal peoples; Minority
    groups; Native Americans (U.S. and
    Canada); Rights
Indonesia, 19, 39n, 56, 62
Interethnic accommodation, 71–72
International Court of Justice, 75n

International Covenant on Civil and Political Rights (1976), 24, 167n
International Covenant on Economic, Social and Cultural Rights (1976), 24
International institutions, 3, 5, 13, 32–33, 37–38, 39n, 71–72, 81, 261. *See also* European Union; United Nations
International law, 1–5, 19–26, 29–30, 35, 38, 39n, 50, 52–54, 56, 58–60, 67, 69–71, 77–79, 81, 83–84n, 89, 115n, 167n, 238, 241–42, 248–55, 257–60, 265, 269n, 276, 306–7n. *See also* United Nations
International mediation, 2, 34–38, 39n
Iraq, 39n, 58, 196, 265
Irian Jaya, 53
Iroquois, 90, 112n
Irredentism, 55–56, 60
Islamic law, 127
Italy, 231n, 235n

Jackson, Andrew, 279, 292
James Bay and Northern Quebec Agreement, 264
Jefferson, Thomas, 287, 294, 298
Judaism, 302
Justice: distributive, 94, 133; rectificatory, 93–97, 99, 110, 113n, 114n

Kansas, 289
Kashmir, 53, 56
Kingsbury, Benedict, 115n
Klaus, Václav, 45n
Koh, Harold Hongju, 85n
Kosovo, 27, 48n, 52–54, 56, 265
Kosovo Liberation Army, 57
Kymlicka, Will, 6, 91–93, 106, 112n, 115n, 119–21, 134–35n, 178–79, 182–85, 187, 189n, 230n

Laforest, Guy, 236n
Lakota Indians, 90
Language rights and policy, 1–2, 7–11, 22–23, 92, 99, 103, 106, 120, 129,

136–39, 141–42, 144–66, 167–73n, 174–84, 187–88, 221, 225; and consent theory, 8–10, 179–81, 183–84, 187–88; language equality policy, 8, 175; language preservation, 149, 159, 169n; "norm and accommodation" policy, 8, 174, 176, 178, 188. *See also* Canada; Cultures and cultural preservation; Education; Minority groups; Quebec; Rights
Lansing, Robert, 75n
Laponce, J., 234n
Latvia, 159
Lau v. Nichols, 175
League of Nations, 21, 40–41n, 51, 60, 78–79
Legitimacy, 14, 26–27, 31–32, 71, 79, 89, 100–101, 110, 213, 240, 249
Levesque, René, 205
Levy, Jacob, 2, 6–7, **119–35**
Liberalism, Community, and Culture (Kymlicka), 134n
Liberal Party (Quebec), 205
Liberal Party (Sudan), 57
Liberator, The, 288
Lijphart, Arend, 76n
Lincoln, Abraham, 12, 29, 44n, 273, 280–88, 292, 295–96, 298, 304, 306n, 308–9n, 311n
Linz, J., 236n
Little, Allan, 47n
Livingston, Edward, 278–79, 308n
Llewellyn, Karl, 70
Locke, John, 29, 299
Lomasney, Kristin, 73n
Lord Acton, 29
Louisiana, 278, 287, 295–97, 312n
Lyons, David, 135n

Maaka, Roger, 112n
Macdonald, John A., 102
Macedonia, 196
Madison, James, 279, 306n, 308n
Malanczuk, Peter, 67
Malaysia, 73n, 90, 127
Manitoba Act, 95

Margalit, Avishai, 100, 114n
Marshall, John, 128, 274, 279, 292, 294
Massachusetts, 287–89
Massachusetts Anti-Slavery Society, 288
Mass media, 140
May, Stephen, 172n
McAuliffe, Billee Elliott, 135n
McCorquodale, Robert, 73n
McIlwain, Charles, 276
Mečiar, Vladimir, 45n, 48n
Meech Lake Accord (1987), 233n
Mercredi, Ovide, 99, 113n
Mexican War, 288–89
Mexico, 104, 116n, 118n
Miller, David, 112n, 270n
Mill, James, 27
Mill, John Stuart, 26, 28, 100, 114n, 203
Minority groups, 4–5, 7–11, 37, 50–51, 55–56, 91–92, 97, 122, 127, 130–31, 138–39, 146, 154, 157, 162, 164, 167–69n, 195–96, 204, 221, 243–46, 248, 261, 280; linguistic, 137, 148; national minorities, 2, 8–10, 20, 26, 92–93, 115n, 119, 163, 178–79, 181–83, 187, 193, 198, 200–202, 204–5, 220–21, 223–29. *See also* Aboriginal peoples; Immigration and immigrants; Indigenous (autochthononous) peoples; Language rights and policy; Native Americans (U.S. and Canada); Rights, of minorities
Mississippi, 278, 290, 295–96, 300
Missouri, 288
Mobutu Sese Seko, 107
Moldova, 52
Monahan, Patrick, 234n
Montenegro, 48n
Moore, Margaret, 2, 6–7, **89–118**, 200–201, 234n
Moses, 311n
Mouser, Denette, 134n
Multicultural Citizenship (Kymlicka), 112n, 178, 189n
Multiculturalism, 164–65
Muravchik, Joshua, 86n

Nationalism, 20, 26, 29, 45n, 82n, 194, 200, 216–17, 219, 226, 253–56, 270–71n, 274, 279, 281–82, 293–94, 312n
Nation-building, 105, 163, 226–27
Native Americans (U.S. and Canada), 92, 95, 99, 102, 116n, 119–20, 122, 125, 129, 135n, 153, 243, 256, 259, 262–67, 273. *See also* Aboriginal peoples; Indigenous (autochthonous) peoples
Netherlands, 102, 232–33n
Nevins, Allan, 309n
New Hampshire, 287
New Zealand, 90, 95, 101–3, 109, 120, 172n
Nielsen, Kai, 231n
Nigeria, 57–58, 61, 127, 174
Nisga'a Treaty, 117n
Norman, Wayne, 2, 11–14, **193–237**
North American Free Trade Agreement, 233n
North Atlantic Treaty Organization, 48n
North Carolina, 296
Northern Ireland, 75n
Norway, 124
Nozick, Robert, 135n
Nullification, 278–80, 292, 296, 308n

On Liberty (Mill), 100, 203
Open Society Institute, 48n
Orentlicher, Diane, 1–5, 12, 14, **19–49**, 59–64, 67–69, **77–86**
Organisation for Economic Co-operation and Development, 80
Organisation for Security and Co-operation in Europe, 80
Organization of African Unity, 51
Organization of American States, 80

Pakistan, 54–55, 57, 62
Palestine, 58
Paris (Versailles) Peace Conference, 21, 24, 40n, 59, 78
Parti Québécois, 205

Pastor, Robert, 86n
Patten, Alan, 2, 7–10, **174–89**
Pellet, Alain, 73n
Perpetuity, 273–74, 282–85, 287, 290, 309n
Pettit, Philip, 133
Philippines, 58, 231n
Phillips, Wendell, 288
Philpott, David, 73n, 231n
Pluralism, 161, 163, 219
Poland, 63
Politics in the Vernacular (Kymlicka), 115n, 134n
Portugal, 48n, 102
Post, Robert, 272, 303, 305–6n
Powell, Thomas Reed, 53
Puerto Rico, 231n

Quebec, 13–14, 25–26, 31–32, 39n, 84n, 121, 127, 149, 154–55, 157, 162, 181, 200, 205–7, 210, 213, 225, 231n, 233–34n, 238–67, 268n, 270–71n. *See also* Canada; Language rights and policy; Minority groups; Secession; Self-determination

Raskin, Jamin, 26
Rawls, John, 131, 183, 222, 236–37n
Raz, Joseph, 100, 114n
Réaume, Dénise, 169n, 171n
Reformation, Protestant, 302
Refugees, 165, 185
Religion, 125
Reparations, 91, 96, 113n
Republicanism, 27–30, 44n, 133, 308n
Requejo, Ferran, 237n
Resnick, Philip, 233n
Revolution, 277–79, 297, 308n
Rhode Island, 287
Rhodesia, 147
Rich, Roland, 46–47n
Richards, David A. J., 312n
Rights: group and cultural, 22–23, 89, 96, 98–99, 121–22, 145, 156–58, 161, 180, 183–84, 187, 256, 265; individual, 223, 251, 302; land and

property, 122, 132–33; liberal democratic, 91, 314n; of indigenous peoples, 7, 92, 94–95, 98, 106, 109, 120–21, 128, 133, 139; of minorities, 3–5, 14, 21–22, 35, 37–38, 53–54, 60, 68, 78, 123, 129, 138, 160, 167n, 194, 213, 239, 247, 250, 262, 264–65, 267; to democratic governance, 3, 23–25, 52, 64, 66, 68–70, 79–81, 82–84n, 123; to political participation, 4, 22–24, 38, 54, 60, 64, 82, 99, 241, 253–54, 258. *See also* Autonomy; Democracy; Human rights; Language rights and policy; Minority groups; Secession, and right to secede; Self-determination, right to
Roth, Brad R., 85–86n
Rousseau, Jean-Jacques, 310n
Royal Commission on Aboriginal Peoples (1996), 104
Rubio-Marín, Ruth, 2, 7–11, **136–73**, 178–83, 187
Rumania, 51
Russia, 40n, 120
Rwanda, 56

Sambanis, Nicholas, 74n
San Andreas Accords (1996), 104–5
Santa Clara Pueblo v. Martinez, 134n
Scandanavia, 90
Schleswig, 21
Schnably, Stephen, J., 85n
Schwartz, Herman, 46n
Scotland, 75n, 200, 225
Secession: alternatives to, 6, 23; as bargaining tool, 12, 29, 45n; and "biased referee problem," 13, 197, 199, 213; and constitutionalism, 1–3, 11–15, 31, 193–95, 197–205, 208–15, 217–25, 227–29, 232n, 234–36n, 238–45, 247–48, 255, 257, 259–60, 262–64, 266–67, 268–69n, 272–76, 278–92, 294–305, 308n, 311n, 313–14n; and democratic principles, 3, 20, 23–39, 59, 77–82, 85n, 197, 302; and effectivity, 248–50;

Secession (*Continued*)
and ethnic conflict, 3–5, 11–12, 36, 50–51, 53, 55–57, 71, 216, 255; and individualism, 289; and international recognition, 3–5, 35–37, 69, 249–50, 252, 258, 262; justifications for, 3, 7, 11–15, 198–202, 250; and linguistic minorities, 149; and moral theory, 197–202, 232n, 276; negotiation/mediation of, 31–38, 46n, 196, 204–5, 207, 209, 213, 225, 227, 232n, 239, 241, 243–44, 248, 250, 256–57, 259–67, 268n; and referendums, 13, 31–33, 36, 193, 200, 205–9, 212, 214, 218, 233–35n, 245, 248, 260, 267, 300; as remedial measure, 3, 7, 12, 14, 22–23, 25, 38, 53, 59, 79, 82n, 120, 241–43, 266, 268n; and revolution, 278, 299, 308–10n; and right to secede, 1–5, 11–12, 25, 50–69, 72, 77–78, 82n, 194, 198, 201–4, 211, 217–18, 224–25, 227, 235n, 238–40, 243, 245–46, 253, 258–59, 267, 271n, 274, 276, 301, 313n; separatist movements and claims, 19–21, 24–39, 39n, 50, 77–79, 81–82, 82n, 196, 200, 205–6, 230–31n, 238–67, 268–70n. *See also* Democracy; International law; Language rights and policy; Rights; Self-determination; Self-government

Second Treatise on Government (Locke), 299

Self-determination: and indigenous peoples, 91, 93, 98–100, 104, 110, 113n, 115–17n, 119–20, 123; external, 42n, 45n, 241; internal, 89; and international law, 20–24, 59; right to, 1, 22, 24, 26, 41–42n, 50–52, 58, 60–68, 78, 84n, 89, 99, 120, 131, 194, 204, 219, 226, 236n, 238, 241–42, 253–55, 259, 269n, 276, 280. *See also* Autonomy; Cultures and cultural preservation; Indigenous (autochthonous) peoples; Minority groups; Rights; Secession; Self-government

Self-esteem, 142, 149–50, 169n

Self-government, 1, 6–8, 20, 24–29, 38, 58, 89, 91–94, 98–101, 104–8, 110, 112n, 114n, 117–18n, 119–21, 123–24, 126, 128–29, 131, 133, 157, 161–63, 215, 219, 226, 229, 265, 296–97, 299. *See also* Autonomy; Cultures and cultural preservation; Minority groups; Rights; Secession; Self-determination

Self-respect, 137

Serbia, 27, 31, 45n, 47–48n, 52, 265

Sherman, William L., 111n

Sierra Leone, 81

Silber, Laura, 47n

Simpson, Audra, 116n

Simpson, Gerry, 73n

Singapore, 73n

Sisk, Timothy D., 39n

Slavery, 90, 273, 275, 278, 280–81, 284, 288–90, 294, 296–97, 301, 303–4, 308n, 312n

Slovakia, 19, 33, 39n, 45n

Slovenia, 30, 34–36, 47–48n, 57, 251

Solana, Javier, 48n

Somalia, 39n, 52, 69

Somaliland, 52

South Africa, 65, 174

South Carolina, 278, 287, 295–98, 311n

Southern People's Liberation Army (Sudan), 57

Soviet Union, 19, 35, 52, 58, 115n, 231n, 237n, 267–68n, 270n, 273

Spain, 11, 39n, 48n, 106, 127, 149, 153, 159, 168n, 172n, 174, 196, 199, 200, 225

Sri Lanka, 39n, 53, 56, 58

Stampp, Kenneth, 278, 284–85

Stannard, D. E., 111n

Stein, Eric, 45n

St. Kitts-Nevis, 230n, 235n, 267n

Story, Joseph, 279

Sudan, 39n, 57, 251, 265
Sudetenland, 60
Suksey, Markku, 235n
Sullivan, John, 112n
Sunstein, Cass, 12, 28, 133, 213,
    215–18, 220, 222, 229, 232–33n,
    235–37n, 273–74
Sweden, 40–41n, 48n, 59, 124
Switzerland, 11, 146, 170n, 174, 196,
    234n

Tamil Tigers, 57
Tamil United Liberation Front, 57
Tamir, Yael, 121
Taney, Roger, 281, 294, 312n
Taylor, Charles, 233n
Tennessee, 278, 290, 298–300
Territorial integrity, 20, 22–23, 41n, 52,
    55, 61, 64–69, 83n, 111n, 258, 283
Texas, 278, 293, 295–97
Texas v. White, 273, 306n
Theory of Justice, A (Rawls), 236n
Thompson, Dennis, 44n
Thoreau, Henry David, 289
Tibet, 132
Tittemore, Brian D., 85n
Toleration, 136
Torture, 81
Touval, Saadia, 74n
Transniestria, 69
Treaties, 95–96, 98, 104, 109, 295
Tribal governments, 7
Tully, James, 113n, 234n, 236n
Turkey, 39n
Turpel, Mary-Ellen, 99, 113n

Uganda, 90
Ukraine, 39n
United Kingdom, 11, 61–62, 64, 75n,
    196
United Nations, 20, 22–23, 34, 45n, 51,
    58, 60–61, 67, 79–80, 83–84n, 111n,
    258; Charter of, 22, 41–42n, 79,
    269n; Security Council, 24, 47n, 69
United States, 14, 20, 36, 61–62, 64, 68,
    80, 90–91, 95, 97, 112n, 116n, 120,

122, 124–25, 128–29, 132, 147, 151,
    153, 158, 173n, 174–75, 180, 196,
    219, 228, 231n, 242, 273–305, 307n,
    309n, 312n; Southern states, 274,
    277–79, 281, 286, 288, 294,
    300–302, 304, 309–10n, 312n;
    Supreme Court, 175, 273, 281, 284,
    304, 308n. *See also* Constitution,
    U.S.
Upper Silesia, 21
Utilitarianism, 27–28, 30
Uti possidetis, 250–52, 270n

Van Parijs, Philippe, 236n
Vermont, 287
Virginia, 278, 290, 296
Voting practices, 147

Waldron, Jeremy, 98, 113n
Wales, 75n
Walters, M., 234n
War of 1812, 287–88
Warsaw Pact, 231n
Washington, George, 111
Washington (state), 90
Waters, Timothy William, 39n
Watts, Ronald, 118n
Webber, Jeremy, 122
Webster, Daniel, 278
Weinstock, Daniel, 188n, 202–4, 209,
    230n, 232n, 235–37n
Wellman, C., 231n
West Virginia, 290
Whelan, Frederick, 42n
Whitman, Walt, 306n
Wilson, Woodrow, 21, 39–40n, 51–52,
    59, 78
Wounded Knee, 90

Young, Iris Marion, 113n
Yugoslavia, 19, 30–31, 34–37, 39n,
    45–49n, 51–52, 54, 57, 196, 250–52,
    270n

Zaire, 90